Anxiety and Cognition
A Unified Theory

Michael W. Eysenck
Royal Holloway
University of London

Psychology Press
a member of the Taylor & Francis group

Psychology Press, Publishers
27 Church Road
Hove
East Sussex, BN3 2FA
UK

British Library Cataloguing in Publication Data

A catalogue record for this book is available from the British Library

   ISBN 0-86377-478-4

Cover design by Joyce Chester
Printed and bound in the UK by TJ Press Ltd., Padstow, Cornwall

To my daughter Fleur with love

Let fear, then, be a kind of pain or disturbance resulting from the imagination of impending danger, either destructive or painful.
(Aristotle)

Contents

Preface

In 1992, I published a research monograph entitled *Anxiety: The cognitive perspective*. That book was based on the assumption that it is valuable to adopt a cognitive approach when attempting to understand individual differences in anxiety among normal and clinical populations. More specifically, it was argued that there are several important similarities between normals high in trait anxiety and clinical patients with generalised anxiety disorder.

This monograph is built to some extent on the foundations provided by that earlier monograph. However, it represents a more ambitious attempt to develop inter-related cognitive theories of anxiety as an emotion, of trait anxiety as a personality dimension, and of clinical anxiety. The author is uncomfortably aware that he really should be an expert on emotion, personality, clinical psychology, and cognitive psychology in order to do this. Unfortunately, he is not. However, various people who are experts in one or more of these areas have very kindly lent their assistance by commenting on some of the draft chapters of this book. Among those to whom I am truly grateful for such assistance are the following: Chris Brewin; Nazanin Derakshan; Elaine Fox; Andy MacLeod; Karin Mogg; Richard McNally; and Brian Parkinson.

I am also very grateful to those within the Psychology Department at Royal Holloway University of London who have been actively involved in the research programme reported here. They include the following: Sukhbeer Bohphal; Sally Caruana; Nazanin Derakshan; Jan de Fockert;

Alison Wheeler; James Walsh, and Josephine Wild. Nazanin Derakshan deserves to be singled out for special thanks, because of the outstanding contributions she has made in every way to the research programme. Without her assistance, it is doubtful that this book could (or would) have been written.

I am also very grateful to Manuel Calvo, who has made an outstanding contribution to our understanding of anxiety and cognition. I have found the research collaboration we have had over the past several years extremely valuable. I have also enjoyed meeting him and his family on the sunny island of Tenerife in the Canary Islands, especially in the middle of inhospitable English winters. Finally, promising research collaboration is being developed with a number of clinical researchers from the Complutense University in Madrid, including Hector Gonzalez-Ordi, Juan-Jose Miguel-Tobal, and Antonio Cano-Vindel.

This book is dedicated to my elder daughter Fleur. She has waited patiently for five years since she last had a book dedicated to her, and I hope that she will not have to wait so long for the next one!

Michael W. Eysenck
Beijing, China

CHAPTER ONE

Theories of trait anxiety

INTRODUCTION

Anxiety has become an increasingly fashionable focus of research in recent years, and it may be wondered whether yet another book on anxiety is needed. However, most books on anxiety are rather limited in scope. More specifically, they generally focus on only one of three main areas of research in which anxiety is of major importance: emotion; personality; and clinical or abnormal psychology. In contrast, an attempt (ambitious or foolish) has been made in this book to consider anxiety in all three areas within a common theoretical framework. It is for this reason that the title of this book refers to a "unified theory of anxiety".

There are numerous theories of emotion, most of which include a list or classification of the basic emotions. Anxiety (or fear) is regarded as one of the basic emotions in nearly all of these theories (e.g., Plutchik, 1980; Russell, 1991). As far as personality research is concerned, trait anxiety (or neuroticism) is included as one of the major dimensions of personality in most contemporary theories (see Digman, 1990, for a review). Finally, anxiety is of major concern in clinical psychology. For example, 12 different anxiety disorders are identified in DSM-IV (1994).

Why have most theorists concentrated on anxiety as an emotional state, or as an aspect of personality, or in connection with clinical disorders? One reason was identified by Eysenck (1992). As he pointed out, the goals of researchers in the clinical and personality areas have been rather different: "Those engaged in clinical research have focused primarily on cognitive factors involved in the aetiology and maintenance of clinical anxiety, whereas those investigating cognition in normal groups have concentrated on the ways in which anxiety affects performance" (p.1).

The starting point for the unified theory of anxiety was previous theory and research on trait anxiety in normal groups. Accordingly, relevant theories of trait anxiety are discussed in this chapter. In subsequent chapters, the new unified theory of anxiety is discussed with reference to an understanding of anxiety as an emotion, personality dimension, and clinical disorder. Four major issues provide recurring themes throughout the book. First, there is the issue of which factors determine the experience of anxiety. Second, there is the issue of the inter-relationships among the cognitive, physiological, and behavioural systems involved in anxiety. Third, there is the issue of why it is that some individuals experience much more anxiety than others. Fourth, there is the issue of the similarities and differences between anxiety in normals and in anxious patients.

TRAIT ANXIETY

Personality theorists have spent several decades disagreeing among themselves about the number and nature of important personality factors or traits. Among the protagonists have been Cattell (e.g., Cattell, Eber, & Tatsouka, 1970), who argues that there are sixteen personality factors, and H. J. Eysenck (1967), who identifies only three. In recent years, however, there has been a developing consensus that there are five major personality factors, which are often called the Big Five. For example, Costa and McCrae (1985) identified the following five factors: extraversion; agreeableness; conscientiousness; neuroticism; and openness. There are minor quarrels about the nature of one or two of these factors (see Digman, 1990, for a review), but there is a large measure of agreement.

Although much has been accomplished at the level of personality description, this has not been matched by commensurate progress at the level of explanation. In other words, relatively little is known of the underlying causal factors and processes producing individual differences in these personality factors. What is missing from contemporary accounts was expressed in the following way by Block (1995):

The Big Five are often called 'the five-factor model of personality' and are referred to as providing an understanding of the 'structure of personality'. As the term 'model' is used in conventional parlance among psychologists, it means a theoretically based, logically coherent, working representation or simulation that, in operation, attempts to generate psychological phenomena of interest. However, no identifiable hypotheses, theories, or models guided the emergence of or decision on this five-fold space (p.188).

Virtually everyone agrees that one of the Big Five is a factor known variously as trait anxiety, neuroticism, or negative affectivity. Since much of this book is concerned with this personality factor, it is important to clarify the inter-relationships of these terms at the outset. Trait anxiety was defined by Spielberger, Gorsuch, and Lushene (1970) as "relatively stable individual differences in anxiety proneness" (p.3). Neuroticism closely resembles trait anxiety, with questionnaire measures of the two personality factors typically correlating approximately +0.70 with each other (Watson & Clark, 1984). However, there is one minor difference between them: trait anxiety correlates approximately −0.30 with extraversion, whereas neuroticism and extraversion are essentially uncorrelated (Watson & Clark, 1984).

In their article, Watson and Clark (1984) reviewed evidence indicating that a wide range of measures of neuroticism, trait anxiety, depression, and so on all inter-correlate highly with each other. They argued that these failures of discrimination indicate that it is inappropriate to assume that the various measures are actually assessing different personality factors. Their preferred solution is to assume that self-report questionnaires allegedly measuring trait anxiety, depression, and so on, are in fact assessing essentially the same personality factor of negative affectivity.

There have been various theoretical attempts to account for individual differences in trait anxiety or the closely related factors of neuroticism or negative affectivity. Some of these theories (e.g., H.J. Eysenck, 1967; Gray, 1982) have emphasised the role of heredity and individual differences in physiological activity. Other theories (e.g., M.W. Eysenck, 1992; Williams, Watts, MacLeod, & Mathews, 1988) have focused primarily on the role of the cognitive system in accounting for individual differences in trait anxiety.

THEORIES OF H.J. EYSENCK AND GRAY

Gray's (1982) theory of trait anxiety and H.J. Eysenck's (1967) theory of neuroticism both involved two major assumptions. The first assumption is that individual differences in the personality dimension of trait anxiety or neuroticism depend to a large extent on genetic factors. According to H.J. Eysenck (1967), "the evidence suggests fairly strongly that something like 50 per cent of individual differences in neuroticism and extraversion ... is accountable for in terms of hereditary influences" (p.210). Subsequently, he revised the figure upwards: "genetic factors contribute something like two-thirds of the variance in major personality dimensions" (Eysenck, 1982, p.28). According to Gray (1982), "studies of the personality traits of neuroticism and extraversion ... estimate the contribution of heredity to these conditions at about 50 per cent of the variance" (p.438).

The second major assumption is that heredity influences the level of trait anxiety or neuroticism via the physiological system. According to H.J. Eysenck (1967), individual differences in neuroticism depend upon the functioning of the so-called "visceral brain". This consists of the hippocampus, amygdala, cingulum, septum, and hypothalamus. Somewhat similar structures were identified by Gray (1982). He argued that individual differences in trait anxiety depend upon the septo-hippocampal system, its neocortical projection in the frontal lobe, and its monoaminergic afferents from the brain-stem. He used the term "behavioural inhibition system" to refer to these structures.

Influence of heredity
The most important evidence relating to the role of heredity in determining trait anxiety and neuroticism comes from twin studies, and only this research will be considered in detail. However, it should be mentioned that the findings from adoption studies are broadly in line with those from twin studies, although they suggest a somewhat lower contribution of heredity than do twin studies (Brody, 1988).

The first relevant twin study seemed to provide remarkably strong support for the importance of heredity. H.J. Eysenck and Prell (1951) studied neuroticism, and found that the correlation between monozygotic twins was +0.85, compared to only +0.22 for dizygotic twins. These findings suggested that 80% of individual differences in neuroticism are due to heredity.

All subsequent studies have indicated that the findings of H.J. Eysenck and Prell (1951) were very anomalous, especially the extremely high correlation for monozygotic twins. Zuckerman (1987) reviewed the evidence from eight other twin studies. The highest correlation for monozygotic twins in any of those studies was +0.67, and the mean correlation was only +0.52. The largest twin study in which neuroticism was assessed was that of Floderus-Myrhed, Pedersen, and Rasmusson (1980). They studied over 12,000 twin pairs, obtaining a correlation of +0.50 for monozygotic twins and of +0.23 for dizygotic twins.

In principle, especially important evidence about the influence of heredity on personality can be obtained from monozygotic twins brought up apart. The reason for this is that they have essentially the same heredity but are brought up in dissimilar environments. However, most studies (e.g., Shields, 1962) are flawed because many of the monozygotic twins were brought up together during the first few years of life. In addition, other monozygotic twin pairs who were brought up apart were placed in different branches of the same family, and sometimes even attended the same school. We will focus on the study by Pedersen, Plomin, McClearn, and Friberg (1988), which is the nearest approach yet to a definitive study. They assessed neuroticism in 95 monozygotic pairs brought up apart, 150 monozygotic pairs brought up together, 220 pairs of dizygotic twins brought up apart, and 204 dizygotic pairs brought up together. Of the twin pairs brought up apart, 48% were separated before their first birthday, and 82% were separated by the age of five.

Pedersen et al. (1988) found that the correlations for neuroticism were as follows: +0.25 for monozygotic twins brought up apart; +0.41 for monozygotic twins brought up together; +0.28 for dizygotic twins brought up apart; and +0.24 for dizygotic twins brought up together. According to Pedersen et al. (1988), these correlations indicate that 31% of individual differences in neuroticism are due to heredity.

In sum, the available evidence indicates that genetic factors contribute approximately 30% of the variance in trait anxiety or neuroticism, but it is difficult to provide a precise figure. However, it is now certain that the contribution to the variance made by genetic factors is considerably less than the 67% claimed by H.J. Eysenck (1982). At the other extreme, it would appear that Torgersen (1990) under-stated the contribution of heredity: "The development of the relatively normally distributed neuroticism or anxiousness may be modestly influenced by genetic factors ... However, by far the most important source of variance seems to be individual environmental factors" (p.285).

Physiological differences

The fact that the contribution of genetic factors to trait anxiety and to neuroticism is less than claimed by H.J. Eysenck (1967) and by Gray (1982) has implications for the relationship between these personality dimensions and physiological functioning. However, as we will see, the actual relationship is much less than would be expected even on the basis that only 30% of the variance in trait anxiety and neuroticism is contributed by genetic factors.

It has not been possible to obtain direct measures of individual differences in the level of activity in the behavioural inhibition system or visceral brain. However, researchers have used a wide range of indirect physiological measures such as the EEG, heart rate, skin conductance, and skin resistance. There have been several large-scale studies, with a very wide range of different physiological measures having been taken in various stressful and non-stressful conditions. All of the available evidence was reviewed by Fahrenberg (1992), who came to the following conclusion: "Over many decades research has failed to substantiate the physiological correlates that are assumed for emotionality and trait anxiety. There is virtually no distinct finding that has been reliably replicated across studies and laboratories" (pp.212–213).

The almost complete failure of psychophysiological studies to find any consistent differences between those high and low in trait anxiety is rather puzzling. Gray (1982) reviewed evidence which indicates strongly that the septo-hippocampal system is centrally involved in anxiety. This evidence comes from two strands of research. First, various anti-anxiety drugs such as the benzodiazepines, barbiturates, and alcohol have been found to exert broadly comparable effects on behaviour. Second, lesions to the septo-hippocampal system in rats and other species produce several behavioural effects. As Gray (1982) pointed out, there are 19 different kinds of behavioural measure for which drug and lesion data are available. On 18 of these measures, drugs and lesions have essentially the same effects. The obvious implication of these findings is that the septo-hippocampal system is of major importance in anxiety.

The reasons why there are so few differences in physiological activity between those high and low in self-report measures of trait anxiety are discussed more fully in Chapter 3. The main reason is that those who score low on self-reported trait anxiety form a heterogeneous group. Weinberger, Schwartz, and Davidson (1979) obtained measures of trait anxiety and of social desirability from their subjects. They argued that high scores on social desirability reflect a defensive or repressive coping style. Those who obtained low scores on social desirability as well as on trait anxiety were categorised as truly low-anxious, whereas those who scored high on social desirability but low on trait anxiety were classified as repressors. When the subjects were exposed to a moderately stressful situation, the repressors responded physiologically much more than the truly low-anxious. In fact, the repressors were more physiologically responsive than the high-anxious subjects on most of the measures.

Similar findings to those of Weinberger et al. (1979) have been obtained in a number of subsequent studies. For example, Brown, Tomarken, Orth, Loosen, Kalin, and Davidson (1996) found that high scorers on trait anxiety did not differ from low scorers in their basal salivary cortisol levels. However, when the low scorers were divided into low-anxious and repressor groups, it was found that high-anxious subjects had significantly higher salivary cortisol levels than the low-anxious subjects. One of the implications of these findings is that there are two rather different types of individuals who obtain low scores on questionnaire measures of trait anxiety. However, the major implication for theories such as those of H.J. Eysenck (1967) and Gray (1982) is as follows: the failure to discover any consistent relationship between trait anxiety and physiological reponsiveness is due mainly to the high level of responsiveness of repressors.

Evaluation

The theoretical approach to trait anxiety and neuroticism advocated by H.J. Eysenck (1967) and by Gray (1982) has only been partially successful. Genetic factors determine individual differences in trait anxiety and neuroticism to some extent, but they are less important than was assumed by H.J. Eysenck (1967) and by Gray (1982). As we have seen, it has proved difficult to demonstrate the theoretically predicted differences in physiological functioning between those high and low in trait anxiety.

In addition to the above problems, the physiological approach is severely limited in many ways. As Eysenck (1992) pointed out, "The various inadequacies of the physiological approach to trait anxiety and neuroticism arise to a large extent because environmental influences and the role of learning are de-emphasised. As soon as one considers learning, then the importance of the cognitive system becomes obvious" (p.42). Evidence suggesting the importance of environmental factors was reviewed by Conley (1984). He averaged the data from several studies, and found that the consistency of trait anxiety or neuroticism from one year to the next (with the intrinsic unreliability of the questionnaire eliminated statistically) was +0.98. This may seem high, but it still implies that fairly large changes in trait anxiety or neuroticism occur over a period of a few years. The level of year-by-year consistency is lower than that of intelligence, which is +0.99 (Conley, 1984).

It is assumed within the physiological approach that individuals with highly responsive physiological systems will be anxious across virtually all stressful situations, whereas low trait-anxious individuals will generally experience rather little anxiety. Eysenck (1992) termed this the "unidimensional view" of trait anxiety, and pointed out that there is evidence against it. Endler (1983) proposed a multi-dimensional approach, according to which the increase in state anxiety produced by a threatening environment will be greater among those high in trait anxiety only when there is *congruence* between the nature of the threat and the dimension or facet of trait anxiety possessed by the individual. This prediction has been confirmed several times when the dimensions of social evaluation and physical danger have been investigated (e.g., Donat, 1983; Kendall, 1978).

In sum, the physiological approach is over-simplified. This is especially apparent in its relative neglect of environmental factors, changes in personality over time, the multi-dimensional nature of trait anxiety, and individual differences in cognitive functioning. However, there is no doubt that the genetic factors emphasised by this approach are of importance. In addition, individual differences in the functioning of the septo-hippocampal system play a role in determining levels of trait anxiety when repressors are excluded.

COGNITIVE APPROACHES

Williams et al. (1988)

In 1988, Williams et al. put forward a theory which was mainly designed to account for clinical anxiety and depression, but which also included some consideration of trait anxiety. In their theory, there is a crucial theoretical distinction between integration or priming and elaboration. Priming is an automatic process in which a stimulus word produces activation of the various components comprising its internal representation, which means that the word will subsequently be accessed more readily when only a fraction of its features is presented.

In contrast, elaboration is a strategic process in which the activation of the internal representation of a presented word leads to the activation of associated internal representations. This spread of activation either strengthens existing inter-connections among words or leads to the formation of new inter-connections. Elaboration has the effect of making the presented word easier to retrieve subsequently. The distinction between priming and elaboration is relevant during retrieval as well as during encoding. Words may be retrieved in a relatively automatic and effortless fashion, as is the case in tests of implicit memory (e.g., word-fragment completion) which do not depend on conscious recollection. Alternatively, words may be retrieved only as a result of an active search of long-term memory, as is the case in tests of explicit memory, which depend on conscious recollection.

Williams et al. (1988) argued that the distinction between priming and elaboration is of great relevance to an understanding of cognitive differences associated with anxiety and depression. In their own words, "Anxiety preferentially affects the passive, automatic aspect of encoding and retrieval, whereas depression preferentially affects the more active, effortful aspects of encoding and retrieval" (pp.173–174).

Williams et al. (1988) discussed in some detail how anxiety affects the processing of threatening information. At the pre-attentive stage, stimulus input is processed by an affective decision mechanism. This mechanism assesses the threat value of the presented stimulus or stimuli, and this information is then passed on to the resource allocation mechanism. This mechanism directs attention towards or away from threatening sources. State anxiety affects the output of the affective decision mechanism by increasing the subjective threat value of presented stimuli. Trait anxiety "may represent a permanent tendency to react to input from the ADM (affective decision mechanism) by directing attention towards or away from the location of threat" (p.175).

One of the main predictions which follows from this theory is that there will often be an interaction between trait and state anxiety. High trait anxiety provides a constant tendency to direct attention to threat, whereas low trait anxiety is associated with a tendency to direct attention away from threat. Both of these directional biases increase in magnitude as the level of state anxiety increases. This interactional pattern has been obtained in a number of studies discussed later in the chapter (e.g., Broadbent & Broadbent, 1988; MacLeod & Mathews, 1988; MacLeod, 1990).

Williams et al. (1988) applied their theory to negative memory bias (the tendency in explicit memory to remember relatively more threat-related than non-threatening words) and to implicit memory bias (the tendency in implicit memory to produce more threat-related than neutral words). According to the theory, depression should be associated with negative memory bias but not with implicit memory bias, whereas anxiety should be associated with implicit memory bias but not with explicit memory bias. They claimed that the available evidence (most of which related to explicit memory rather than to implicit memory) tended to support their predictions.

As far as the development of anxiety disorders is concerned, the theory predicts that those high in trait anxiety are more vulnerable than those low in trait anxiety because of their cognitive processing of threat-related stimuli. However, this vulnerability will typically lead to psychopathology only when the level of state anxiety is high, because this increases the attentional bias towards threat. According to this version of the diathesis–stress model, a high level of trait anxiety forms the diathesis, and the stress is provided by life events or other factors producing high levels of state anxiety. More specifically, the strong attentional bias towards threat found in those high in both trait and state anxiety makes the environment appear very threatening, and this could play a part in raising anxiety to clinical levels.

Evaluation

The theory proposed by Williams et al. (1988) was a pioneering attempt to provide a coherent account of the role of cognitive processes and biases in trait anxiety and in clinical anxiety, as well as in depression. As such, it has had a considerable impact on subsequent theory and research. For example, it is now generally accepted that various cognitive biases are typically associated with anxiety in both normal and clinical populations. In addition, there is reasonable evidence that anxiety affects pre-attentive and attentional processing of threat-related stimuli more often than explicit memory for threat, whereas the opposite pattern is found with depression. These contrasting patterns can be accounted for to some extent by invoking the distinction between priming or integration and elaboration.

On the negative side, the theory is rather limited in various ways. First, it is unlikely that more than a small fraction of the processes involved in cognitive functioning can meaningfully be categorised as involving either priming or elaboration. It is claimed within the theory that anxiety affects priming rather than elaboration, but there is convincing evidence that anxiety influences the elaborative processes involved in the recall of threat-related information (e.g., Breck & Smith, 1983; Claeys, 1989; Kennedy & Craighead, 1988; Martin, Ward, & Clark, 1983; Mayo, 1983, 1989; Young & Martin, 1981).

Second, there is increasing evidence (discussed in more detail in Chapter 3) that the selective attentional and interpretive biases shown by high-anxious individuals do not depend on automatic processes in the simple fashion assumed by Williams et al. (1988). So far as selective attentional bias is concerned, there is evidence that it depends on postconscious automatic processes rather than on preconscious automatic processes (Fox, 1996). In other words, automatic processes underlying selective attentional bias may only produce a biasing effect when there has been prior activation of relevant knowledge stored in long-term memory. However, in unpublished research, Mogg and Bradley have found evidence of an anxiety-congruent attentional bias for masked threat stimuli that were not previously activated by supraliminal stimuli (Mogg, pers. comm.).

So far as interpretive bias is concerned, the evidence indicates that it probably does not depend on automatic processes (Calvo & Castillo, in press; Calvo, Eysenck, & Castillo, in press; Richards & French, 1992). More specifically, the processes underlying interpretive bias take longer to be completed than would be expected if they were automatic.

Third, the theory is limited in that it is assumed that the main cognitive difference between those high and low in trait anxiety is in the allocation of attentional resources to threatening environmental stimuli. In fact, there are also cognitive biases associated with the interpretation of ambiguous stimuli and the retrieval of threatening information (Eysenck, 1992). Furthermore, as is discussed in Chapter 3, those high in trait anxiety apply their cognitive biases to their own physiological activity, behaviour, and cognitions as well as to threat-related environmental stimuli.

Williams et al. (1997)

Williams, Watts, MacLeod, and Mathews (1997) have put forward a modified version of their earlier theory. In general, they argued that most of the research published since 1988 supports their theory, but that there were some findings which were difficult to account for within it. More specifically, the predicted implicit memory bias in anxiety is sometimes not found, and unexpectedly an explicit memory bias in anxiety has been reported in a number of studies.

According to Williams et al. (1997), the distinction between perceptual and conceptual processing is of more fundamental importance than the one between explicit and implicit. They pointed out that these two distinctions are often confounded: most tests of explicit memory involve conceptual processing, and most tests of implicit memory involve perceptual processing. More specifically, they argued in favour of the Multiple-Entry Memory (MEM) model proposed by Johnson and Multhaup (1992) and Johnson and Hirst (1993). According to this model, there are two perceptual subsystems designed to extract perceptual information from the environment, and there are two reflective subsystems for the manipulation of information, for the anticipation of events, and so on. The perceptual subsystems assign priority to processing threat-related stimuli in anxious individuals.

The reflective subsystems are used for elaborative processing. Of particular importance is the distinction between memorial elaboration (refreshing, rehearsing, reactivating, and retrieving) and non-memorial elaboration (noting, discovering, shifting, and initiating). As the terms imply, memorial elaboration typically enhances memory, whereas non-memorial elaboration does not. According to Williams et al. (1988), generalised anxiety disorder patients do not engage in elaborative processing of threatening stimuli, and so do not show a negative memory bias. However, it is hard to reconcile this viewpoint with the fact that excessive worrying about threatening events is the central symptom of generalised anxiety disorder. According to Williams et al. (1997), the worrying of generalised anxiety disorder patients represents non-memorial elaboration, and this can disrupt and prevent memorial elaboration. This provides a more plausible account of the phenomena than the earlier version of the theory.

Evaluation

The revised version of the Williams et al. (1988) theory is an improvement on the original theory. It is able to account for a wider range of experimental findings than the original theory, for two main reasons. First, it is a more flexible theory which includes additional theoretical assumptions. Second, it incorporates recent developments in theorising on cognitive processing. The revised version of the theory shares with the original version the strength of providing a plausible account of the different ways in which the cognitive system functions in anxiety and in depression.

On the negative side, it can be argued that some important issues are relatively neglected in both versions of the theory. For example, the emphasis is on ways in which the cognitive processes of normals high in trait anxiety and patients with the various anxiety disorders are similar, with little consideration of differences in cognitive processing in the various groups. Another issue that is not discussed fully concerns the relationship between the functioning of the cognitive system and the functioning of the behavioural and physiological systems. More generally, Williams et al. (1997) tend to treat the cognitive system in isolation from the other systems involved in anxiety and depression.

EYSENCK'S (1992) THEORY

Eysenck (1992) put forward a cognitive theory of trait anxiety. This theory had as its starting point the assumption that the most important function of anxiety is to facilitate the early detection of impending danger in potentially threatening environments. It follows from this assumption that individuals high and low in trait anxiety should differ in terms of their pre-attentive and attentional functioning, since it is the attentional system which is involved in threat detection.

This part of the overall theory is known as hypervigilance theory, and was originally proposed by Eysenck (1991b). According to hypervigilance theory, there are several ways in which individuals high in trait anxiety demonstrate hypervigilance. There is general hypervigilance or distractibility, "which is demonstrated by a propensity to attend to any task-irrelevant stimuli which are presented" (Eysenck, 1992, p.43). There is also specific hypervigilance, which involves a propensity to attend selectively to threat-related rather than neutral stimuli. This is commonly referred to as selective attentional bias. It was assumed that this bias applies to both social-threat and physical-threat stimuli. In addition, the hypervigilance of high-anxious individuals involves a high rate of environmental scanning, a broadening of attention prior to the detection of a threat-related or task-relevant stimulus, and a narrowing of attention when such a stimulus is being processed.

Eysenck, MacLeod, and Mathews (1987) argued that another important difference between those high and low in trait anxiety is in their interpretation of ambiguous stimuli and situations. More specifically, those high in trait anxiety have an interpretive bias which leads them to interpret ambiguous stimuli in a threatening fashion. This bias was assumed to apply to ambiguous stimuli having either a social-threat or physical-threat interpretation. Eysenck (1992) also assumed that high-anxious individuals possess a negative memory bias in explicit memory. This is defined as the tendency to remember disproportionately more threat-related than non-threatening information, and this bias was also assumed to apply to social-threat and physical-threat stimuli.

In sum, Eysenck (1992) proposed that individuals high in trait anxiety possess a range of cognitive biases which are applied to ambiguous or threat-related stimuli. These biases include selective attentional bias, interpretive bias, and negative memory bias. It was assumed that these biases would be greater when high trait-anxious individuals are stressed or high in state anxiety than when they are non-stressed or low in state anxiety.

Eysenck (1992) also attempted to relate trait anxiety to clinical anxiety. The key theoretical assumptions bridging the gap between normal and clinical anxiety were expressed in the following way by Eysenck (1992):

> Generalised anxiety disorder can appropriately be considered within the framework of the hypervigilance theory ... According to that theory, it is assumed that the attentional functioning of patients with generalised anxiety disorder resembles that of normal individuals with high trait anxiety. It is also assumed that hypervigilance forms part of a cognitive vulnerability factor for generalised anxiety disorder. Other cognitive processes and structures (e.g.,

those involved in learning and memory) may also contribute
to a cognitive vulnerability factor, but they are of subsidiary
importance to those involved in hypervigilance (p.45).

In addition to identifying the cognitive biases which characterise
generalised anxiety disorder patients, it is important to consider the
causality issue. In other words, why are these cognitive biases found in
generalised anxiety disorder patients? According to Eysenck (1992),
there are three possible reasons for the existence of these cognitive
biases. The first possibility is that the biases may simply reflect, or be
a secondary consequence of, the patient being in a clinically anxious
mood state. The second possibility is that the biases form part of a
manifest vulnerability factor, in which case they will be found in
vulnerable individuals regardless of their current state of anxiety. The
third possibility is that the biases are part of a latent vulnerability
factor, in which case they will be found in vulnerable individuals only
when they are in an anxious state.

The general research strategy for deciding among these three
possibilities involved collecting information on cognitive biases from
four groups: normals high in trait anxiety in non-stressed conditions;
normals high in trait anxiety in stressed conditions; current generalised
anxiety disorder patients; and recovered generalised anxiety disorder
patients. The predictions from the three positions identified above are
relatively straightforward. If the cognitive biases shown by current
generalised anxiety disorder patients reflect clinically anxious mood
state, then normals high in trait anxiety will not exhibit these biases,
and neither will recovered generalised anxiety disorder patients. If
there is a manifest vulnerability factor, then the cognitive biases of
current generalised anxiety disorder patients should be found in high
trait-anxious normals regardless of situational stress, and they should
also be found in patients who have recovered from generalised anxiety
disorder. Finally, if there is a latent vulnerability factor, then the
cognitive biases of current patients should also be found in high
trait-anxious normals when in a stressful situation, but should not be
found in high trait-anxious normals when they are not stressed or in
recovered generalised anxiety disorder patients.

Experimental evidence

Since the experimental evidence relevant to his theory was discussed at
length by Eysenck (1992), it would be superogatory to provide a detailed
account here. However, some of the evidence relating to the selective
attentional, interpretive, and negative memory biases will be discussed,
because these biases are of central importance, both to Eysenck's (1992)

theory and to the theory developed later in this book. The coverage here will focus mainly on research with normal groups, with research on clinical patients being discussed at more length in Chapter 5. In most of the studies discussed below, social-threat words (e.g., stupid; inept) and physical-threat words (e.g., paralysed; crippled) were presented. Unless otherwise stated, any biases were found with both types of threat-related stimuli. The attempt has been made to provide representative rather than comprehensive coverage of relevant recent studies.

Selective attentional bias

Eysenck et al. (1987) reported the first study on selective attentional bias in high-anxious subjects, with the full details being given in Eysenck (1991a). They used a dichotic listening task, in which pairs of words were presented concurrently, one to each ear. Each word presented to the attended ear had to be shadowed (i.e., repeated back aloud), but the words on the unattended ear were to be ignored. All of the words on the unattended ear were affectively neutral, whereas the words on the attended ear consisted of a mixture of neutral, socially threatening, and physically threatening words. A tone was sometimes presented to one ear very shortly after a pair of words had been presented, and the subjects were instructed to respond to this tone as rapidly as possible. It was assumed that the faster the speed of responding to the tone, the greater was the allocation of attentional resources to that ear. Subjects completed the Facilitation–Inhibition Scale (Ullmann, 1962), which correlates highly with standard measures of trait anxiety.

As can be seen in Fig. 1.1, the facilitators (i.e., those high in trait anxiety) attended closely to the ear at which a threatening word had just been presented, as revealed by their rapid responding to the tone when it followed a threatening word to the same ear, coupled with rather slow responding when it followed a threatening word to the other ear. Inhibitors (those low in trait anxiety) had the opposite pattern of responding, indicating that they avoided devoting attention to the ear on which a threatening word had just been presented.

These findings have been replicated and extended in a number of subsequent studies. MacLeod and Mathews (1988) used a visual analogue of the auditory task used by Eysenck et al. (1987). They found that high and low trait-anxious students had no selective attentional bias towards examination-relevant stress words well before an important examination. However, there were significant effects in the week before the examination. High trait-anxious subjects showed selective attentional bias for the examination-related threatening

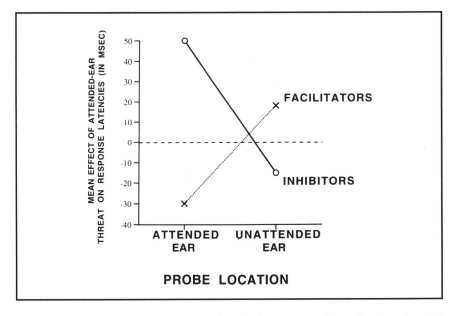

FIG. 1.1. Mean differences in probe reaction time between conditions (threat and neutral attended word) as a function of facilitation–inhibition and ear to which probe was presented. Data from Eysenck (1991a).

words, whereas low trait-anxious subjects showed the opposite bias. Further support for the notion that the selective attentional bias depends interactively on trait and state anxiety was obtained using the same task by Broadbent and Broadbent (1988).

Interpretive bias

Interpretive bias was investigated by Eysenck et al. (1987). Homophones having a threat-related and a neutral interpretation (e.g., die, dye; pain, pane) were presented auditorily, and the subjects were instructed to write down each word as it was presented. There was a significant correlation coefficient of +0.60 between trait anxiety and the number of threat-related homophone interpretations, suggesting that individuals high in trait anxiety possess an interpretive bias.

Byrne and Eysenck (1993) used the homophone task with groups of varying levels of trait anxiety. The high trait-anxious group produced more threatening homophone interpretations than did the medium or low trait-anxious groups. MacLeod and Cohen (1993) studied interpretive bias by recording the length of time taken to read a continuation sentence that followed an ambiguous sentence. They confirmed the existence of an interpretive bias in high trait-anxious individuals.

Russo, Patterson, Roberson, Stevenson, and Upward (1996) have cast doubt on the interpretation of the above findings. They replicated the finding that high trait-anxious subjects have an interpretive bias for threat-related homophones. However, they also found that high trait anxiety was associated with a tendency to select the emotional interpretation of homophones even when this interpretation was not threat-related. They concluded that "cognitive interpretive biases in anxiety may not be specific to threatening information ... but, rather, that the emotional value of target items is an important determinant in inducing processing bias" (p.219). For reasons which are unclear, they did not refer to the earlier study by Byrne and Eysenck (1993), in which high trait-anxious subjects showed a bias for threat-related homophones but not for homophones having a positive emotional interpretation.

Calvo and Eysenck (1995) investigated interpretive bias in a study in which ambiguous sentences were followed by words which had to be named as rapidly as possible. The crucial condition was one in which a possible ego-threat interpretation of the sentence was confirmed or disconfirmed by the subsequent sentence. Only high-anxious subjects had significantly slower naming latencies to disconfirming words than to confirming ones, indicating that they tended to interpret the ambiguous sentences in an ego-threatening fashion (see Fig. 1.2). However, they did not show an interpretive bias with ambiguous sentences having a possible physical-threat interpretation (see Fig. 1.2).

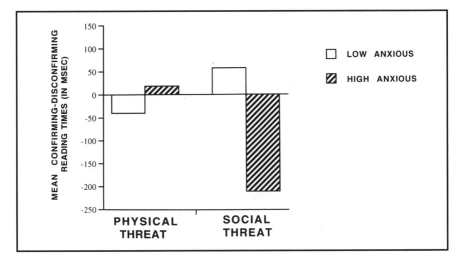

FIG. 1.2. Mean differences in reading time between confirmatory and disconfirmatory conditions for the last word of disambiguating sentences as a function of test anxiety and sentence type (physical threat vs. social threat). Data from Calvo and Eysenck (1995).

MacLeod (1990) discussed three studies in which he investigated the extent to which interpretive bias depends on the prevailing level of state anxiety or arousal. In two of these studies, the homophone task used by Eysenck et al. (1987) was performed under normal conditions or under high arousal created by physical exercise. In both studies, there was an interaction between trait anxiety and arousal, with high arousal increasing the tendency of high trait-anxious subjects to produce threatening interpretations of homophones, but decreasing the tendency of low trait-anxious subjects to do so.

In his third study, MacLeod (1990) presented a series of ambiguous sentences, each of which was followed by a word strongly associated with one of the possible interpretations. The subjects' task was to name this final word as rapidly as possible, it being assumed that naming would be faster when its meaning was congruent with their interpretation of the preceding sentence than when it was not. Those high in trait anxiety were faster to name words related to threatening interpretations if they were high in state anxiety than if they were low in state anxiety. In contrast, low trait-anxious subjects exhibited the opposite pattern. Thus, MacLeod (1990) obtained strong evidence that the interpretive bias depends interactively on trait anxiety and on the current level of state anxiety or arousal.

Negative memory bias

There have been several studies of negative memory bias in high-anxious subjects. In order to demonstrate that negative memory bias is due to anxiety, it is necessary to rule out the alternative possibility that it is due to depression. Measures of anxiety and of depression usually correlate highly with each other, and there is a large body of evidence indicating the existence of a negative memory bias associated with depression (see Blaney, 1986, for a review)

Negative memory bias for recall of negative trait words by those high in neuroticism was reported by Young and Martin (1981) and by Martin, Ward, and Clark (1983), with a self-referent task being used in both studies. In addition, Martin et al. (1983) discovered that high-neuroticism scorers did not have a negative memory bias when the encoding task involved deciding whether the trait words described a "typical undergraduate from your college". This finding indicates that the negative memory bias found with the self-referent task did not occur simply because those high in neuroticism had greater familiarity with the negative trait words. Martin et al. (1983) also found that the negative memory bias was associated with neuroticism rather than depression.

Kennedy and Craighead (1988) obtained estimates of the amount of positive and negative feedback received during a learning task from anxious and non-anxious groups. The groups did not differ in their estimates of positive feedback. However, in the first of two experiments the anxious subjects estimated the amount of negative feedback as greater than did the non-anxious subjects, even though it was actually the same. An important feature of this research was that the two groups did not differ in their level of depression.

Claeys (1989) conducted a study of incidental recall in subjects high and low in social anxiety. The high-anxious subjects recalled more self-descriptive unlikeable trait words than did the low-anxious subjects. However, the two groups did not differ in their recall of likeable trait words.

One of the most important studies on negative memory bias in anxiety was reported by Breck and Smith (1983). Their subjects, who were high or low in social anxiety, decided which of a set of positive and negative trait adjectives were self-descriptive. State anxiety was manipulated by instructing the subjects that the experiment would or would not be followed by social interaction. On the subsequent unexpected test of recall, there was a highly significant interaction between social anxiety and the valence (positive or negative) of the trait adjectives. In this interaction, a higher proportion of negative self-descriptive adjectives was recalled by the socially anxious subjects, but the opposite was found for recall of the positive self-descriptive adjectives. It is important to note that the interaction was significant only when the subjects had been informed that the experiment would be followed by social interaction. In other words, there seemed to be an interactive relationship between trait and state anxiety.

Additional relevant evidence was reported by Bradley and Mogg (1994) and by Bradley, Mogg, Galbraith, and Perrett (1993). It was found in both studies that negative memory bias was determined interactively by neuroticism and by current negative mood.

Eysenck (1992) discussed other studies in which there was no evidence of negative memory bias in individuals high in trait anxiety or neuroticism. Eysenck and Byrne (1994) tried to clarify the conditions in which high trait-anxious individuals demonstrate an implicit memory bias. They made use of the distinction between data-driven processes (those triggered directly by external stimuli) and conceptually driven processes (those initiated by past experience, knowledge, or expectations). According to Roediger and Blaxton (1987), explicit memory depends mainly on conceptually driven processes. Roediger and Blaxton (1987) also assumed that long-term memory is better when there is a match between the type of processing at the time of learning and the type of processing required by the memory test, than when there is a mismatch. Eysenck and Byrne (1994) found that high trait-anxious individuals showed an explicit memory bias in free recall when the encoding task depended mainly on conceptually driven processes (each list word had to be generated from a cue). However, they did not do so when the encoding task depended mainly on data-driven processes (each word was simply read by the subject) (see Fig. 1.3).

Implicit memory bias

In recent years, there has been greatly increased interest in the distinction between implicit memory and explicit memory (Eysenck & Keane, 1995). These terms were defined in the following way by Schachter (1987): "Implicit memory is revealed when previous experiences facilitate performance on a task that does not require conscious or intentional recollection of those experiences; explicit memory is revealed when performance on a task requires conscious recollection of previous experiences" (p.501). All of the studies on negative memory bias discussed in the previous section were concerned with explicit memory rather than implicit memory. The existence of a negative memory bias in explicit memory does not necessarily imply

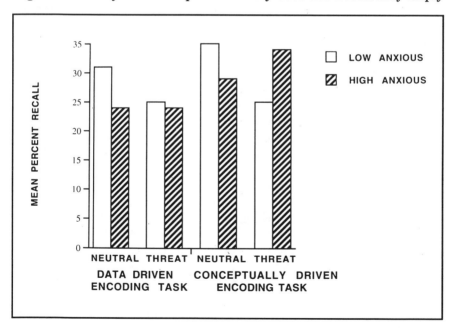

FIG. 1.3. Free recall as a function of trait anxiety, encoding task, and word valence (threat vs. neutral). Data from Eysenck and Byrne (1994).

that a similar bias exists in implicit memory, because different processes are involved in the two kinds of memory. For example, amnesic patients are typically greatly impaired on tests of explicit memory, but perform at normal levels on tests of implicit memory (see Eysenck & Keane, 1995).

The first study on anxiety and implicit memory bias was by Mathews, Mogg, May, and Eysenck (1989), using groups of generalised anxiety disorder patients, recovered generalised anxiety disorder patients, and normal controls. Only the current patients exhibited an implicit memory bias. However, this finding was not replicated by Mathews, Mogg, Kentish, and Eysenck (1995).

Additional analysis of the data obtained by Mathews et al. (1989) indicated that there was no relationship between trait anxiety and implicit memory bias. In contrast, Richards and French (1991) found an implicit memory bias in high trait-anxious subjects (but not those low in trait anxiety) when a self-referenced imagery task was performed at the time of acquisition. However, there was no evidence for an implicit memory bias when the list words were simply read at the time of learning. Nugent and Mineka (1994) failed to demonstrate any implicit memory bias for threat-related material in high trait-anxious subjects in two separate experiments.

Eysenck and Byrne (1994) studied implicit memory bias on a word-completion task using the same data-driven and conceptually driven encoding tasks used to investigate free recall. Roediger and Blaxton (1987) argued that implicit memory typically depends on conceptually driven processes. This led to the prediction that high-anxious subjects would show an implicit memory bias when the same type of processing was required by the encoding task. In fact, however, high trait-anxious individuals had an implicit memory bias regardless of the processes required by the encoding task.

Evaluation

One of the most fundamental assumptions made by Eysenck (1992) was that individual differences in trait anxiety depend at least in part on various cognitive biases. There was reasonably convincing evidence in support of this assumption in 1992, and since then much additional empirical support has been forthcoming. Thus, individual differences in the functioning of the cognitive system are clearly of major importance in the attempt to understand how those high in trait anxiety differ from those low in trait anxiety. Furthermore, the main cognitive biases assumed by Eysenck (1992) to be present in those high in trait anxiety (i.e., selective attentional bias; interpretive bias; negative memory bias) have been reported repeatedly.

The theory proposed by Eysenck (1992) did not explicitly have its origins in any broader theory of emotion. However, the general theoretical approach is consistent with Lazarus's (1966, 1991) cognitive appraisal theory. According to that theory, emotional experience depends on a process of cognitive appraisal applied to the situation. Initially, there is primary appraisal, in which an evaluative judgement is made as to whether or not the situation is dangerous. Then there is secondary appraisal, in which the situation is considered in relation to the individual's available resources (e.g., coping strategies). Finally, there is a process of reappraisal, which is activated when actions have been initiated and are starting to affect the threatening situation.

Within that framework, it could be argued that selective attentional bias and interpretive bias both affect the processes involved in cognitive appraisal. More specifically, the fact that individuals high in trait anxiety selectively attend to threat-related aspects of the situation and that they interpret ambiguous aspects of the situation as threatening means that their cognitive appraisal of most situations will be more threatening than that of individuals low in trait anxiety.

There is at least one fundamental limitation of Lazarus' theoretical approach. He assumed that cognitive appraisal is of central importance in determining emotional experience, physiological activity, and action tendencies and behaviour. As a consequence, the natural assumption from his theory is that there would be reasonable agreement or concordance among these three different response systems. In fact, a lack of concordance is typically found. For example, Craske and Craig (1984) studied competent pianists under the stressful condition of performing in public. In essence, they discovered that measures belonging to the same response system mostly correlated with each other, whereas measures from different response systems did not.

As was discussed earlier in the chapter, there is generally very little agreement between self-report measures of anxiety and physiological measures (see Fahrenberg, 1992). There is consistent empirical evidence for a significant association between self-reported and rated trait anxiety or neuroticism, which indicates some agreement or concordance between the verbal and behavioural response systems. However, the strength of the association is usually relatively modest. McCrae (1982) reported a correlation coefficient of +0.47 between self-reported neuroticism and spouses' ratings for neuroticism. White and Nias (1994) compared self-report and relative (parent or spouse) ratings of neuroticism on the Eysenck Personality Questionnaire. There was a correlation coefficient of +0.48 for female subjects, and one of +0.37 for male subjects.

As Eysenck (1992) pointed out, "A complete theory of anxiety would need to account for the dynamic interrelationships among these systems (the three response systems), and in so doing would explain the typical failures of concordance of response measures across systems" (p.3). Eysenck (1992) did not do this, in part because failures of concordance cannot readily be explained within a Lazarus-type approach.

There is another problem with the general theoretical approach adopted by Lazarus (1966, 1991) and by Eysenck (1992). It is assumed that emotional experience is determined primarily by cognitive appraisal of the situation. The weakness in this assumption is that it de-emphasises the possibility that the experience of anxiety may depend on internal sources of information (e.g., perception of one's own physiological activity) as well as on external sources of information. This issue is discussed at greater length in Chapter 2.

One final problem with the theory put forward by Eysenck (1992) will be addressed. It was pointed out earlier in the chapter that there are good reasons for sub-dividing low scorers on trait anxiety into separate low-anxious and repressor groups. In spite of the comparably low trait-anxiety scores of the two groups, repressors are typically much more physiologically aroused than the low-anxious in moderately stressful situations (Weinberger, 1990; Weinberger et al., 1979). In Eysenck's (1992) theory, however, these two groups were not distinguished. In other words, no account was taken of the heterogeneity within the group of low scorers on trait anxiety.

WEINBERGER'S REPRESSOR THEORY

The new theory of trait anxiety which is put forward in Chapter 3 has been influenced in various ways by the important theoretical and research contributions of Weinberger (e.g., 1990). In the first place, his proposal that those scoring low on trait anxiety should be divided into separate repressor and low-anxious groups has simply been incorporated into the new theory. Second, an especially important part of Weinberger's contribution is the explanation that it provides for some of the failures of concordance among the different response systems involved in anxiety. More specifically, the notion that some of these concordance failures are due to the coping strategies adapted by repressors has influenced the new theory.

The new theory has also been influenced by Weinberger's views on the processes used by repressors. According to Weinberger (1990):

> Repressors are likely to use a variety of strategies to avoid awareness of affects and impulses that are incompatible with their self-images. They should not only repress threatening memories ... but also recruit several related neurotic-level defences ... such as intellectualisation and denial. Paradoxically, repressors' preoccupation with avoiding awareness of anxiety may interfere with effective coping and actually heighten behavioural and physiological indications of distress (p.343).

In spite of the above similarities between the new theory and that of Weinberger, there are a number of important differences. First, while Weinberger has done much to elucidate the characteristics of repressors, he has not considered in detail the processes used by high-anxious individuals. In contrast, much of the emphasis within the new theory is on the various cognitive biases exhibited by the high-anxious. Second, the new theory is based on a reasonably explicit theory of emotion which attempts to identify the major sources of information leading to the experience of anxiety. In contrast, Weinberger's repressor theory is not related in a coherent fashion to any theory of emotion.

Third, although Weinberger (1990) discussed some of the cognitive processes which might be used by repressors, he did not systematically identify those processes, nor did he specify clearly the kinds of information to which the distinctive cognitive processes of repressors are applied. In contrast, it is assumed in the new theory that the repressors' cognitive biases may apply to four different sources of information: environmental stimuli; their own action tendencies and behaviour; their own physiological activity; and information stored in long-term memory.

SUMMARY AND CONCLUSIONS

Anxiety is of importance in theories of emotion, in personality theories, and in clinical theories. In contrast to most previous theories, the unified theory put forward in this book is designed to integrate the areas of emotion, personality, and clinical psychology within a common theoretical framework. The origins of this new theory lie in research and theory on the personality dimension of trait anxiety or neuroticism, and this is the main focus of the chapter.

The physiological approach to trait anxiety or neuroticism was proposed by H.J. Eysenck (1967) and by Gray (1982). This approach has been partially successful, in that it has established the importance of genetic factors and the likelihood that the septo-hippocampal system plays a role in determining individual differences in trait anxiety. However, this approach neglects environmental influences on trait anxiety, and does not readily account for some of the phenomena (e.g., the multi-dimensional nature of trait anxiety; changes in trait anxiety over time).

More recently, cognitive approaches to trait anxiety have been proposed by Williams et al. (1988, 1997), and by Eysenck (1992). These approaches have succeeded in establishing consistent differences in various cognitive biases between individuals high and low in trait anxiety. However, these approaches have shed little light on the important issue of the frequent lack of concordance among self-report, behavioural, and physiological measures of anxiety. Weinberger's (1990) repressor theory, with its crucial distinction between low-anxious individuals and repressors, provides a partial account of failures of concordance. More specifically, he argued that repressors have much lower self-reported than physiological anxiety because of their defensive coping style.

In sum, the available evidence indicates that a satisfactory theoretical account of trait anxiety must include a detailed consideration of the functioning of the cognitive system. Previous theories have only had limited success in this direction, which is why a new theory of trait anxiety is presented in Chapter 3.

CHAPTER TWO

A four-factor theory of anxiety

INTRODUCTION

Numerous theories of emotion have been proposed over the years, and they differ considerably in terms of their focus. It would not be possible to provide a detailed account of all of these theories in this chapter. What will be done instead will be to consider some of the key theoretical controversies within the field of emotion. After that, a new theory of emotion of particular relevance to anxiety is put forward.

It is possible to identify two diametrically opposed viewpoints concerning the relationship between physiological activity and emotional experience. One viewpoint is that physiological activity, especially heightened arousal or activity of the sympathetic nervous system, generally or always has a causal role in determining emotional experience. The other extreme viewpoint is that physiological activity does not play a causal role at all in producing emotional experience. There are two somewhat different versions of this viewpoint. According to a commonsensical perspective, physiological activity is caused by emotional experience (e.g., we feel frightened, and this makes our heart beat faster). According to a somewhat different perspective (e.g., Lazarus, 1991), physiological arousal and emotional experience occur essentially in parallel, with neither having a significant impact on the other.

The James–Lange theory of emotion is the best-known approach based on the notion that emotional experience depends on prior physiological arousal. The central thrust of this theory was expressed in the following terms by William James (1898):

> The bodily changes follow directly the perception of the exciting fact, and ... our feeling of the same changes as they occur IS the emotion. Common sense says, we lose our fortune, are sorry and weep; we meet a bear, are frightened and run; we are insulted by a rival, are angry and strike. The hypothesis here to be defended says that this order of sequence is incorrect ... and that the more rational statement is that we feel sorry because we cry, angry because we strike, afraid because we tremble, and not that we cry, strike, or tremble because we are sorry, angry, fearful, as the case may be (p.449).

The James–Lange theory has been regarded as inadequate for a long time. For example, it is stated within the theory that an emotional stimulus produces a series of bodily changes. However, remarkably little is said about the processes involved. Another difficulty for the theory is that we often seem to experience emotion before the bodily changes have occurred, rather than afterwards as the theory predicts.

Another major criticism of the James–Lange theory concerns its assumption that there is a distinctive pattern of bodily changes associated with each and every emotional state. According to Parkinson (1994), "One of the main problems with James's theory ... is that the physiological changes that accompany a wide variety of emotions are actually very similar, and certainly not distinct enought to differentiate widely contrasting subjective states such as euphoria and anger" (p.495).

This criticism is generally valid. However, some evidence for distinctive patterns is available in the fact that smiling is associated with happiness, crying with misery, and running away with anxiety. There is also evidence that emotions differ in terms of autonomic activity. Ekman, Levenson, and Friesen (1983) asked their subjects to recreate the facial expressions of anger, fear, sadness, happiness, surprise, and disgust. Anger, fear, and sadness all produced much greater increases in heart rate than did happiness, surprise, or disgust. Hand temperature increased considerably with anger, and it increased slightly with happiness, but it decreased with disgust. The existence of differential physiological patterning among emotions does not, of course, demonstrate that distinctive emotional feelings depend on such physiological differences.

SCHACHTER'S TWO-FACTOR THEORY

One of the most influential theories of emotion was put forward by Schachter and Singer (1962) and Schachter (1964). In some ways, their two-factor theory can be regarded as a development and extension of the James–Lange theory. As can be seen in Fig. 2.1, emotional experience depends on three factors. First, the situation must be interpreted as being an emotional one. Second, and reminiscent of the James–Lange theory, there must be a state of physiological arousal. Third, the emotional situation must be perceived to be the cause of the physiological arousal. If any of these three factors is missing, then little or no emotion will be experienced.

The major problem with testing the theory is that the different factors contributing to emotional experience are difficult to disentangle. In everyday life, physiological arousal is normally attributed to an emotional situation, and this attribution is relatively direct and automatic. In order to test the theory, Schachter and Singer (1962) attempted to arrange matters so that arousal could plausibly be attributed to more than one cause. Some subjects were injected with the stimulant drug adrenaline, which increases the level of physiological arousal. Some of these subjects were informed accurately that the injection would produce arousal, whereas others were misinformed that the injection would have no side-effects or side-effects unrelated to arousal. Other subjects were injected with a saline placebo. The subjects were then put into a situation designed to provide a plausible context for anger or euphoria.

It follows from two-factor theory that those subjects experiencing high arousal (those injected with adrenaline) who were likely to

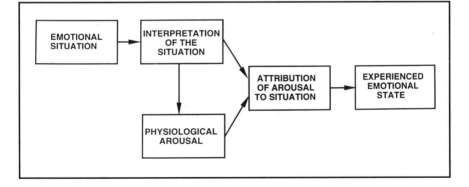

FIG. 2.1. The theory of emotion put forward by Schachter and Singer (1962) and Schachter (1964).

attribute this arousal to the situation (those misinformed about the effects of the injection) should have had the greatest emotional reactions. In contrast, subjects who were injected with adrenaline but informed accurately about its effects should have experienced little emotion because they should have attributed their arousal to the injection. In fact, the findings produced only modest support for the two-factor theory.

Some of the evidence used by Schachter and Singer (1962) to support their theory came from Maranon (1924). In his study, the subjects were injected with adrenaline. Since they understood that the symptoms they subsequently experienced were produced by the drug rather than by the situation, they should not have experienced any emotion. When the subjects were asked how they felt, 71% simply reported their physical symptoms without any emotional overtones. Most of the remaining subjects reported "as-if" or "cold" emotions. Thus, the findings seemed to be consistent with the prediction from two-factor theory.

Later studies resembling that of Maranon (1924) have produced findings suggesting that individuals can experience much emotion even when they know that their bodily sensations are caused by a drug. For example, van der Molen, van den Hout, Vroemen, Lousberg, and Griez (1986) investigated the effects of sodium lactate, which produces many of the symptoms associated with panic attacks. Those subjects who were told that the infusion might cause unpleasant bodily sensations similar to those experienced during periods of anxiety reported high levels of anxious tension after having the sodium lactate. In other words, a substantial amount of emotion was experienced even though the subjects presumably attributed their internal state to the sodium lactate rather than to the situation. Similar findings were reported by Clark and Hemsley (1982).

General evaluation

This is not the place to provide an exhaustive evaluation of the two-factor theory, especially since this has been done very competently by Reisenzein (1983). It seems reasonable to conclude that the theory is interesting and important. For example, Parkinson (1995) argued that, "Schachter's approach inspired a large body of valuable research by proposing that emotion is far more flexible than straightforward physiological theories seemed to imply" (p.113). However, it is generally assumed that the empirical support for Schachter's theory is weak. According to Parkinson (1994), "If Schachter's theory is correct, then it is possible to change the emotions that people experience simply by modifying the way that they interpret their arousal reactions; in a famous experiment, this is exactly what Schachter and Singer (1962) tried to do ... these predicted differences in emotional experience failed to emerge as clearly as Schachter and Singer might have hoped ... Subsequent attempts to replicate the study have been similarly inconclusive" (p.498). Reisenzein (1983) came to a rather similar conclusion: "The frequently weak effects of arousal manipulations on the intensity of emotional states suggest ... that beyond the point of zero arousal, the link between arousal and emotion is much weaker than implied by Schachter's theory" (p.258).

The conclusions of Parkinson (1994) and of Reisenzein (1983) may be appropriate in general terms. However, they did not consider in much detail the possibility that manipulations of arousal may have more impact on the intensity of some emotional states than on others. More specifically, some negative emotional states (such as anxiety) may be more affected by manipulating physiological arousal than are some positive emotional states (e.g., contentment). For example, Maslach (1979) produced physiological arousal in some of her subjects under hypnosis, and ensured that they were unaware of the cause of their arousal by means of post-hypnotic suggestions of amnesia. These subjects experienced more negative emotional states than those subjects who did not experience arousal or those who had no post-hypnotic suggestions. What is especially notable is that these findings were obtained regardless of whether subjects were placed in a situation designed to produce anger or one designed to produce euphoria.

Similar findings were reported by Marshall and Zimbardo (1979). They injected some of their subjects with the stimulant drug adrenaline, and tried to make the subjects misattribute their high level of arousal to the euphoric situation in which they were placed. In fact, these subjects actually experienced more negative feelings than control subjects, and this effect was greater with larger doses of adrenaline.

More evidence that arousal manipulations affect some negative mood states more than some positive ones was reported by Reisenzein and Gattinger (1982). Their subjects were exposed to a mood-induction procedure designed to induce either a positive or a negative mood state. Half of them were physiologically aroused because of prior physical exercise. The findings of most relevance relate to the control subjects, who did not have a large mirror in front of them during the mood-induction procedure. Among these subjects, high physiological arousal increased mood negativity in the negative mood-induction condition, but it had no effect on mood in the positive mood-induction condition.

There are grounds for arguing that Schachter's two-factor theory is more applicable to anxiety (and perhaps anger) than to some other negative emotions (e.g., depression). The role of physiological arousal in emotion is emphasised in two-factor theory, but there is evidence that physiological arousal is of more relevance to anxiety than to depression. Clark and Watson (1991) put forward a tripartite model of anxiety and depression. According to this model, anxiety is characterised mainly by general distress and by somatic anxiety (e.g., trembling; shaky hands; racing or pounding heart; dry mouth; cold or sweaty hands). In contrast, depression is characterised by general distress and by anhedonia or a lack of positive emotional experiences (e.g., lacking energy; feeling that nothing is enjoyable; having no fun in life).

Watson, Weber, Assenheimer, Clark, Strauss, and McCormick (1995) made use of the Mood and Anxiety Symptom Questionnaire, which was explicitly designed to provide scales assessing general distress, anxious arousal, and anhedonia. They found in several groups of subjects that anxious arousal was more associated with anxiety than with depression, and that the anhedonia scale was more associated with depression than with anxiety. The fact that anxious arousal is of much more central relevance to anxiety than to depression suggests that two-factor theory is more likely to account for the experience of anxiety than of depression. Accordingly, we turn to studies on two-factor theory that have focused on anxiety.

Anxiety research

Convincing evidence that experienced anxiety can be affected by an arousal manipulation was obtained by Gerdes (1979). All of her subjects received a local anaesthetic prior to undergoing dental surgery. In the crucial condition, an arousal-inducing dose of adrenaline was included as part of the anaesthetic, but the subjects were told nothing about the source of the arousal. As can be seen in Fig. 2.2, these subjects (males only) experienced more anxiety than subjects who did not receive any adrenaline. They also experienced more anxiety than subjects injected with adrenaline who were told that any arousal which they experienced would probably be due to the anaesthetic.

Schachter and Singer (1962) assumed that actual physiological arousal is needed in order for emotion to be experienced. However, Valins (1966) argued that what is important is the perception or cognition that one is aroused. Actual and perceived physiological activity are generally positively correlated, but often only fairly modestly. Pennebaker (1982) discussed several studies which addressed this issue, concluding that, "the mean between-subjects symptom-physiology measure correlations have hovered around +0.30" (p.60). He also reviewed within-subjects' studies, and concluded that the accuracy of perceived physiological functioning was also low in such studies.

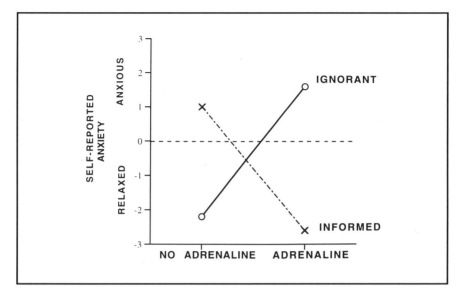

FIG. 2.2. Self-reported anxiety as a function of drug condition (adrenaline vs. no adrenaline) and instructions (ignorant vs. informed). Data from Gerdes (1979).

In order to adjudicate between the views of Schachter and Singer (1962) and Valins (1966), it is possible to manipulate perceived arousal independently of actual arousal. In a study by Borkovec, Wall, and Stone (1974), speech-anxious subjects received false feedback about their heart rate during a speech. Some of them were informed that their heart rate had increased, whereas others were told either that it had decreased or that it had not changed. Borkovec et al. (1974) discovered that those subjects told that their heart rate had increased had higher self-reported anxiety, more overt signs of anxiety, and less fluent speech than the other two groups when giving their next speech. These findings depended on perceived rather than actual arousal, because actual heart rate did not vary across conditions.

Perceived arousal was also manipulated independently of actual arousal in the study by Gerdes (1979) discussed earlier. False feedback was provided after heart rate and blood pressure had been measured. One-third of the subjects were informed that they were highly aroused, another one-third were told they were unaroused, and the remainder were given no feedback. This manipulation had no effect on those subjects who were told that their state of arousal was probably attributable to the anaesthetic, but it had clear-cut effects on subjects who were uninformed about the source of the arousal. Those given feedback that they were highly aroused reported much higher levels of anxiety than those told that they were unaroused and those given no feedback. As with the study by Borkovec et al. (1974), the absence of actual differences in physiological arousal among the conditions indicates that the findings depended on perceived rather than actual arousal.

Evidence apparently indicating that actual physiological feedback is important for emotion was reported by Hohmann (1966). He studied people who had suffered damage to the spinal cord, as a consequence of which they had lost some of their ability to experience autonomic arousal. The patients reported reduced emotional intensity, especially those with the most severe spinal damage. In the words of one of the patients, "It's sort of cold anger...it just doesn't have the heat to it that it used to. It's a mental kind of anger" (p.151).

More recent studies have not replicated Hohmann's (1966) findings. Bermond, Nieuwenhuyse, Fasotti, and Schwerman (1991) found that most of their patients with spinal damage reported increased rather than decreased intensity of emotions. Rather surprisingly, the patients even reported that the somatic symptoms of emotion remained at the same level after injury. This suggests that perceived physiological arousal can influence emotional experience even when actual autonomic feedback is absent.

It is important to note that the processes involved in the studies by Borkovec et al. (1974) and by Gerdes (1979) on the one hand, and by Bermond et al. (1991) may not be as similar as is implied here (Parkinson, pers. comm.). Borkovec et al. (1974) and Gerdes (1979) found that telling subjects that they were aroused increased their self-reported emotional states, whereas Bermond et al. (1991) demonstrated that the feeling of emotion derives in part from perceived bodily feedback.

Conclusions

One of the crucial issues is whether physiological arousal can make an independent contribution to experienced emotion. The evidence indicates clearly that the extent to which this is possible varies from emotion to emotion. Positive emotional states are rarely increased by increasing the level of physiological arousal, although sexual excitement is a possible exception. In contrast, negative emotional states, especially anxiety, can be enhanced when the level of physiological arousal is increased independently of the situation (e.g., Borkovec et al., 1974; Gerdes, 1979; Marshall & Zimbardo, 1979; Maslach, 1979). However, it is important to distinguish between actual physiological arousal and perceived physiological arousal. The evidence indicates that experienced levels of anxiety depend more on perceived than on actual physiological arousal (e.g., Borkovec et al., 1974; Gerdes, 1979).

In sum, the two-factor theory is reasonably successful when applied to the emotion of anxiety, but is less applicable to positive emotional states. However, as we will see later in the chapter, the two-factor theory provides a rather limited view of the factors causing anxiety.

COGNITIVE APPRAISAL

According to Parkinson (1994), "The first and most central factor in the causation of emotion relates to the evaluation of some situation or event, based on the process of appraisal. Appraisal theorists suggest that emotions are rarely direct reactions to stimulus qualities. Rather what gives an object emotional impact is its relevance to the individual's personal concerns" (p.493).

Lazarus (e.g., 1966, 1982, 1991) is the most prominent appraisal theorist. According to his theory, cognitive appraisal of situations can be subdivided into three more specific forms of appraisal. First, there is primary appraisal, in which the situation is regarded as being positive, stressful, or irrelevant to well-being. Second, there is secondary appraisal, in which account is taken of the resources which the individual has available to cope with the situation. Third, there is reappraisal, in which the primary and secondary appraisals are modified if necessary.

A more detailed version of this appraisal theory was put forward by Smith and Lazarus (1993). They argued that there are six appraisal components, two of which involve primary appraisal and four of which involve secondary appraisal. The two primary appraisal components are motivational relevance (related to personal commitments?) and motivational congruence (consistent with the individual's goals?). The four secondary appraisal components are as follows: accountability (who deserves the credit or blame?); problem-focused coping potential (can the situation be resolved?); emotion-focused coping potential (can feelings about the situation be handled?); and future expectancy (how likely is it that the situation will change?). Within this framework, anxiety possesses the primary appraisal components of motivational relevance and motivational incongruence, and the secondary appraisal component of low or uncertain emotion-focused coping potential.

Some of the key evidence was provided by Lazarus and his colleagues during the the 1960s. The crucial ingredient in their studies was to study the effects on emotional reports and behaviour of systematically manipulating subjects' cognitive appraisals of films. For example, Speisman, Lazarus, Mordkoff, and Davison (1964) showed a film of a Stone Age ritual in which adolescent boys had their penises deeply cut.

They found that the physiological and psychological stress reactions to the film were reduced when the accompanying soundtrack encouraged the subjects to use denial (the film did not show a painful operation) or intellectualisation (consider the film from the perspective of an anthropologist viewing strange native customs).

Further support for Lazarus's cognitive appraisal theory was reported by Koriat, Melkman, Averill, and Lazarus (1972) and by Holmes and Houston (1974). In the study by Koriat et al. (1972), subjects watched an industrial safety film after being given involvement or detachment instructions. Self-reported emotional arousal was considerably lower after the detachment instructions. In the study by Holmes and Houston (1974), self-reported anxiety to threatened electric shocks was lower when the shocks were re-interpreted as interesting new physiological sensations than when no specific interpretation was provided.

Evaluation

In spite of the impact of appraisal theory, its empirical support is less secure than is generally assumed. One reason for this is that it is often very difficult to assess an individual's appraisals, because they may not be accessible to consciousness. In the words of Lazarus (1991):

> Appraisal implies nothing about rationality, deliberateness, or consciousness. A central postulate for dealing with this issue is to say that there is more than one way of knowing, and in the generation of an emotion these ways may be in conflict or may be contributed to simultaneously by two kinds of appraisal processes — one that operates automatically without awareness or volitional control, and another that is conscious, deliberate, and volitional (p.169).

It is not clear whether even such a broad conceptualisation of cognitive appraisal can accommodate findings such as those of Le Doux (1990). He found that there is a direct neural pathway from the thalamus to the amygdala. This pathway bypasses the normal route via the cortex in eliciting conditioned fear. Presumably no appraisal or extremely limited appraisal is possible on this direct pathway.

Parkinson and Manstead (1992) argued that there are several problems of interpretation with studies such as the one by Speisman et al. (1964). In essence, the soundtrack manipulations may not have had a direct impact on the appraisal process. Changing the soundtrack changed the stimulus information presented to the subjects, and different soundtracks may have influenced the direction of attention rather than the interpretive process itself. In addition, the films used by Speisman et al. (1964) and by others may have been considerably more ambiguous than everyday social situations. As a consequence, it may be much harder to alter emotional reactions in everyday life than with the films used in laboratory research.

According to Parkinson and Manstead (1992), the appraisal theory put forward by Lazarus represents a rather limited view of emotion. As they pointed out, "Appraisal theory has taken the paradigm of emotional experience as an individual passive subject confronting a survival-threatening stimulus" (p.146). From this perspective, it is reasonable to assume that there are associations between cognitive appraisals and emotional reactions because the former cause the latter. However, it is probably more realistic to assume that people are rarely in a completely unemotional state, and that emotions can influence the cognitive appraisal process as well as being influenced by it.

The greatest weakness of Lazarus's appraisal theory is that it does not provide an explanation of the lack of concordance typically found across self-report, physiological, and behavioural measures of anxiety (e.g., Craske & Craig, 1984; Weinberger et al., 1979). The reason for this is that Lazarus (1991) assumes that all of these measures are determined by cognitive appraisal of the situation (see Fig. 2.3). Thus, a threatening cognitive appraisal of a situation should produce anxious responses of all kinds, whereas a non-threatening appraisal should produce minimally anxious self-report, physiological, and behavioural measures. As Lazarus (1991) argued, "Each kind of emotion comprises a distinctive cognitive, motor, and physiological response configuration that is defined by the common adaptational (psychological and physiological) requirement of the person–environment relationships as these are appraised" (p.202). However, Lazarus (1991) also argued in favour of what appears to be a somewhat different theoretical position: "It is possible to imagine an arrangement of the components of the emotion process as relatively independent and responsive to the particular adaptational requirements connected with an ongoing transaction ... In this view, which I favour, each component would function in a more flexible way" (p.196).

Lazarus and Folkman (1984) responded to the lack of concordance in the following way: "When studies are done across measurement levels, what is commonly produced from one method is largely uncorrelated with findings from another method and, in effect, method variance overwhelms everything else" (p.323). According to this argument, differences among self-report, behavioural, and physiological measures should be essentially random or unsystematic. Very different assumptions are incorporated into the new theory of emotion discussed

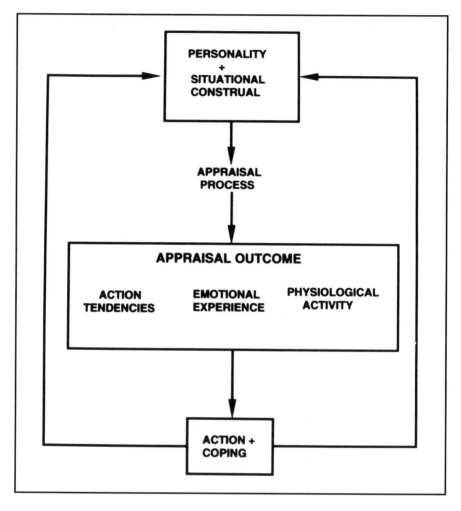

FIG. 2.3. A simplified version of the theory of emotion put forward by Lazarus (1991).

later in the chapter. According to that theory, the various components of anxiety are less independent of each other than is assumed by Lazarus (1991). Nazanin Derakshan and Eysenck (in press) carried out a study which provides relevant evidence on this issue; this study is discussed later in the chapter.

There is a considerable amount of evidence from personality studies to indicate that the differences among different types of measures of anxiety are systematic rather than random (e.g., Weinberger, Schwartz, & Davidson, 1979). The relevant studies are discussed fully in Chapter 3. These studies indicate that there are groups of people who show systematic and theoretically predictable differences across anxiety measures, and convincingly disprove the notion that method variance alone is responsible.

FOUR-FACTOR THEORY OF ANXIETY

Parkinson (1994, 1995) argued persuasively that a synthesis of the appraisal and feedback theories can provide a superior theoretical approach to emotion than either theory or its own. As Parkinson (1995) pointed out, "Appraisal and feedback theories could be seen as interlocking rather than mutually exclusive. For example, the bodily reactions which constitute the substance of emotional feedback may themselves often be caused by appraisal of the situation, and the effects that these reactions have on emotion may in turn reflect the way that they influence the appraisal process in many cases" (pp.150–151).

The new four-factor theory of anxiety, which owes much to the views of Parkinson (1994, 1995), is shown in Fig. 2.4. This framework is specifically designed to be applicable to anxiety, but it may be of some relevance to other emotions. The key theoretical assumption is that the

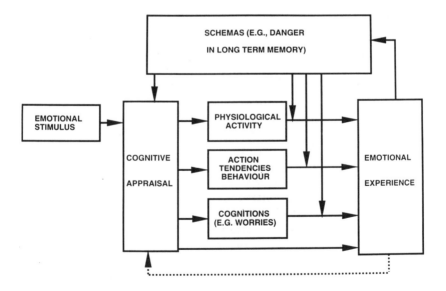

FIG. 2.4. A new four-factor theory of anxiety, based in part on the theory of emotion put forward by Parkinson (1994, 1995).

emotional experience of anxiety is influenced by four different sources of information. One source is based directly on cognitive appraisal of the situation, and is the one which has been emphasised by Lazarus (1966, 1991). It is undoubtedly the most important determinant of anxiety. The three other sources of information, which depend only indirectly on cognitive appraisal of the situation, will now be discussed in turn.

The level of physiological activity is influenced by cognitive appraisal of the situation. However, the impact of physiological activity on the level of experienced anxiety depends on two kinds of cognitive processes: (1) selective attention which may be directed towards or away from physiological activity; and (2) interpretation of perceived physiological activity as threatening or non-threatening. In other words, as was implied by Schachter and Singer (1962), the influence of physiological activity on emotion depends on what is perceived to be its cause.

It is likely that there are factors other than cognitive appraisal which influence the level of physiological activity. For example, Le Doux (1990) reviewed findings from studies of conditioned emotional responses indicating that there is a direct neural pathway from the thalamus to the amgydala. This pathway bypasses the cortex in eliciting conditioned fear.

It is important to note that the four-factor theory of anxiety presented here differs from two-factor theory in two ways in its account of the effects of physiological arousal on emotion. First, the theory is somewhat more cognitive than that of Schachter and Singer (1962), in that it is assumed that the attributional or interpretive processes are applied to the perceived level of physiological activity or arousal. In contrast, Schachter and Singer (1962) seem to have assumed that attributional processes are applied to the *actual* level of physiological arousal.

Second, it is assumed that high physiological arousal can lead to the experience of anxiety, even if the source of the arousal is not attributed to the situation. All that is required is for the physiological arousal itself to be interpreted as threatening. This is very different from the predictions of two-factor theory.

Another source of information for the experience of anxiety consists of cognitions based on information stored in long-term memory. Worries are especially significant cognitions with respect to the emotion of anxiety. What is important for experienced anxiety is not so much the number of worries and other threat-related pieces of information and schemas contained in long-term memory; rather, it is the tendency to attend selectively to such information in conjunction with its interpretation.

The final source of information influencing the experience of anxiety is based on the individual's own action tendencies and behaviour. For the purpose of the theory, behaviour is defined in a broad fashion. It consists essentially of all the overt evidence which can be used by someone else to infer a person's level of anxiety. Thus, it includes facial expressions, other forms of non-verbal behaviour, verbal behaviour, and purposeful actions. Behaviour *per se* has some influence on the experience of anxiety; however, what is more important is the extent to which an individual selectively attends to his or her own behaviour, combined with how that behaviour is interpreted.

The theory may need future refinement in its approach to action tendencies and behaviour. Parkinson (1995) argued for a distinction between expressions and actions: "Expressions are manifestations that provide information to other people about your emotional state, whereas actions are oriented to more instrumental goals" (p.118). This distinction may be important, but Parkinson (1995) admitted that it is not always possible to draw the distinction in a clear-cut fashion. For example, a smile may be regarded as an expression. However, someone may smile in order to achieve the instrumental goal of being liked by another person. According to the theory being presented here, perceived expressions and actions both contribute in similar ways to experienced anxiety.

The final aspect of the new theory of anxiety shown in Fig. 2.4 concerns the broken line running from emotional experience back to cognitive appraisal of the situation. This line is broken because there is apparently inconsistent evidence on the issue of whether emotional experience generally affects cognitive appraisal. Arntz, Rauner, and van den Haut (1995) presented threat-related scenarios to their subjects, and also provided information indicating that there was an anxious or a non-anxious response to each scenario. Various groups of anxious patients rated the perceived danger of the scenarios as significantly greater when there was an anxious response than when there was not. However, the presence vs. absence of an anxious response had no effect on the danger ratings provided by normal controls.

Alison Wheeler and Eysenck (unpubl.) carried out a study that was similar to the one of Arntz et al. (1995). They used threat-related scenarios that were more ambiguous in terms of the threat involved than were those of Arntz et al. (1995). Normal groups had perceived danger ratings that were much higher (41 vs. 26 on a 101-point scale) when anxiety was experienced than when it was not; this difference was significant beyond the $p < 0.00001$ level. Thus, their findings were very different from those of Arntz et al. (1995). The broken line connecting emotional experience and cognitive appraisal is there because it is not clear when cognitive appraisal is, and is not, affected by emotional experience.

There are three other aspects of the theory which need to be clarified at this point. First, it is assumed that the attentional and interpretive biases affecting the influence of each of the four sources of information on anxious experience normally depend on processes operating below the level of conscious awareness, although these processes may well not be automatic. Accordingly, it is only the products of these cognitive biases that normally enter conscious awareness. However, this does not exclude the possibility that at least some cognitive biases can be produced by manipulations (e.g., instructions) designed to affect conscious awareness.

Second, it is assumed that the extent to which the cognitive biases influence processing within the emotional system depends on the prevailing level of state anxiety. More specifically, cognitive biases become greater as state anxiety increases. This produces the possibility of a positive feedback mechanism, in which cognitive biases increase state anxiety, which leads to enhanced cognitive biases, which further increase the level of state anxiety. State anxiety was defined by Spielberger, Gorsuch, and Lushene (1970) as "characterised by subjective, consciously perceived feelings of tension and apprehension, and heightened autonomic nervous system activity" (p.3). It is generally assumed that measures of trait anxiety should show greater stability over time than measures of state anxiety. However, as Usala and Hertzog (1991) pointed out, conventional assessment of the test-retest reliability of trait and state anxiety measures confounds reliability and stability. Usala and Hertzog (1991) unconfounded these factors, and found "significantly higher stability in trait anxiety which ... cannot be attributed to differential reliability in the state and trait scales themselves" (p.477).

Third, it is assumed that schemas stored in long-term memory play an important role in the operation of cognitive biases. According to Beck and Clark (1988):

> Schemas are functional structures of relatively enduring representations of prior knowledge and experience. The cognitive structures guide the screening, encoding, organising, storing and retrieving of information ... Stimuli consistent with existing schemas are elaborated and encoded, while inconsistent or irrelevant information is ignored or forgotten ... The maladaptive schemas in the anxious patient involve perceived physiological or psychological threat to one's personal domain as well as an exaggerated sense of vulnerability (pp.24–26).

It is assumed that normal individuals possess danger- and threat-related schemas which resemble in some ways those possessed by anxious patients. However, as we will see in Chapter 3, it is also assumed that there are substantial individual differences among normals in the nature and extent of such schemas.

Relevance to other theories

Several other theorists have also argued that there are a number of different systems involved in anxiety. For example, Lazarus (1991) distinguished among action tendencies, emotional experience, and physiological responses, and Lang (1971, 1985) identified separate behavioural, physiological, and verbal response systems. In line with such theorists, it is assumed here that physiological activity, behaviour, and negative cognitions are all consequences of being in threatening situations; in that sense, they can be regarded as responses or dependent variables. However, there is a crucial difference between most previous theories and the one presented here. It is assumed that physiological activity, behaviour, and negative cognitions can all then influence emotional experience. The notion that physiological activity, behaviour, and negative cognitions fulfil a dual function is at the centre of the proposed theory. In other words, what is being proposed is that there is a system of interdependent variables and processes underlying anxiety. As Lazarus (1991) pointed out, the notion of a system implies that any variable can act as an antecedent, mediator, or consequent.

There are various points of similarity between the proposed four-factor theory of anxiety and Lang's (1985) three-systems model. It is assumed in both theories that various systems or components are involved in anxiety. It is also assumed that lack of concordance among these systems or components is of crucial importance. In the words of Lang (1985), "The three data subsystems in anxiety are only loosely coupled. This apparent disarray in the data base is also the primary challenge to the theorist who seeks to explain the nature of anxiety" (p.134).

One of the most obvious differences between Lang's (1985) approach and the one advocated here concerns the importance of self-report data. It is assumed within the four-factor theory that self-report data are important, and that they are meaningfully related to other measures of anxiety. In contrast, Lang (1985) seemed to regard self-report measures as being of little or no consequence: "Feeling states are completely private and represent a poor data source for the clinician preparing to undertake treatment" (p.131).

According to Lang (1985), what is of crucial importance is the emotion memory structure for anxiety. This memory structure contains three categories of information: "(1) information about prompting external stimuli and the context in which they occur; (2) information about responding in this context, including expressive facial or verbal behaviour, overt acts of approach or avoidance, and the visceral and somatic events that support attention and action; and (3) information that elaborates or defines the meaning of the stimulus and response data" (p.158). The extent to which there is concordance among the three response systems in anxiety depends on coherence, which is defined by the strength of the associative connections with this memory structure. The assumptions of the four-factor theory are very different. As will become clearer in Chapter 3, it is assumed that the degree of concordance among the components of anxiety depends mainly on the extent of any cognitive biases applied to threat-related internal and external sources of information.

Evidence

Much of the evidence relevant to the new theory of emotion is discussed in Chapter 3. In general terms, the evidence discussed in this chapter focuses on the effects of experimental manipulations of selective attentional bias and interpretive bias on experienced anxiety. In contrast, the emphasis in the next chapter is on individual differences in cognitive biases which depend on the dimensions of trait anxiety and social desirability.

At a very general level, the four-factor theory of anxiety is based on the assumption that the anxious emotional state is associated with attention to external and internal sources of information. More specifically, anxiety creates additional attention to information about an individual's own physiological activity, his or her action tendencies and behaviour, and his or her cognitions. This theoretical approach is consistent with the evidence that negative affective states such as anxiety and depression are associated with high levels of self-focused attention (see Ingram, 1990).

Cognitive appraisal

According to the theory, emotional experience depends to a large extent on the cognitive appraisal of the situation. Cognitive appraisal sometimes takes place at the conscious level, but often it does not. Several studies demonstrating that manipulating the interpretation of the situation influences experienced emotion were discussed earlier in the chapter (Holmes & Houston, 1974; Koriat et al., 1972; Speisman et al., 1964). Because this part of the theory closely resembles aspects of

Lazarus' (1966, 1991) theorising, it is assumed that much of the evidence supporting his cognitive appraisal theory also supports the new theory.

According to the theory, experienced anxiety depends on perceived rather than on actual physiological arousal. Two relevant studies were discussed earlier in the chapter. Borkovec et al. (1974) and Gerdes (1979) compared conditions in which perceived arousal differed, but actual physiological arousal did not. In both studies, self-reported anxiety was systematically affected by the perceived level of arousal.

Physiological activity

According to the theory, the effects of physiological arousal on experienced levels of negative affect depend on selective attentional bias and interpretive bias. So far as selective attentional bias is concerned, it has been reported in several studies that attention to pain increases the pain experience, and that distraction reduces it (Arntz & Schmidt, 1989; Beers & Karoly, 1979; Tan, 1982; Turk, Meichenbaum, & Genest, 1983). It has also been reported that anxiety increases sensitivity to pain (Cornwall & Donderi, 1988; Dougher, Goldstein, & Leight, 1987; Haslam, 1966). As Arntz, Dreessen, and Merckelbach (1991) pointed out, the latter finding might occur in a direct fashion because anxiety increases pain, or in an indirect fashion because anxiety increases attention to pain, which then produces enhanced pain sensitivity. They manipulated anxiety and attention to pain, and discovered that subjective pain was affected directly by attention but not by anxiety. This is consistent with the view that the effects of anxiety on subjective pain are mediated by attentional processes.

Evidence that the impact of physiological arousal on experienced anxiety depends on interpretive bias was reported by van der Molen et al. (1986), in a study referred to earlier in the chapter. Normal subjects were given either a lactate infusion or a placebo. They were instructed either that they would experience unpleasant bodily sensations, or that they would experience feelings of pleasant tension. With lactate infusion, subjects instructed to expect aversive symptoms experienced a considerable amount of anxious tension, whereas on average those expecting positive affect remained emotionally neutral (see Fig. 2.5). However, there was no evidence of interpretive bias when subjects were given the placebo.

Similar findings were reported by Salkovskis and Clark (1989). Their subjects were provided with a negative or a positive interpretation of the sensations produced by voluntary hyperventilation. The negative interpretation informed them that there was a possibility that they might pass out during hyperventilation, whereas the positive

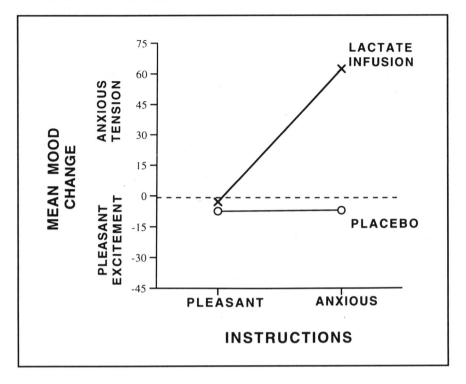

FIG. 2.5. Amount of anxious tension experienced in response to a lactate infusion or a placebo as a function of instructions. Data from van der Molen et al. (1986).

interpretation stated that dizziness and tingling are "indications of unusually good psychological adjustment" (p.54). The two groups did not differ in their experience of bodily sensations, but the subjects given the negative interpretation scored substantially higher on self-reported negative affect (including anxiety) than did those given the positive interpretation.

Action tendencies and behaviour
According to the theory, experienced anxiety depends in part on action tendencies and behaviour, and on the selective attentional and interpretive biases applied to this behaviour. Evidence that emotional experience can be influenced by expressive behaviour was reported by Strack, Martin, and Stepper (1988). The subjects were asked to rate the funniness of cartoons while holding a pen in their mouth. Some subjects were asked to hold the pen between their teeth, which produces an expression resembling a smile. Other subjects were told they could only use their lips to hold the pen, which produced more of a frowning face.

Those subjects who held the pen between their teeth rated their amusement at the cartoons as significantly greater than did those who held the pen using their lips.

Evidence that expressive behaviour can influence negative emotional states was reported by Larsen, Kasimatis, and Frey (1990). Subjects were asked to move golf tees taped to their foreheads to produce a furrowed brow. This created a sad-looking expression, and the subjects reported increased sadness. Zajonc, Murphy, and Inglehart (1989) instructed their subjects to produce a sound like the German "ü" repeatedly. This produced a facial expression like disgust, and caused the subjects to report less pleasant feelings.

Laird and Bresler (1992) concluded their review of studies on expressive behaviour and emotion as follows:

> Dozens of published studies demonstrate that manipulating facial expressions produces corresponding changes in emotional experience or related measures. These studies demonstrate effects of facial expressions on a wide variety of emotions, including happiness, anger, sadness, fear, humour, and pain. These effects are quite specific as well …
> The evidence with respect to facial expressions seems quite convincing: people do feel the emotions their faces are induced to express (p.216).

Evidence that selective attentional bias to one's own behaviour and other symptoms can influence anxiety was obtained by Woody (1996). Each subject stood close to a speaker, who described his own behavioural and other symptoms (or those of the subject) in front of other people. There was evidence that the subjects paid more attention to their own behaviour and symptoms when the speaker was talking about them rather than about himself. As would be predicted by the theory, the subjects reported significantly higher levels of anxiety when they were attending to themselves than when they were not.

Scheier and Carver (1977) manipulated selective attentional bias to behaviour by using a mirror. Subjects received a Velten mood-induction procedure to produce negative affect. The self-focused attention produced by the mirror led to higher levels of negative affect than occurred in a control condition.

Bandler, Madaras, and Bem (1968) conducted a study which is of relevance to the notion that interpretive bias applied to one's own behaviour can influence emotional experience. All the subjects were exposed to electric shocks of the same intensity. Some of the subjects were instructed to endure the shocks, whereas other subjects were encouraged to escape from them. It was assumed that those subjects who escaped from the shocks would interpret their escape behaviour as indicating that the shocks were very severe. As predicted, subjects in the escape condition produced significantly higher discomfort ratings than did those in the endurance condition.

Additional evidence that emotional experience is affected by the way in which people interpret their own behaviour was reported by McAllister (1980). The subjects wrote two essays about themselves, one of which was high in self-disclosure and the other of which was low. The subjects gave the high self-disclosure essay to another person, having been led to believe either that they could choose which essay to hand over or that they could not. Those subjects who believed they had chosen to behave as they did felt more positive about themselves than did those who believed they had no choice.

Long-term memory

According to the theory, negative information in long-term memory can increase anxiety. One way of studying the effects on self-reported anxiety of attending to negative information in long-term memory is to consider the emotional consequences of worrying. This was done by Borkovec, Robinson, Pruzinsky, and DePree (1983). They asked their subjects to indicate the extent to which they experienced each of 14 emotional states when worrying. Anxious feelings were the most intensely experienced reaction to worrying, followed by anxiety-related feelings such as tension, apprehension, and nervousness.

More direct evidence that attending to worries can cause anxiety was reported by Borkovec and Inz (1990). Patients with generalised anxiety disorder and normal controls relaxed and then worried in their usual fashion. Both groups showed substantial increases in rated anxiousness and unpleasantness between the relaxation and worry conditions. East and Watts (1994) essentially replicated these findings among normal high-trait worriers. Albersnagel (1988) found that a mood-induction procedure was successful in producing a significant increase in anxious mood.

Wells and Morrison (1994) carried out a more naturalistic study. Normal subjects were asked to record detailed information about two spontaneously occurring worries in a diary. These worries were rated as being moderately distressing to the subjects.

Derakshan and Eysenck

Some of the predictions of the new theory of emotion were tested by Derakshan and Eysenck (in press), in a study which is reported in more detail in Chapter 3. In essence, they asked their subjects to give a public talk, obtaining several measures of anxiety during and after it. Half-way through the talk, subjects indicated their self-reported anxiety on three adjective scales (uncomfortable; nervous; apprehensive) to provide a measure of state anxiety. They also provided measures of self-reported behavioural anxiety, physiological anxiety, and cognitive anxiety (anxiousness of their thoughts). Heart rate was recorded throughout, and afterwards the subjects rated the extent to which their increased heart rate was due to the talk being stressful or threatening; this will be referred to as perceived physiological anxiety. Finally, several days later, the subjects watched a videotape of themselves delivering the talk, and rated their symptoms of behavioural anxiety on several scales; this will be referred to as perceived behavioural anxiety. The videotapes were also rated by judges to provide an approximate measure of actual behavioural anxiety; this will be referred to as rated behavioural anxiety.

Some of the key findings are shown in Fig. 2.6. According to Lazarus (1991), action tendencies or behaviour, emotional experience, and physiological responses are all determined by cognitive appraisal. The obvious implication is that all three kinds of measures should be highly inter-correlated. As can be seen in Fig. 2.6, the correlation between self-reported anxiety and actual physiological responding was a non-significant +0.18, the correlation between self-reported anxiety and rated behavioural anxiety was a statistically significant +0.44, and the correlation between actual physiological responding and rated behavioural anxiety was +0. 37 and significant. In other words, the three types of measures mostly inter-correlated significantly with each other, but the correlations were modest in size.

According to the new theory, experienced or self-reported anxiety is determined by perceived behavioural anxiety, perceived physiological anxiety, and perceived cognitive anxiety. Self-reported anxiety correlated +0.78 with self-reported physiological anxiety rated half-way through the talk, +0.77 with self-reported cognitive anxiety, and +0.80 with self-reported behavioural anxiety. It could be argued that these inter-correlations are inflated because all the measures were collected at the same time, and all involved self-report measures. However, comparable correlations were obtained when measures taken some time after the measure of self-reported anxiety were considered. The subjects indicated the extent to which their heart rate had increased because of the stressfulness and threateningness of the talk approximately two minutes after providng the measure of self-reported anxiety, and their self-assessment of behavioural anxiety based on viewing the videotape was assessed several days later. Self-reported anxiety correlated +0.77 with this measure of perceived physiological anxiety, and it correlated +0.75 with this measure of perceived behavioural anxiety.

	RATED BEHAVIOURAL ANXIETY	ACTUAL PHYSIOLOGICAL ANXIETY	SELF-REPORTED ANXIETY	PERCEIVED BEHAVIOURAL ANXIETY	PERCEIVED PHYSIOLOGICAL ANXIETY	SELF-REPORTED BEHAVIOURAL ANXIETY	SELF-REPORTED PHYSIOLOGICAL ANXIETY	SELF-REPORTED COGNITIVE ANXIETY
1. RATED BEHAVIOURAL ANXIETY	-	.37	.44	.36	.37	.42	.28	.34
2. ACTUAL PHYSIOLOGICAL ANXIETY	.37	-	.18	.11	.30	.21	.13	.06
3. SELF-REPORTED ANXIETY	.44	.18	-	.75	.77	.80	.78	.77
4. PERCEIVED BEHAVIOURAL ANXIETY	.36	.11	.75	-	.82	.69	.66	.69
5. PERCEIVED PHYSIOLOGICAL ANXIETY	.37	.30	.77	.82	-	.76	.68	.73
6. SELF-REPORTED BEHAVIOURAL ANXIETY	.42	.21	.80	.69	.76	-	.80	.66
7. SELF-REPORTED PHYSIOLOGICAL ANXIETY	.28	.13	.78	.66	.68	.80	-	.62
8. SELF-REPORTED COGNITIVE ANXIETY	.34	.06	.77	.69	.73	.66	.62	-

FIG. 2.6. Inter-relationships among self-reported anxiety, actual and self-reported physiological anxiety, and rated and self-reported behavioural anxiety. Based on data from Derakshan and Eysenck (in press).

These findings indicate that experienced or self-reported anxiety is much more closely related to self-reported perceived physiological, behavioural, and cognitive anxiety than it is to actual physiological and behavioural anxiety. The findings also indicate that there are important differences between actual and perceived physiological and behavioural anxiety. Actual physiological responding correlated +0.13 with self-reported physiological anxiety, and it correlated +0.30 with perceived physiological anxiety. Actual behavioural anxiety based on judges' ratings correlated +0.42 with self-reported behavioural anxiety, and it correlated +0.36 with self-assessed behavioural anxiety based on the videotape. These correlations are sufficiently low that it cannot be assumed that actual and perceived measures are equivalent.

The data obtained by Derakshan and Eysenck (in press) are correlational in nature, and so care needs to be taken when attempting to infer causality. The finding that self-reported anxiety correlated highly with several measures of self-reported and perceived behavioural, physiological, and cognitive anxiety could be due to effects of self-reported anxiety on these other measures rather than to effects of perceived behavioural, physiological, and cognitive anxiety on self-reported anxiety.

However, there are two points that need to be made. First, it is improbable that the measure of perceived behavioural anxiety was influenced by state anxiety, since it was obtained several days later in non-stressful conditions. Second, it is assumed within the theory that there are bidirectional influences between perceived behavioural, physiological, and cognitive anxiety on the one hand and experienced anxiety on the other hand.

In sum, the findings obtained by Derakshan and Eysenck (in press) are more consistent with the predictions of the new theory than with the predictions from appraisal theories (e.g., Lazarus, 1966, 1991). However, it is intrinsically difficult to establish directions of influence within a complex system such as that underlying anxiety.

SUMMARY AND CONCLUSIONS

Major theories of emotion (e.g., James–Lange theory; Schachter and Singer's two-factor theory; Lazarus's cognitive appraisal theory) have focused on some of the main processes and factors involved in emotional states including anxiety. Some theories have emphasised the role of the environment in determining emotion, whereas others have emphasised feedback from bodily and other sensations.

Parkinson (1994, 1995) pointed out that the major theories are limited because some key factors are neglected. In general terms, emotional experience can be determined both by information available in the environment and by feedback from internal processes.

The new four-factor theory of anxiety is based on four major assumptions. First, four sources of information determine the level of experienced anxiety: cognitive appraisal of the situation; perceived level of behavioural anxiety; perceived level of physiological anxiety; and negative cognitions from long-term memory. Second, the effects of these four sources of information on experienced anxiety depend on attentional and interpretive biases normally operating below the level of conscious awareness. Third, these cognitive biases become greater as state anxiety increases. Fourth, schemas or organised packets of knowledge stored in long-term memory affect the operation of these cognitive biases.

The theory proposed in this chapter represents an attempt to indicate how the above four sources of information interact with each other to produce experienced anxiety. This theory may be over-simplified in some respects. In particular, there must be a suspicion that there is actually more interaction among the four factors than is allowed for within the theory.

CHAPTER THREE

A new theory of trait anxiety

THEORETICAL FRAMEWORK

A new theory of emotion, based in part on a synthesis of the theories put forward by Lazarus (1966, 1991) and by Schachter and Singer (1962), was proposed in Chapter 2. As was pointed out in that chapter, the theory is more applicable to anxiety than it is to other negative emotional states or to positive emotional states. The main focus in this chapter is on the extension of that theory to provide a theoretical account of trait anxiety.

The key ingredients in the four-factor theory of trait anxiety can be seen in Fig. 3.1. The fundamental assumption added to the theory of anxiety presented in Chapter 2 is that there are fairly consistent individual differences in the cognitive biases operating at four different points within the emotional system. The main cognitive biases which are of relevance are the selective attentional bias and the interpretive bias discussed in Chapters 1 and 2.

The four-factor theory of trait anxiety is designed to apply to four groups of individuals based on the terminology introduced by Weinberger et al. (1979): low-anxious; repressors; high-anxious; and defensive high-anxious. As is discussed by Weinberger (1990), these groups have usually been identified by taking account of scores on a measure of trait anxiety (e.g., Taylor's Manifest Anxiety Scale; Spielberger's State–Trait Anxiety Inventory) and the Marlowe–Crowne

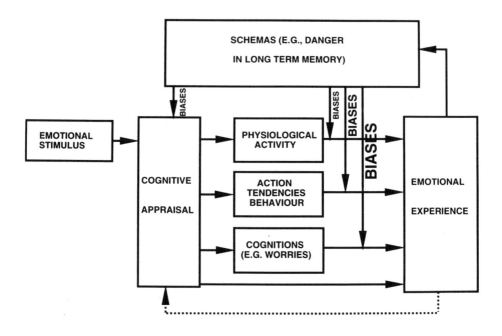

FIG. 3.1. A new four-factor theory of trait anxiety.

Social Desirability Scale (Crowne & Marlowe, 1964). Low-anxious individuals and repressors both score low on trait anxiety, but the two groups differ in their social desirability scores: low-anxious individuals score low, whereas repressors score high. High-anxious individuals and defensive high-anxious individuals both score high on trait anxiety, with high-anxious individuals scoring low on social desirability, and the defensive high-anxious scoring high. It is assumed that the Marlowe–Crowne Social Desirability Scale provides a measure of defensive coping style or protection of self-esteem.

Other measuring instruments have been proposed. For example, there is the Weinberger Adjustment Inventory (Weinberger & Schwartz, 1990), which assesses the dimensions of distress, self-restraint, and repressive defensiveness. Repressors are defined as low scorers on distress and high scorers on self-restraint and repressive defensiveness. As yet, there is no convincing evidence that the Weinberger Adjustment Inventory is a superior way of identifying repressors than the method based on trait anxiety and social desirability scores. Evidence that the two approaches are comparable was obtained by Derakshan and Eysenck (in press). They found that Weinberger's distress scale correlated +0.79 with trait anxiety, his self-restraint scale correlated +0.47 with social desirability, and his repressive defensiveness scale correlated +0.68 with social desirability. There was $p < 0.001$ associated with each of these correlations.

Additional evidence indicating that the two approaches are similar was reported by Turvey and Salovey (1993). They found that there were fairly large correlations among the three scales of the Weinberger Adjustment Inventory, the Manifest Anxiety Scale, and the Marlowe–Crowne Social Desirability Scale.

The major predictions of the four-factor theory of trait anxiety are straightforward (see Eysenck & Derakshan, submitted b). It is assumed that high-anxious individuals have selective attentional and interpretive biases leading them to exaggerate or magnify the threateningness of external and internal stimuli. More specifically, high-anxious individuals have cognitive biases associated with the cognitive appraisal of the situation, as well as with the processing of information about their own physiological activity, action tendencies and behaviour, and cognitions. It is assumed that repressors have opposite selective attentional and interpretive biases, leading them to minimise the threateningness of external and internal stimuli. In other words, repressors tend to avoid attending to threat-related external and internal stimuli, and they tend to interpret ambiguous external and internal stimuli in a non-threatening fashion. More specifically, repressors have opposite cognitive biases associated with the cognitive appraisal of the situation, as well as with the processing of information about their own physiological activity, action tendencies and behaviour, and cognitions (see Derakshan & Eysenck, submitted d).

It is assumed that low-anxious individuals generally do not have either cognitive biases or opposite cognitive biases. It is more difficult to make any specific predictions about the defensive high-anxious group. In most populations, there are significantly fewer defensive high-anxious individuals than members of any of the other three groups, so that this group is often omitted from experimental studies. As a consequence, less is known about the defensive high-anxious than about the other groups. However, they can be characterised as individuals who adopt a defensive coping style (as indicated by their high levels of social desirability), but do so unsuccessfully (as indicated by their high levels of trait anxiety). As Kohlmann (1993) pointed out, an implication of this characterisation is that defensive high-anxious individuals are possibly even more anxious in some sense than high-anxious individuals. It would appear to follow that defensive high-anxious individuals are likely to exhibit the same cognitive biases as high-anxious individuals, and might even show these biases to a greater extent.

There are some additional predictions which follow from the assumption that the activation of danger- or threat-related schemas in long-term memory is influenced by the level of experienced or state anxiety (see Fig. 3.1). It is predicted that the cognitive biases in high-anxious individuals and the opposite cognitive biases in repressors will be greater when the level of experienced anxiety is high than when it is low. In other words, there are bi-directional influences, with cognitive biases influencing the level of experienced anxiety, and the level of experienced anxiety influencing the operation of cognitive biases (see Eysenck & Derakshan, submitted b).

It is also assumed in Fig. 3.1 that experienced emotion can have a direct effect on cognitive appraisal of the situation (see the broken line at the bottom of the figure). The relevant evidence was discussed in Chapter 2. Arntz et al. (1995) obtained no evidence that experienced anxiety influences cognitive appraisal in normal individuals. However, Alison Wheeler and Eysenck (unpubl.) found with more ambiguously threatening situations that there were powerful effects of experienced anxiety on cognitive appraisal. They found that these effects were of comparable magnitude in low-anxious, repressor, high-anxious, and defensive high-anxious groups. As a consequence, it is tentatively proposed that the impact of experienced anxiety on cognitive appraisal does not depend on group differences in cognitive biases.

Finally, it is assumed that the various cognitive biases and opposite cognitive biases normally depend on processes operating below the level of conscious awareness, although these processes may well not be fully automatic in nature. McNally (1995) discussed some of the relevant evidence, and concluded that "biases are automatic in the sense of being involuntary (and sometimes unconscious), but not in the sense of being capacity-free" (p.747). In general terms, it is only the products of those cognitive biases and opposite cognitive biases which normally enter conscious awareness. However, it is also assumed that cognitive biases and opposite cognitive biases can be produced by manipulations (e.g., instructions) designed to affect conscious processing.

The ultimate value of any theory depends importantly on the extent to which its predictions are supported by empirical evidence, and the relevant evidence will be considered in detail later in the chapter. However, it is appropriate at this stage to consider the potential advantages of this four-factor theory over the theory of anxiety proposed by Eysenck (1992). Some of these advantages are considered below.

The first advantage of the current theory of trait anxiety is that it is firmly based on a theory of emotion, whereas Eysenck's (1992) theory of trait anxiety was not. The different sources of information associated with the experience of anxiety are clearly delineated within the theory of emotion, as a consequence of which the task of accounting for individual differences in the experience of anxiety is facilitated.

The second advantage of the new theory of trait anxiety is that it provides a much more comprehensive account than was provided by the circumscribed theory of Eysenck (1992). More specifically, Eysenck (1992) focused only on individual differences in cognitive biases applied to external threat-related stimuli, whereas the new theory also considers cognitive biases applied to various internal stimuli (physiological activity; action tendencies and behaviour; and cognitions based on information in long-term memory).

The third advantage, and one of major importance, is that the current theory offers a partial explanation for failures of concordance among self-report, physiological, and behavioural measures of anxiety. The theory predicts that high-anxious individuals and repressors will tend to exhibit discrepancies between self-reported or experienced anxiety on the one hand, and physiological anxiety and behavioural anxiety on the other hand. High-anxious individuals should exhibit relatively higher self-reported anxiety than physiological or behavioural anxiety, whereas repressors should have higher physiological and behavioural anxiety than self-reported anxiety (see Derakshan & Eysenck, submitted d).

An important study providing strong evidence that some failures of concordance are consistent with this general approach was reported by Newton and Contrada (1992). Low-anxious, high-anxious, and repressor subjects gave a talk in private and in public conditions, and the effects of these conditions on self-reported negative affect and heart rate were assessed. The most striking findings were obtained in the public condition. As can be seen in Fig. 3.2, there were marked discrepancies between the self-report and physiological measures. Repressors had by far the greatest increase in heart rate, but this was accompanied by only a small increase in self-reported negative affect. In contrast, high-anxious individuals had a very large increase in self-reported negative affect, but only a modest increase in heart rate.

Similar findings were reported by Gudjonsson (1981). Subjects were asked a series of questions, and self-reported arousal and actual physiological arousal were recorded. Those who were below the median on the self-report measure and above the median for the physiological measure were termed "repressors", whereas those above the median for self-report and below the median for the physiological measure were termed "sensitisers". Repressors as so defined had low neuroticism scores and high social desirability scores, whereas sensitisers had high neuroticism scores and low social desirability scores. In other words,

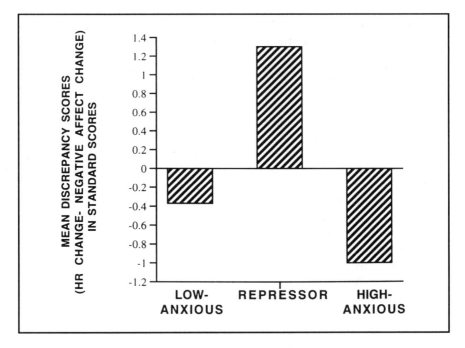

FIG. 3.2. Mean discrepancy scores (heart rate change–negative affect change) in standard scores in the public condition for low-anxious, repressor, and high-anxious groups. Data from Newton and Contrada (1992).

most of those who were defined as repressors on the basis of high physiological reactivity and low self-reported arousal would have been classifed as repressors on the basis of Weinberger's criteria.

Additional relevant evidence has been obtained by Calvo and Eysenck (submitted) in a study in which the subjects were required to give a speech. They used the Cognitive and Somatic Anxiety Scale to obtain measures of cognitive and somatic state anxiety. They also used physiological measures and measures of rated behavioural anxiety. They then calculated z scores for each of these measures for a sample including individuals high, intermediate, and low in trait anxiety. Some of the findings from the high and low extremes of trait anxiety are shown in Figs. 3.3, 3.4, and 3.5. The remarkably consistent finding was that high-anxious individuals had significantly higher z scores for self-report measures than for aspects of behavioural anxiety (Figs. 3.3 and 3.4) and various physiological measures (Fig. 3.5). In contrast, those low in trait anxiety had significantly lower z scores for self-report measures than

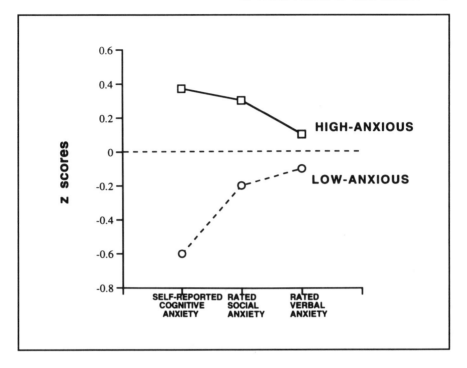

FIG. 3.3. Mean z scores for high and low trait-anxious groups for self-reported cognitive anxiety and rated social and verbal anxiety when required to give a speech. Data from Calvo and Eysenck (submitted).

for measures of behavioural anxiety or physiology. No measure of social desirability was obtained, so it is not possible to divide the low scorers on trait anxiety into low-anxious and repressor groups. However, it is generally the case that more low scorers on trait anxiety are repressors than are truly low-anxious, and theoretically it would be predicted that the discrepancies between self-report scores and behavioural and physiological measures would be found in repressors rather than in low-anxious individuals.

The fourth advantage is that the new theory of trait anxiety is more realistic than Eysenck's (1992) theory in its approach to those scoring low on trait anxiety. The previous theory treated all low scorers on trait anxiety as a homogeneous group, in spite of strong empirical evidence that they should be subdivided into low-anxious and repressor groups (see Weinberger, 1990, for a review; also Derakshan & Eysenck, submitted d).

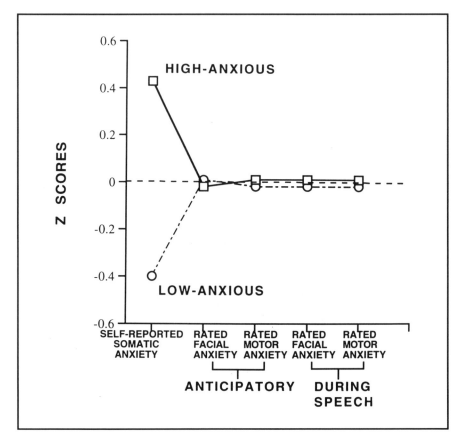

FIG. 3.4. Mean z scores for high and low trait-anxious groups for self-reported somatic anxiety and rated facial and motor anxiety in anticipation of giving a speech and during the speech. Data from Calvo and Eysenck (submitted).

ENVIRONMENTAL THREAT

In this section, the central focus is on individual differences in selective attentional bias and interpretive bias as these biases apply to environmental stimuli. It is predicted that high-anxious individuals will show both kinds of bias for environmental stimuli (whether related to social or physical threat), whereas repressors will show opposite selective attentional and interpretive biases. It is also predicted that these biases and opposite biases will tend to be greater in stressful conditions. Much of the relevant research on high-anxious individuals was discussed in Chapter 1, and so the main emphasis here will be on

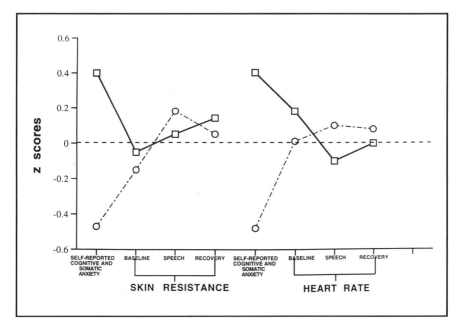

FIG. 3.5. Mean z scores for high and low trait-anxious groups for self-reported cognitive and somatic anxiety and skin resistance (a) and heart rate (b) before, during, and after giving a speech. Data from Calvo and Eysenck (submitted).

studies involving repressors. Any biases reported were obtained with both social-threat and physical-threat stimuli unless otherwise stated.

Selective attentional bias

Schill and Althoff (1968) compared auditory perception in repressors, high-anxious, and low-anxious groups when presented with sexual, aggressive, and neutral sentences masked by noise. The three groups did not differ in their ability to perceive the neutral sentences, indicating that there were no group differences in basic auditory perception. However, the repressors correctly perceived significantly fewer of the sexual sentences than either of the other two groups.

Bonanno, Davis, Singer, and Schwartz (1991) made use of a dichotic listening task, and found that repressors were less disrupted than were high-anxious subjects by threat-related (social and physical) words presented on the unattended channel. On a subsequent test of recognition memory, high-anxious subjects recognised 71% of the threat-related words which had previously been presented on the unattended channel, compared to 61% for the low-anxious subjects, and

46% for the repressors. According to Bonanno et al. (1991), these findings indicate that the repressors attended less than the other groups to the threatening words on the unattended channel.

The most direct test of the prediction that repressors should exhibit an opposite selective attentional bias was reported by Fox (1993) in a study in which she presented a mixture of social-threat and physical-threat words. The repressors responded slower to the probe when it replaced a social-threat word than when it replaced a neutral word. This provides evidence for an opposite selective attentional bias in repressors for social-threat stimuli but not for physical-threat stimuli. In contrast, low-anxious subjects showed no bias at all, and high-anxious individuals showed an attentional bias for social-threat and physical-threat stimuli.

Two studies have investigated opposite selective attentional bias in repressors. Dawkins and Furnham (1989) found that both repressors and high-anxious subjects were significantly slower at naming the colours of emotional words than of neutral words, but there was no difference for low-anxious subjects. These findings suggest that attentional processes in repressors were affected by threat, but do not provide clear evidence of avoidance of threat. In a similar study, Myers and McKenna (in press) also used the modified Stroop. Their findings were very different to those of Dawkins and Furnham (1989). The high-anxious, defensive high-anxious, and low-anxious groups were all significantly slower at naming the colours of socially emotional words than neutral words, but the repressors' colour naming was unaffected by threat.

It is difficult to interpret the findings of Dawkins and Furnham (1989) and of Myers and McKenna (in press), in part because they obtained different findings with repressors. In addition, however, it is likely that the modified Stroop does not provide a good measure of selective attentional bias or of opposite selective attentional bias. As De Ruiter and Brosschot (1994) pointed out, "The increased Stroop interference might ... be the result of an attempt to avoid processing the stimulus because it contains emotionally valenced information ... Attentional bias occurs in the early stages, and cognitive avoidance at later stages" (p.317).

Pre-attentive versus attentional processes

The issue of whether selective attentional bias depends on pre-attentive or on conscious processes was investigated by Mogg, Bradley, and Hallowell (1994) using the dot-probe task under conditions of no stress, laboratory-induced stress, and examination-induced stress. In the supraliminal condition, high trait-anxious subjects showed a selective attentional bias only in the examination-stress condition. In the subliminal condition, high trait-anxious subjects showed a bias only in the no-stress condition.

Somewhat clearer findings have been found in a number of studies using the modified Stroop task. For example, MacLeod and Rutherford (1992) considered high and low trait-anxious subjects who were in a state of low or high stress. The two groups did not differ in their performance on the modified Stroop when the threat-related words were presented supraliminally. However, there was a significant interaction of trait-anxiety group, stress, and word valence (threat-related vs. neutral) in the subliminal condition. In this interaction, high trait-anxious subjects showed a selective attentional bias only when highly stressed, and low trait-anxious subjects showed evidence of an opposite attentional bias only when stressed. Thus, the selective attentional bias depended interactively on trait and state anxiety, and it appeared to be based on processes operating below the level of conscious awareness.

Further evidence that the selective attentional bias may depend on pre-attentive processes was reported by Mogg, Kentish, and Bradley (1993) in a study on the modified Stroop task. There was a selective bias associated with high trait anxiety when the threat-related stimuli were presented subliminally, but not when they were presented supraliminally.

A particularly interesting study was reported by MacLeod and Hagan (1992). They administered the modified Stroop task to female subjects awaiting colposcopy investigation. There was no evidence for selective attentional bias in the high trait-anxious subjects in the supraliminal condition. In the subliminal condition, however, there was a bias which was associated with both trait and state anxiety. The best predictor of the seriousness of emotional distress caused subsequently by receiving a diagnosis of cervical pathology was the size of the bias effect on the subliminal version of the modified Stroop task.

Van den Hout, Tenney, Huygens, Merckelbach, and Kindt (1995) attempted to replicate the findings of MacLeod and Hagan (1992) on non-stressed subjects. They found that trait and state anxiety both correlated significantly with the bias effect on the subliminal version of the modified Stroop task. In addition, the size of the bias effect on the subliminal task was the best predictor of emotional vulnerability to stressful life events. The one consequential difference between the findings of the two studies is that van den Hout et al. (1995) found that high trait-anxious subjects had a selective attentional bias in the supraliminal condition.

Fox (1996) has obtained evidence indicating that one cannot simply conclude that high-anxious subjects will consistently exhibit a selective bias with subliminal presentation of threat-related stimuli. She made use of Bargh's (1989) distinction between preconscious and postconscious automatic processes. Preconscious automatic processes occur provided that the individual notices the presence of the triggering stimulus in the environment. In contrast, postconscious automatic processes occur only after certain kinds of recent, conscious processing. Postconscious automatic processes depend on the prior activation of relevant knowledge structures (e.g., danger schemas).

Fox (1996) addressed the issue of whether any selective bias in high-anxious subjects involves preconscious or postconscious automatic processes in three experiments, in which the task was to classify a central number as odd or even while ignoring spatially separate threat-related or neutral words. The flanking stimuli were presented either supraliminally or subliminally. In the first experiment, as in nearly all previous studies, supraliminal and subliminal trials were randomly mixed. In line with previous findings, high-anxious subjects showed a selective bias in the subliminal condition, but not in the supraliminal condition.

As Fox (1996) pointed out, such findings could be due either to preconscious automatic processes or to postconscious automatic processes. Accordingly, subliminal and supraliminal trials were presented in separate blocks in the second experiment, and the subliminal block of trials was always presented first. This was done to prevent the possibility of postconscious automatic processes being instigated by the subjects because of their exposure to supraliminally presented threatening words. There was no evidence of a selective bias in the high-anxious subjects on either subliminal or supraliminal trials. In the third experiment, half of the subjects received a block of subliminal trials followed by a block of supraliminal trials, whereas the other half received the reverse order. As can be seen in Fig. 3.6, high-anxious subjects showed a selective bias on subliminal trials when the subliminal trials followed the supraliminal trials, but not when the subliminal trials came first. As in the previous experiments, there was no evidence for a selective bias on supraliminal trials. The findings suggest that this selective bias requires relevant information to have been activated in long-term memory beforehand, and thus that it depends on postconscious automatic processes rather than preconscious automatic processes. However, Mogg (pers. comm.) has not replicated these findings in an unpublished study with Bradley using the dot-probe task.

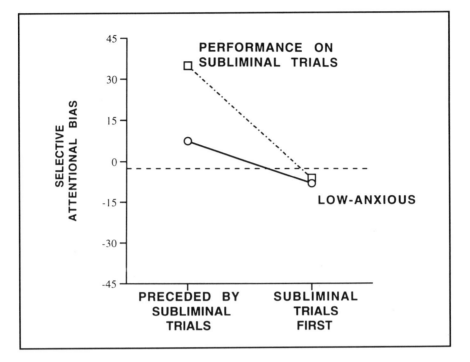

FIG. 3.6. Selective attentional bias on subliminal trials either preceded or not preceded by supraliminal trials as a function of trait anxiety. Data from Fox (1996, exp. 3).

Interpretive bias

A study on opposite interpretive bias in repressors was reported by Mogg, Bradley, Millar, Potts, Glenwright, and Kentish (1994). Subjects varying in levels of trait anxiety and social desirability provided interpretations of homophones having a threatening and a neutral interpretation. The interpretive bias was positively associated with trait anxiety and negatively associated with social desirability, and the association was greater in the first half of the task for trait anxiety, but in the second half of the task for social desirability. These findings provide limited support for the prediction that repressors should exhibit an opposite interpretive bias. However, it should be pointed out that there have been a number of unpublished studies (e.g., by Eysenck and by Fox) which have failed to obtain any evidence of an opposite interpretive bias for repressors on the homophone task.

Myers and Vetere (unpubl.) made use of the Coping Resources Inventory, which measures resources in five different domains: cognitive; physical; social; emotional; and spiritual/philosophical. The repressors scored significantly higher than the low-anxious, high-anxious, and defensive high-anxious groups on total scores on the Coping Resources Inventory and on the the cognitive and physical sub-scales. In addition, the repressors scored significantly higher on the social and emotional sub-scales than the high-anxious and defensive high-anxious groups. These findings suggest that repressors are overly positive in their cognitive appraisals, and this can be regarded as evidence for an opposite interpretive bias.

Time course

As we have seen, there is convincing evidence for the existence of an interpretive bias in high-anxious individuals exposed to ambiguous stimuli. However, it is not clear from the studies discussed so far whether the biased processing occurs on-line or whether it occurs in subsequent stages of processing. Richards and French (1992) provided some relevant evidence. On half of the trials, they presented homographs, followed 500, 750, or 1250ms thereafter by a target word with either a neutral or a threatening meaning related to one of the meanings of the homograph. On the other half of the trials, the target was a non-word rather than a word. The subjects' task was to make a lexical decision about the target stimulus as rapidly as possible. The key finding was that high-anxious subjects made faster responses to threatening target words and slower responses to neutral target words than subjects low in trait anxiety at the 750 and 1250ms intervals, but not at the 500ms interval. These findings suggest that interpretive bias does not occur automatically, but rather depends on post-lexical strategic processes.

Convincing support for the notion that interpretive bias depends on strategic processes occurring some time after the presentation of ambiguous stimuli was reported by Calvo, Eysenck, and Castillo (in press) and by Calvo and Castillo (in press). In the study by Calvo et al. (in press), ambiguous sentences concerned with ego threat, physical threat, or neutral events were followed by disambiguating sentences in which a target word either confirmed or disconfirmed the consequences implied by the initial sentence. The sentences were read in a self-paced fashion, and the speed of reading the confirming and disconfirming sentences provided a measure of interpretive bias. High-anxious subjects showed interpretive bias for ego-threat sentences, but not for physical threat sentences. Of particular relevance, the evidence for interpretive bias was not observed on the disambiguating target word itself, but only subsequently.

The study by Calvo and Castillo (in press) resembled that of Calvo et al. (in press) in that ambiguous sentences concerned with ego threat, physical threat, or neutral events were followed by a disambiguating sentence containing a target word which either confirmed or disconfirmed the consequence implied by the ambiguous sentence. However, the task was different, in that the subjects had to name the target word, which was presented either 500ms or 1200ms after the preceding context. Another difference is that stress level was manipulated to produce high and low stress conditions. As can be seen in Fig. 3.7, high-anxious subjects showed an interpretive bias for ego threat but not for physical threat, under high stress but not low stress

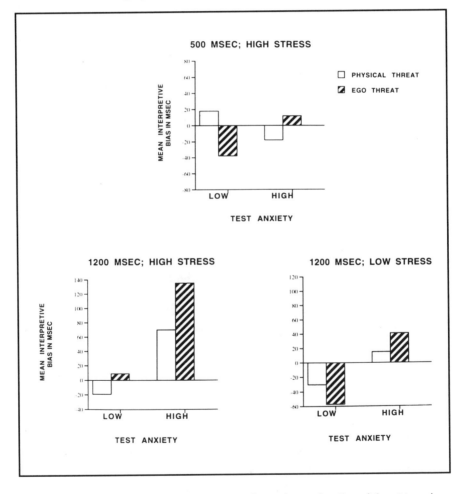

FIG. 3.7. Mean interpretive bias in ms on a naming task as a function of threat type (ego vs. physical), delay (500 vs. 1200ms), stress (high vs. low), and test anxiety. Data from Calvo and Castillo (in press).

conditions, and at 1200ms but not at 500ms. Thus, their findings fit very well with those of Richards and French (1992) and of Calvo et al. (in press) in indicating that interpretive bias does not occur rapidly and automatically, but rather that it involves subsequent strategic processes.

BEHAVIOURAL ANXIETY

In this section, we will be concerned with individual differences in attention to, and interpretation of, information from the individual's own behavioural system. According to the theory of trait anxiety, high-anxious individuals should attend selectively to their own behaviour, and they should tend to interpret their own behavioural information in a threatening fashion. As a consequence, high-anxious individuals should typically have greater self-reported than rated behavioural anxiety, and this should be especially the case in stressful situations. In contrast, repressors should selectively avoid attending to their own behaviour, and they should tend to interpret their own behavioural information in a non-threatening fashion. As a consequence, repressors should typically have less self-reported than rated behavioural anxiety, and this should be especially the case in stressful situations (see Eysenck & Derakshan, submitted b).

Selective attentional bias

The research on selective attentional bias is limited to studies in which low scorers on trait anxiety were not divided into low-anxious and repressor sub-groups. However, the findings are of some relevance to the theory. Indirect evidence that high-anxious individuals attend more to their own behaviour than do low scorers on trait anxiety was reported by Matthews and Wells (1988). They made use of a scale devised by Fenigstein, Scheier, and Buss (1975) to assess public self-consciousness, which is essentially a measure of the tendency to attend to one's own behaviour in social situations. Trait anxiety correlated +0.39 with this measure of public self-consciousness. In similar fashion, Lennox and Wolfe (1984) reported a correlation of +0.31 between social anxiety and the same measure of public self-consciousness.

Asendorpf (1987) investigated attention to their own behaviour and interpretation of their own behaviour in subjects high and low in dispositional shyness. The subjects watched videotapes of their interaction with a confederate of the experimenter, and recalled their thoughts and feelings. Shy subjects did not have more thoughts than non-shy subjects about their own behaviour and the impression they were making, suggesting that they did not attend more to their own behaviour.

Daly, Vangelisti, and Lawrence (1989) found that speech-anxious subjects paid slightly (but non-significantly) more attention to themselves and their behaviour than did non-speech-anxious subjects when giving a talk in public. However, there was a considerable difference between the groups in the proportion of their cognitions during the speech which were both self-focused and negative: 49% versus 24% for those high and low in speech anxiety, respectively.

In ongoing research, Derakshan and Eysenck are investigating the effects of manipulating the focus of attention towards, or away from, the subject's own behaviour. In contrast to previous studies, repressor and defensive high-anxious groups are being studied in addition to low-anxious and high-anxious groups.

Interpretive bias

Discrepancies between self-reported and rated behavioural measures were investigated by Clark and Arkowitz (1975). They used high and low scorers on the Social Avoidance and Distress scale (Watson & Friend, 1969), a measure which was found by Watson and Friend (1969) to correlate +0.54 with trait anxiety. The socially anxious subjects rated their own overall level of social skill in two social situations as lower than did judges, whereas those low in social anxiety rated their own level of social skill as higher than did judges. The socially anxious subjects' self-reported social anxiety was highly significantly greater than the judges' rated social anxiety, whereas there was no difference between self-reported and rated social anxiety for the low-anxious subjects.

Beidel, Turner, and Dancu (1985) obtained self-report and rating measures of anxiety in three different social situations. There were non-significant differences between the self-report and rating measures in all situations for the non-anxious subjects. For the anxious subjects, their self-reported anxiety was considerably greater than rated anxiety in the two most stressful conditions (talking to an opposite-sexed person; giving an impromptu talk), but there was no difference in the least stressful condition (talking to a same-sexed person).

Behavioural aspects of speech anxiety in the low-anxious and in repressors were studied by Harrigan, Suarez, and Hartman (1994). Transcripts of what subjects had said in a moderately stressful situation were evaluated for state anxiety by judges. Repressors were judged to be the most anxious group, with the low-anxious being the least anxious group. The two intermediate groups were the high-anxious and the defensive high-anxious. All of these findings were much stronger when the subjects were high in state anxiety than when they were low in state anxiety.

Similar findings were reported by Harrigan, Harrigan, Sale, and Rosenthal (submitted). Judges assessed the anxiety levels of subjects who had been videotaped under moderately stressful conditions. The judges were presented with either auditory or visual information from the videotape. Rated anxiety was much higher for repressors than for the low-anxious when visual information only was available, and there was a small effect in the same direction when auditory information was available.

The findings of Harrigan et al. (1994) and of Harrigan et al. (submitted) are of interest, because repressors consistently report experiencing low levels of anxiety (Weinberger, 1990). In spite of these self-reports, it appears that repressors have high behavioural anxiety in stressful situations. This discrepancy is in line with predictions from the theory of trait anxiety.

Nazanin Derakshan and Eysenck (in press) tested the predictions of the theory in a more direct fashion. They argued that all of the published work suffered from the limitation that the self-reports and ratings may not have been based on the same evidence. For example, the subjects' self-reported social anxiety in the study by Clark and Arkowitz (1975) may have been based on information (e.g., negative thoughts about poor performance) not available to those rating the subjects' level of social anxiety. As a consequence, there are two possible explanations for the discrepancies between self-reports and ratings reported in the literature: (1) they may be due to systematic biases in the ways in which different groups of individuals interpret their own behaviour; or (2) they may be due to individual differences in the non-behavioural evidence that is used to produce self-reports of anxiety.

In order to investigate interpretive bias and opposite interpretive bias properly, it is important to try to ensure that the subjects and the raters are using the same information. Accordingly, Derakshan and Eysenck (in press) asked their subjects and raters to view the same videotapes as the subjects. Subjects and raters were both instructed to assess the subjects' level of behavioural anxiety solely on the basis of the videotape evidence. Each subject provided two short videotapes, one based on talking about those aspects of their personality they liked most, and the other based on those aspects of their personality they disliked most.

As there were no differences in behavioural anxiety between the positive and negative videotapes, the data were pooled across videotapes.

In the repressor group, as predicted, rated behavioural anxiety was highly significantly higher than self-reported behavioural anxiety. In the high-anxious group, also as predicted, rated behavioural anxiety was significantly lower than self-reported behavioural anxiety.

In their second experiment, Derakshan and Eysenck (in press) carried out a replication and extension of their first experiment. They asked low-anxious, repressor, high-anxious, and defensive high-anxious groups of psychology students to give a short talk on a topic within psychology in front of a small audience. They were videotaped throughout, and their heart rate was monitored (the heart rate data are discussed later). Approximately two weeks later, the subjects viewed the videotape of themselves, and rated their behavioural anxiety on the Timed Behavioural Checklist (Paul, 1966). They were explicitly instructed to base their ratings on the evidence of the videotape alone, and to ignore any thoughts they might have had during the talk. Two independent judges also viewed the videotapes, and completed the Timed Behavioural Checklist.

The main analysis involved a comparison between the aggregated scores on the Timed Behavioural Checklist produced by the subjects and by the judges. As can be seen in Fig. 3.8, the high-anxious and defensive high-anxious groups exhibited an interpretive bias, in that their self-rated behavioural anxiety was significantly higher than the judges' ratings of behavioural anxiety. In contrast, the repressor group

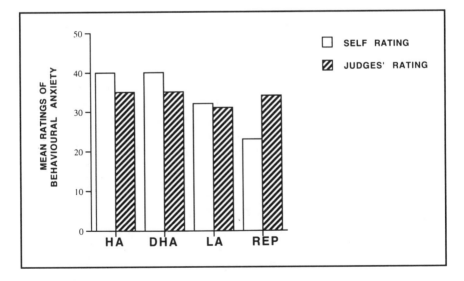

FIG. 3.8. Mean rated and self-reported behavioural anxiety in stressful conditions in low-anxious (LA), repressor REP), high-anxious (HA), and defensive high-anxious (DHA) groups. Data from Derakshan and Eysenck (in press, exp. 2).

exhibited an opposite interpretive bias, with their self-rated behavioural anxiety being considerably lower than the judges' ratings.

Further, more detailed, analyses indicated that the interpretive bias for high-anxious subjects was found in speech-related symptoms and facial symptoms, but not for bodily symptoms or lack of eye contact. The repressors exhibited an opposite interpretive bias for speech-related symptoms, bodily symptoms, and lack of eye contact, but not for facial symptoms.

There are at least two possible ways of accounting for the findings discussed so far. One possibility is that the interpretive bias of high-anxious individuals and the opposite interpretive bias of repressors extend beyond ratings of their own behavioural anxiety to encompass ratings of the behavioural anxiety of others. The other possibility is that the high-anxious and repressor groups misinterpret their own bodily symptoms, but do not misinterpret the bodily symptoms of others. All of the subjects rated a number of other subjects' videotapes, and the evidence from these ratings indicated that the interpretive and opposite interpretive biases were specific to self-rated behavioural symptoms.

The findings of Derakshan and Eysenck (in press) are also relevant to the issue of the weak relationship between trait anxiety and rated behavioural anxiety. Lamb (1978) found very few differences in specific behavioural symptoms of anxiety between those high and low in public speaking anxiety when giving a talk, and high- and low-anxious individuals did not differ in rated anxiety in the studies of Clark and Arkowitz (1975) and Beidel et al. (1985). The reason that the relationship between trait anxiety and rated behavioural anxiety is surprisingly weak is because repressors score low on trait anxiety but relatively high on rated behavioural anxiety (Derakshan & Eysenck, in press). As Derakshan and Eysenck (in press) found, high-anxious individuals in a stressful situation are rated as significantly more behaviourally anxious than low-anxious individuals, but do not differ from repressors.

LONG-TERM MEMORY

In this section we will be concerned with individual differences in attention to, and interpretation of, negative information stored in long-term memory. Some of this information refers to past events involving danger or loss. However, some of it (e.g., worries) has a future orientation. Worrying typically has a strongly repetitive quality to it, with the same or similar negative thoughts about the future being rehearsed frequently. It is assumed that this repetitiveness depends to a large extent on the fact that certain future-oriented information in long-term memory is being re-accessed. Selective attentional bias to external stimuli is shown when threat-related stimuli are processed preferentially, or when threat-related stimuli can be located faster than neutral stimuli. In similar fashion, selective attentional bias to negative information stored in long-term memory is shown when such information is more readily accessed than neutral information stored in long-term memory.

According to the new theory, high-anxious individuals should attend selectively to negative information stored in long-term memory, and they should also interpret such information as being highly threatening. As a consequence, they should have greater self-reported than rated cognitive anxiety, especially in stressful situations. In contrast, repressors should selectively avoid attending to negative information stored in long-term memory, and they should interpret such information as being relatively non-threatening. As a consequence, repressors should tend to have lower self-reported than rated cognitive anxiety, especially in stressful situations.

Some of the relevant evidence on negative memory bias, i.e., disproportionate recall of threat-related material compared to neutral material, was discussed in detail in Chapter 1, and so will only be mentioned here. In essence, there are several studies in which high and low scorers on trait anxiety were compared, and in which the high-anxious group provided evidence of a negative memory bias (Bradley & Mogg, 1994; Bradley, Mogg, Galbraith, & Perrett, 1993; Breck & Smith, 1983; Claeys, 1989; Kennedy & Craighead, 1988; Martin, Ward, & Clark, 1983; Young & Martin, 1981). However, it is difficult in some of these studies to decide whether the negative memory bias was mediated by anxiety rather than by depression.

Selective attentional bias

There are at least two main ways in which selective attentional bias to negative information in long-term memory can be assessed. First, there is the relatively naturalistic approach of attempting to obtain information about the frequency with which negative information (e.g., worries) is thought about at the conscious level during everyday life. Second, there is the experimental approach of comparing the relative ease with which negative and positive information can be retrieved from long-term memory.

There is evidence from the naturalistic approach that high-anxious individuals attend disproportionately to threat-related information stored in long-term memory, perhaps in part because they have more such information stored. Borkovec, Robinson, Pruzinsky, and DePree (1983) obtained a correlation of +0.67 between trait anxiety and the amount of time which people reported that they spent worrying. In a similar fashion, Tallis, Eysenck, and Mathews (1992) correlated trait anxiety with scores on two slightly modified versions of the Worry Domains Questionnaire; the correlations were +0.78 and +0.84.

Eysenck and van Berkum (1992) used the naturalistic approach with the Worry Questionnaire. This was administered to 113 individuals, along with the Spielberger State–Trait Anxiety Inventory and the Marlowe–Crowne Social Desirability Scale. Overall, worry frequency correlated +0.65 with trait anxiety, and it correlated –0.26 with social desirability. As a consequence, high-anxious subjects had easily the highest level of worry frequency, and repressors had the lowest.

Eysenck and Derakshan (in press) also used the naturalistic approach. However, unlike the approach adopted in most previous studies, they studied worry in groups of subjects faced by the same future threat-related event, namely, important university examinations. They asked psychology students approaching their examinations to indicate on average the amount of time per day they spent worrying about their performance on each examination. They were also asked to provide an estimate of the same information with respect to a friend who was sitting the same examinations. The high-anxious subjects reported spending significantly more time worrying about the examinations than would a friend, whereas repressors reported spending significantly less time worrying about the examinations than would a friend.

We turn now to evidence from the experimental approach. Nearly all the studies on the accessibility of threat-related information from long-term memory in repressors have involved explicit memory. Davis (1990) discussed her series of studies on this issue. In one experiment (Davis, 1987), some subjects were asked to recall childhood events in which they felt happy, sad, angry, or fearful, whereas other subjects were asked to recall events in which those emotions were experienced by someone else. Repressors recalled fewer experiences in which they themselves felt happy, sad, angry, or fearful than did low-anxious and high-anxious subjects. This was not due to a generally poor ability to retrieve childhood memories, because repressors actually remembered substantially more events than the other two groups in which someone else experienced the various emotional states. In other experiments, Davis (1987) used various retrieval cues, and found that repressors experienced greater difficulty than other groups in recalling fear, anger, and self-conscious experiences.

Myers and Brewin (1994) pointed out that there was no strong evidence that repressors had had as many negative emotional childhood experiences as other groups in the studies reported by Davis (1987). As a consequence, her findings could be due to repressors having smaller numbers of personal negative childhood memories than other groups stored in long-term memory, rather than to repressors retrieving personal negative memories in an inefficient fashion. Myers and Brewin (1994) used an interview technique which indicated that repressors had experienced childhoods which were probably less happy than those of low-anxious, high-anxious, and defensive high-anxious individuals. In spite of the apparent availability of negative childhood memories, repressors were considerably slower than the other three groups of subjects to recall such memories. In contrast, the four groups did not differ in their speed of recall of positive childhood memories, indicating that repressors do not have a general inability to retrieve distant memories.

So far, all of the studies we have discussed have involved the recall of autobiographical events. Evidence that repressors have an opposite memory bias that extends to other kinds of negative information was reported by Myers and Brewin (1995). Their subjects read a story concerning a woman's childhood with both positive and negative information about each parent, and personal relevance was increased by requiring them to process the material in relation to the self. The repressors remembered significantly fewer negative phrases than the control group, but the two groups did not differ in their recall of positive information.

Eysenck (submitted) carried out a study on implicit memory bias and opposite implicit memory bias in groups of repressors, low-anxious, and high-anxious subjects. The subjects were presented with a mixture of threat-related and neutral words, followed by a word-completion task. There was a significant interaction between groups and word valence, which was due to the fact that the repressors showed an opposite implicit memory bias whereas the other two groups did not show any bias.

Interpretive bias

Myers and Brewin (in press) studied interpretive bias and opposite interpretive bias as they apply to some of the beliefs stored in long-term memory. There were five groups of subjects in their first experiment: low-anxious; repressors; high-anxious; defensive high-anxious; and non-extreme on either trait anxiety or social desirability. These groups of subjects were asked to indicate the relative likelihood of negative and positive events happening to them compared to their fellow students.

The repressors rated the likelihood of negative future events happening to them as significantly less than all four other groups. Only the repressors' ratings were significantly below the point at which the probability of events happening to them and to their fellow students was the same.

Similar, but smaller, differences were found for ratings of future positive events. The repressors rated the likelihood of positive events happening to them relative to fellow students higher than any other group, but the difference was only statistically significant with respect to the non-extreme group. Only the repressors rated themselves as significantly more likely to experience positive events relative to their peers.

In their second experiment, Myers and Brewin (in press) asked their student subjects to rate how true of themselves and of the average college student were positively and negatively valenced trait adjectives. There were two groups: repressors and a mixed group of non-repressors. Only the repressors showed a significant self–other discrepancy for negative trait adjectives: they rated negative words as less descriptive of themselves than of others. The two groups did not differ with respect to positive trait adjectives, since both groups rated positive words as more descriptive of themselves than of other people.

Butler and Mathews (1987) focused on the real-life worries of students in the period before examinations. They made use of the Subjective Probability Questionnaire, which contains several items referring to positive and negative examination-related events. Half of the items refer to the self and the other half to some other person. They found that high trait-anxious students were more pessimistic than low trait-anxious students about the forthcoming examinations, and that estimates of the likelihood of examination failure were higher one day before the examinations than one month before.

The above findings may seem to indicate the existence of an interpretive bias or unrealistic worry on the part of high trait-anxious students. However, Butler and Mathews (1987) did not assess actual examination performance, and it is known that test anxiety (which correlates fairly highly with trait anxiety) is often negatively related to examination performance (e.g., Morris & Liebert, 1970; Spielberger, Gonzalez, Taylor, Algaze, & Anton, 1978). As a consequence, it is not clear whether the greater pessimism about the forthcoming examinations shown by high trait-anxious students was realistic or unrealistic.

In a study already mentioned, Eysenck and Derakshan (in press) studied interpretive bias in the form of unrealistic worry in students approaching important examinations. They asked the students to predict their level of examination performance some weeks before the examinations, and then compared these predictions against actual examination performance. As can be seen in Fig. 3.9, the high-anxious and defensive high-anxious groups both performed significantly better than they had predicted. This is strong evidence for an interpretive bias, because we have a precise measure of the discrepancy between expectations and what actually happened. In contrast, repressors showed a slight, but non-significant, tendency in the opposite direction.

Eysenck and Derakshan (in press) also administered the Subjective Probability Questionnaire. One of the key measures they calculated was the discrepancy between self and other negative expectations for performance-related (or controllable) examination events. As can be seen in Fig. 3.10, high-anxious and defensive high-anxious subjects had significantly more negative expectations for self than for other, indicating the existence of an interpretive bias with respect to themselves. In contrast, repressors had a highly significant discrepancy in the opposite direction, indicating the existence of an opposite interpretive bias for themselves. Similar findings were obtained for repressors (but not for high-anxious or defensive high-anxious groups) for negative non-performance-related (or non-controllable) examination events.

We have seen that high-anxious and defensive high-anxious individuals sometimes exhibit an interpretive bias with respect to their beliefs and worries about the future, and repressors sometimes exhibit an opposite interpretive bias. So far as repressors are concerned, it seems from the study by Eysenck and Derakshan (in press) that an important factor is whether their expectations can be based on fairly detailed information (e.g., the students had mostly received feedback on previous examinations and on assessed course work). In general, repressors do not seem to show an opposite interpretive bias for their expectations when some detailed information is available, but they do have an opposite interpretive bias for expectations when such information is not available.

PHYSIOLOGICAL ANXIETY

In this section, we will be dealing with individual differences in attention to, and interpretation of, negative information about the individual's own physiological activity or bodily sensations. According to the theory, high-anxious individuals should selectively attend to information about their own physiological activity and should interpret that information as being rather threatening. In contrast, repressors

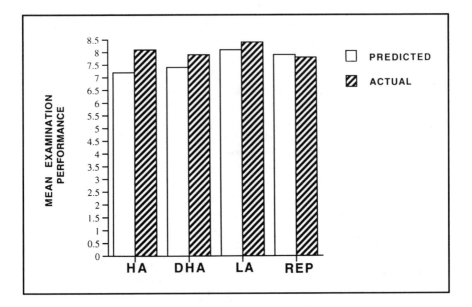

FIG. 3.9. Mean predicted and actual examination performance on a 12-point scale in low-anxious (LA), repressor (REP), high-anxious (HA), and defensive high-anxious (DHA) groups. Data from Eysenck and Derakshan (in press).

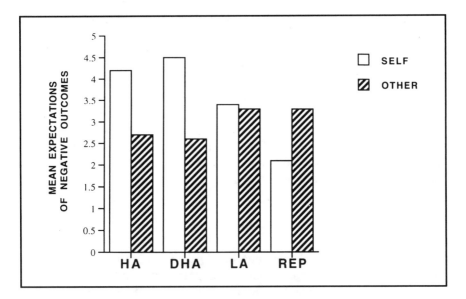

FIG. 3.10. Mean expectations for negative performance-related examination events in low-anxious (LA), repressor (REP), high-anxious (HA), and defensive high-anxious groups for themselves and for a friend. Data from Eysenck and Derakshan (in press).

should selectively avoid attending to their own bodily sensations, and should interpret such sensations in a non-threatening fashion.

Selective attentional bias

Walsh, Eysenck, Wilding, and Valentine (1994) manipulated attention to physiological activity by instructing some subjects falsely that they would be exposed to ultrasonic sound, and that they should attend to their internal state during its presentation. Perceptions of physiological activity in this condition were compared with those in a control condition in which the instructions did not refer to direction of attention. Those high in trait anxiety had smaller differences in perceptions in the two conditions, presumably because they were attending to their internal state in both conditions.

Another way of assessing the extent to which individuals attend to their own physiological activity is to use the mental-tracking task. In essence, subjects simply try to count their heartbeats over a period of time, and their estimate of the number of heartbeats is compared with the actual number. The great majority of subjects under-estimate the number of heartbeats, presumably because failures of attention cause some of the beats to be missed. This approach was used by Schandry (1981), who found that those who were good and poor at estimating their own heartbeats did not differ in their actual heart rate. Those who were most accurate were higher in emotional lability (i.e., higher in trait anxiety) and higher in state anxiety than those who were least accurate. This suggests that those high in trait anxiety attended more closely to their heartbeats.

Related findings were reported by Naring and van der Staak (1995). Their subjects carried out several one-minute tasks, and provided estimates of heart rate after each task. Accuracy of heartrate perception was greater among those high in state anxiety.

Derakshan and Eysenck (submitted a) studied heart beat perception in low-anxious, repressor, high-anxious, and defensive high-anxious groups. They asked their subjects to indicate on a 100-millimetre line their estimated heart rate speed in mental-tracking conditions in which they were required to attend to their own heartbeats, and in control conditions in which there was no requirement to attend to their heartbeats. It was assumed that this manipulation might affect the extent to which subjects would attend to their heartbeats. As can be seen in Fig. 3.11, only the repressors estimated their heart rate speed to be significantly slower in the control conditions than in the mental-tracking conditions. An implication of these findings is that repressors are the individuals who are least likely to attend to their own

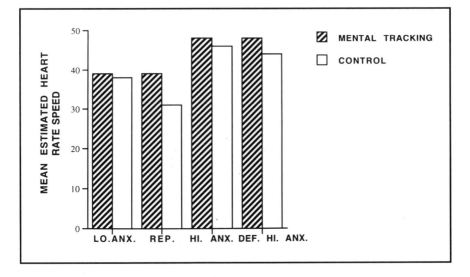

FIG. 3.11. Mean estimated heart rate speed (ex 100) for four personality groups in mental tracking and control conditions. Data from Derakshan and Eysenck (submitted a).

heart rate in the control conditions (i.e., only repressors exhibit an opposite attentional bias for their own heart rate).

Interpretive bias

Most studies on interpretive bias with respect to physiological symptoms have made use of some form of biological challenge. For example, Clark and Hemsley (1982) investigated individual differences in the response to hyperventilation. Those high in neuroticism experienced more negative affect than those low in neuroticism as a consequence of hyperventilation.

McNally (1989) referred to some unpublished findings obtained by a student of his, some of which were published by Holloway and McNally (1987). The effects of hyperventilation were assessed, and it was found that the anxiety caused by hyperventilation was greater in those high in trait anxiety, as was the number of bodily sensations produced. The Anxiety Sensitivity Index was also administered, and found to correlate +0.55 with trait anxiety. Further analyses indicated that anxiety sensitivity was a better predictor than trait anxiety of the effects of hyperventilation. However, Lilienfeld, Jacob, and Turner (1989) argued that it is difficult to interpret the findings because measures of anxiety sensitivity are contaminated by trait anxiety.

Veltman, van Zijderveld, and van Dyck (1994) studied the effects of an injection of adrenaline on normals high and low in trait anxiety. The adrenaline produced a significantly larger increase in state anxiety in the high-anxious group than the low-anxious one, and the same was the case for the number and intensity of symptoms experienced during the experiment. However, there was evidence that these findings occurred because of a lower level of aerobic fitness in the high-anxious group.

Similar findings have been reported in two other studies. Rapee and Medoro (1994) found that responses to hyperventilation were predicted much better by anxiety sensitivity than by trait anxiety. Eke and McNally (1996) found that trait anxiety correlated only +0.09 with the symptoms produced by carbon dioxide challenge, whereas anxiety sensitivity correlated +0.40.

Part of the reason for the weak relationship between trait anxiety and bodily symptoms produced by biological challenge may be that low scorers on trait anxiety were not divided into low-anxious and repressor groups. According to the four-factor theory of trait anxiety, the lowest level of bodily symptoms should be found in repressors rather than in low-anxious individuals. Derakshan and Eysenck (submitted b) found that hyperventilation produced significantly more bodily symptoms in high-anxious individuals than in repressors, but the difference between the high-anxious and low-anxious groups was not significant.

In their second experiment, Derakshan and Eysenck (in press) obtained heart rate measures from all of their subjects while they were giving a public talk. The mean heart rate of the repressor (114 beats per minute), high-anxious (115bpm), and defensive high-anxious groups (108bpm) were comparable, but significantly higher than the heart rate of the low-anxious (91bpm). At the end of the experiment, the subjects were told that their heart rate increased substantially during their talk, and they were asked to indicate the extent to which they agreed with that fact. The repressors showed some evidence of an opposite interpretive bias, in that they were significantly less willing than any other group to accept the statement. However, it is possible that an opposite attentional bias was also involved, with repressors attending less than other groups of subjects to their own physiological acitvity during the talk.

The subjects were then asked to indicate the extent to which they attributed their heart rate increase to the situation being exciting and challenging, and the extent to which it was attributable to the talk being stressful and threatening. As can be seen in Fig. 3.12, the repressors showed a very strong tendency to attribute their increased heart rate to excitement and challenge rather than to stress and threat. In contrast, the high-anxious and defensive high-anxious groups were much more inclined to attribute their increased heart rate to stress and threat than to excitement and challenge. These findings are consistent with the

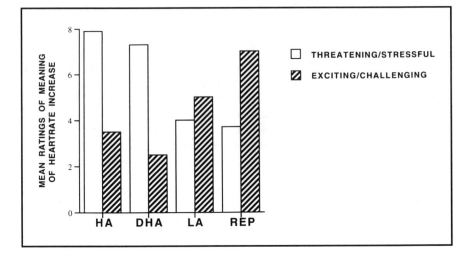

FIG. 3.12. Mean interpretation of heart rate increases in low-anxious (LA), repressor (REP), high-anxious (HA), and defensive high-anxious (DHA) groups. Data from Derakshan and Eysenck (in press, exp. 2).

notion that the repressors have an opposite interpretive bias for their own bodily sensations, whereas high-anxious individuals have an interpretive bias for theirs.

HIGH-ANXIOUS AND
DEFENSIVE HIGH-ANXIOUS INDIVIDUALS

The four-factor theory of trait anxiety does not make specific predictions about defensive high-anxious individuals. However, the steady accumulation of evidence about such individuals means that it is now possible to compare them with high-anxious individuals. At a general level, it has been found (e.g., Derakshan & Eysenck, in press) that defensive high-anxious and high-anxious individuals are comparable in terms of their levels of physiological and behavioural anxiety in stressful situations. Further relevant evidence was obtained by Eysenck and Derakshan (submitted a). They obtained ratings of trait anxiety from friends and relatives of high-anxious, defensive high-anxious, repressor, and low-anxious individuals. High-anxious and defensive high-anxious individuals were rated comparably high in trait anxiety, and significantly higher than either low-anxious individuals or repressors.

Derakshan and Eysenck (in press) identified further similarities between defensive high-anxious and high-anxious groups. Both groups showed an equivalent interpretive bias for their own behaviour and for their own physiological responses; they also showed the same attentional bias for their own physiological responses. In addition, both groups were found by Eysenck and Derakshan (in press) to be similar in their interpretive bias for future examination performance. However, some differences have also been found. Eysenck and Derakshan (in press) found that high-anxious individuals worried more than did defensive high-anxious individuals about negative future events. Derakshan and Eysenck (submitted c) found on the modified Body Sensation Interpretation Questionnaire (Clark, Salkovskis, Ost, Breitholz, Koehler, Westling, Jeavons, & Gelder, in press) that high-anxious individuals (but not defensive high-anxious individuals) had an interpretive bias for panic body sensations. However, the two groups showed equivalent interpretive bias for social ambiguous events.

The findings so far are by no means conclusive. However, they do cast doubt on Kohlmann's (1993) speculation that defensive high-anxious individuals may be even more anxious than high-anxious individuals. This has not been supported by behavioural or physiological evidence, and some of the evidence from cognitive biases and assessment of worries indicates that defensive high-anxious individuals are, if anything, less anxious than high-anxious individuals. It appears that defensive high-anxious and high-anxious individuals are broadly similar in most respects, but that the defensive coping style of defensive high-anxious individuals provides them with limited protection from worry.

ISSUES RELATING TO THE NEW THEORY

According to the four-factor theory of trait anxiety, high-anxious individuals should exhibit a wide range of cognitive biases and repressors should display a similar range of opposite cognitive biases. However, there is some evidence that these cognitive biases and opposite cognitive biases are somewhat less extensive than predicted by the theory. In evaluating such evidence, it must be remembered that the theory predicts that cognitive biases and opposite cognitive biases should be more apparent when the level of state or experienced anxiety is high than when it is low. Most of the failures to demonstrate the predicted biases occurred in situations in which no attempt was made to produce high levels of state anxiety.

Another reason for some of the failures of prediction is that most measures of trait anxiety (including the Spielberger State–Trait Anxiety Inventory) are predominantly measures of responsiveness to social threat rather than physical threat. Endler, Magnusson, Ekehammar, and Okaka (1976) factor analysed data from Spielberger's State–Trait Anxiety Inventory, the Behavioural Reactions Questionnaire, and the S–R Inventory of Anxiousness. They obtained two major factors which they labelled interpersonal threat and physical danger. Trait anxiety as assessed by the State–Trait Anxiety Inventory loaded +0.80 on the interpersonal threat factor, but it loaded only +0.25 on the physical danger factor. The somewhat restricted scope of most measures of trait anxiety could account for the fact that trait anxiety is only weakly related to the number and intensity of physical symptoms produced by hyperventilation (Derakshan & Eysenck, submitted b; Eke & McNally, 1996; McNally, 1989; Rapee & Medoro, 1994; Veltman et al., 1994).

The situation is rather more complicated with respect to repressors. It is probable that the range of threat-related stimuli producing cognitive biases is narrower in repressors than in high-anxious individuals. As is discussed below, the repressive coping style may often develop in response to an unhappy childhood. As a result, it might be expected that repressors would tend to display opposite cognitive biases primarily with respect to certain threat-related stimuli possessing significant personal social relevance. Evidence consistent with this notion was reported by Davis (1987, 1990). She found that repressors had difficulty in retrieving negative childhood memories to some retrieval cues, but not to others. This suggests some selectivity in the operation of opposite cognitive biases in repressors. Additional evidence consistent with this view was reported by Fox (1993). She found evidence for an opposite attentional bias in repressors for social threat stimuli but not for physical threat stimuli.

The notion that repressors show opposite cognitive biases mainly to personally relevant stimuli may help to explain the various failures to obtain evidence for an opposite interpretive bias on the homophone and other tasks. The words used in these studies cover a wide range of threats, and may generally lack personal relevance to repressors.

There is another important reason why repressors sometimes fail to exhibit opposite cognitive biases. As Nazanin Derakshan (pers. comm.) has pointed out, there is the following pattern of results in most studies in which repressors fail to show an opposite cognitive bias: high-anxious and defensive high-anxious individuals show a cognitive bias which is significantly greater than that of repressors and low-anxious individuals, who do not differ from each other. The evidence from such studies reveals a lack of opposite cognitive bias only on the assumption that it is appropriate to consider low-anxious individuals as a suitable non-biased control group. In view of the fact that low-anxious individuals are often very low in physiological and behavioural anxiety, whereas repressors, high-anxious, and defensive high-anxious individuals all have comparable levels of physiological and behavioural anxiety, this may often not be an appropriate assumption.

There has been some controversy about the precise meaning of high and low scores on the Marlowe–Crowne Social Desirability Scale and other similar measures. According to Crowne and Marlowe (1964), their scale reflects the need to gain approval and the need to avoid disapproval. In contrast, it is assumed here that high scorers on social desirability are motivated mainly by the need to avoid disapproval by means of a defensive coping style. Relevant evidence was reported by Jacobson and Ford (1966). They found that high social desirability scorers were less sensitive to cultural nuances than were low scorers. They argued that high scorers adopted a defensive denial style of coping in which they "gated out" threatening stimuli.

It is assumed within the theory that repressors are basically honest when they claim that they experience relatively little anxiety, and that the discrepancy between their self-reported levels of anxiety and their behavioural and physiological anxiety is due to opposite cognitive biases. However, there is an alternative explanation of this discrepancy. It is possible that repressors do experience high levels of anxiety, but that they choose to report only low levels. Some aspects of this issue were addressed by Millham and Kellogg (1980). They used the bogus pipeline technique, in which subjects are assured that a monitoring device can assess when they are lying. They also used the Jacobson–Kellogg Scale, which measures need for approval and is similar to the Marlowe–Crowne Social Desirability Scale. This Scale was completed under neutral condition and under bogus pipeline conditions. Self-deception was assessed by the score obtained on the Jacobson–Kellogg Scale under bogus pipeline conditions, and other-deception (i.e., the tendency to deceive other people deliberately) was assessed by the difference between the Jacobson–Kellogg scores obtained under the two conditions.

Millham and Kellogg (1980) found that there was a very low, non-significant correlation of −0.06 between self-deception and other-deception, indicating that these are almost entirely independent constructs. They obtained Marlowe–Crowne scores under neutral conditions, and related these scores to the self-deception and other-deception scores: "Partialing out other-deceptive score, the correlation between M–C (Marlowe–Crowne) and self-deception score was 0.80; partialing out self-deception score, the correlation between M–C and other-deception score was 0.64" (p.454). These findings suggest that most repressors are deceiving themselves, but that some may only be deceiving others.

ORIGINS OF HIGH-ANXIOUS AND
REPRESSOR STYLES

We have now discussed a considerable amount of experimental evidence indicating that high-anxious individuals have selective attentional and interpretive biases for a wide range of threat-related information, whereas repressors have opposite selective attentional and interpretive biases for the same information. High-anxious individuals and repressors can both be regarded as anxious in general terms, since repressors exhibit high behavioural and physiological anxiety in stressful situations (e.g., Derakshan & Eysenck, in press; Harrigan et al., 1994; Weinberger et al., 1979). As a consequence, it may appear paradoxical that these two groups have developed diametrically opposed cognitive strategies for handling their anxiety. It is not possible to provide any definite answers, but some speculations will be offered.

One approach to understanding the differing cognitive strategies of high-anxious individuals and repressors is to consider the functional value of these strategies. The attentional and interpretive biases of high-anxious individuals can be considered in terms of Eysenck's (1992) analysis of the function of anxiety: "It is clear that rapid detection of the early warning signs of danger possesses considerable survival value. It can be fatal, for example, if one ignores the smell of burning in a house or the initial malfunctioning of a car. The key purpose or function of anxiety is probably to facilitate the detection of danger or threat in potentially threatening environments" (p.4). The cognitive biases possessed by high-anxious individuals help to ensure that threat-related stimuli are detected rapidly, and this strategy facilitates avoidance of, or escape from, potential danger.

What about the functional value of the defensive coping style adopted by repressors? The most obvious advantage of the opposite attentional and interpretive biases possessed by repressors is that they reduce repressors' conscious experience of anxiety. As a consequence, repressors tend to experience fewer negative mood states than would be the case if they did not have these opposite cognitive biases. There is another incidental advantage which accrues from the development of opposite cognitive biases as a self-protective device in childhood. According to the cultural norms in most societies, it is regarded as preferable to be relatively free of anxiety. The opposite cognitive biases possessed by repressors make it easier for them to conform to such cultural norms.

As is perhaps apparent from what has been said so far, there are also significant disadvantages associated with the cognitive strategies adopted by high-anxious individuals and by repressors. High-anxious individuals have the disadvantage of experiencing a considerable amount of anxiety; in extreme cases, this can turn into clinical levels of anxiety. Repressors have the disadvantage that they may ignore important threat-related stimuli or dangers. One of the consequences of such an approach may be an enhanced susceptibility to psychosomatic disorders (see Schwartz, 1990, for a review).

It is assumed that genetic factors play a role in producing individual differences in susceptibility to anxiety (e.g., Pedersen et al., 1988). However, early attachment experiences may be important in determining whether a given child becomes high-anxious or adopts an avoidant or defensive coping style. Ainsworth and Bell (1970) identified three different styles of attachment between an infant and its mother on the basis of observations of infants with their mother and separated from their mother.

One of the attachment styles identified by Ainsworth and Bell (1970) is anxious/resistant attachment. Infants with anxious and resistant attachment are anxious in the presence of their mother, become very distressed when the mother leaves, and resist contact with her when she returns. This style of behaviour resembles that of high-anxious adults. Another attachment style is avoidant attachment. Infants with this attachment style do not seek contact with the mother, show little apparent distress when separated from her, and avoid contact with her upon her return. This style of behaviour resembles that of adult repressors. The notion that an avoidant attachment style in infants can form the basis for an adult defensive coping style receives additional support from the findings of Sroufe and Waters (1977). They found that infants with an avoidant style who appeared unconcerned upon the return of their caregiver nevertheless displayed an accelerated heart rate.

Additional evidence linking childhood avoidant attachment to adult repressiveness comes from studies by Dozier and Kobak (1992) and Myers and Brewin (1994). Dozier and Kobak (1992) gave adult subjects the Adult Attachment Interview, in which they were asked to remember occasions of separation and threatened separation from their parents. Those subjects who appeared to have adopted an avoidant attachment style had large increases in skin conductance for several questions (e.g., those concerning separation from parents, rejection by parents, and how they were affected by their upbringing). In the study by Myers and Brewin (1994), their female subjects were given a semi-structured interview concerning their childhood. Repressors indicated that they had experienced significantly more paternal indifference and antipathy than the high-anxious, defensive high-anxious, and low-anxious groups. However, these interview-based findings were not found when a less sensitive questionnaire-based approach was adopted. The groups did not differ in terms of maternal indifference and antipathy. As a consequence, it is difficult to relate these findings directly to those of Ainsworth and Bell (1970), since they focused specifically on the mother–child relationship.

In sum, it seems likely that young children who experience indifference and antipathy from one or both parents develop an avoidant attachment style, combining apparent behavioural calmness with high physiological arousal. A related possibility (C. Brewin, pers. comm.) is that parental inconsistency plays a role in the development of an avoidant attachment style. An avoidant attachment style in children often develops into the adult defensive coping style characteristic of repressors.

SUMMARY AND CONCLUSIONS

According to the four-factor theory of trait anxiety presented in this chapter, high-anxious individuals have selective attentional and interpretive biases associated with the cognitive appraisal of the situation, as well as with the processing of information about their own physiological activity, action tendencies and behaviour, and cognitions. In contrast, repressors have opposite selective attentional and interpretive biases for all of those sources of information. The various biases are predicted to be greater when the level of experienced anxiety is high than when it is low. Finally, it is assumed within the theory that the cognitive biases usually depend on processes operating below the level of conscious awareness.

In general terms, the experimental evidence supports the various predictions of the four-factor theory of trait anxiety. However, there have been fewer relevant studies on repressors than on high-anxious individuals, and more research is needed on opposite cognitive biases in repressors. More specifically, it is currently unclear whether the opposite cognitive biases of repressors apply to as extensive a range of external and internal stimuli as the cognitive biases of high-anxious individuals. It is also unclear whether the cognitive biases of high-anxious individuals are as great for stimuli related to physical threat as for stimuli related to social threat.

Little is known of the environmental factors associated with the development of the high-anxious and repressive coping styles. However, there are interesting parallels between the anxious and resistant attachment style of infants and the characteristics of high-anxious adults, and between the anxious and avoidant attachment style of infants and the characteristics of adult repressors.

CHAPTER FOUR

Theoretical approaches to clinical anxiety

INTRODUCTION

The theorist attempting to understand clinical anxiety is immediately faced by the fact that there are a number of different anxiety disorders. According to DSM-IV, there are 12 discriminably different anxiety disorders: panic disorder without agoraphobia; panic disorder with agoraphobia; agoraphobia without history of panic disorder; specific phobia; social phobia; obsessive–compulsive disorder; post-traumatic stress disorder; acute stress disorder; generalised anxiety disorder; anxiety due to a medical condition; substance-induced anxiety disorder; and anxiety disorder not otherwise specified.

There are other problems standing in the way of producing a clear theoretical account of clinical anxiety. One obvious problem is that of comorbidity, which inevitably reduces the likelihood of finding clear-cut cognitive or behavioural differences between patients classified as suffering from different anxiety disorders. Evidence that there is a considerable amount of comorbidity was reported by Barlow, Di Nardo, Vermilyea, and Blanchard (1986) on a sample of 108 consecutive anxious patients presenting at their clinic. Across the entire sample, 34% of the patients were assigned only a primary diagnosis, 36% received one additional diagnosis, 22% received two additional diagnoses, and 8% received three or or more additional diagnoses. The number of additional diagnoses depended to some extent on the primary diagnosis. Additional diagnoses were typically assigned to cases of panic disorder, generalised anxiety disorder, and obsessive–compulsive disorder, but were less frequent with cases of social phobia and agoraphobia.

A much larger study, which also found considerable evidence of comorbidity, was reported by Goisman, Goldenberg, Vasile, and Keller (1995a). They studied 711 patients with one of the following current or past DSM-III-R index anxiety diagnoses: panic disorder without agoraphobia; panic disorder with agoraphobia; agoraphobia without a history of panic disorder; generalised anxiety disorder; social phobia. These 711 patients had received a total of 998 index diagnoses in their lifetime. In 29% of cases, patients with an index diagnosis had never received an additional anxiety diagnosis. In 39% of the cases, there had been one additional diagnosis, in 18% there had been two additional diagnoses, and in 14% there had been three or more additional anxiety diagnoses.

Goisman et al. (1995a) reported that the percentage of patients having no additional lifetime anxiety diagnoses varied considerably from one anxiety disorder to another. Only 11% of those with an index diagnosis of generalised anxiety disorder had no additional diagnosis, and the figure was only 17% of those with social phobia. At the other extreme, 43% of those with panic disorder without agoraphobia had no additional diagnosis, as did 40% of panic disorder patients with agoraphobia.

Another potential problem, related to the issue of comorbidity, is the possibility that the symptoms of anxiety exhibited by patients with the various anxiety disorders may be rather similar. The most direct way of investigating symptom specificity is to make use of appropriate self-report questionnaires. This strategy was followed by Miguel-Tobal and Cano-Vindel (1995), who administered the Inventory of Situations and Responses of Anxiety to anxious patients who were classified on DSM-III-R as suffering from simple phobia, social phobia, agoraphobia, generalised anxiety disorder, or obsessive–compulsive disorder. The Inventory of Situations and Responses of Anxiety assesses cognitive, physiological, and motor response systems of anxiety in four types of situations (evaluative; interpersonal; phobia-related; and daily).

Miguel-Tobal and Cano-Vindel (1995) found that there were some group differences in the number of symptoms, with agoraphobics tending to report the greatest number of symptoms and simple phobics the fewest. However, in spite of the fact that the patients were carefully selected as relatively "pure" cases of each anxiety disorder, there was little evidence of symptom specificity. In contrast, there were predictable group differences in anxiety responses across situations. For example, agoraphobics reported high levels of anxiety in phobic situations, and social phobics reported considerable anxiety in interpersonal situations.

Stronger evidence of symptom specificity was obtained by Beck, Steer, and Beck (1993). The Beck Anxiety Inventory was administered to 655 clinically anxious patients, and the resultant scores were calculated for sub-scales representing subjective, somatic, and panic symptoms. On the basis of these sub-scale scores, six types of patients were identified: above average on all sub-scales; below average on all sub-scales; low on the subjective sub-scale only; high on the subjective and somatic sub-scales only; high on the panic and subjective sub-scales only; and high on the subjective and somatic sub-scales only. Those below average on all sub-scales were more likely to have obsessive–compulsive disorder and social phobia than to have panic disorder, agoraphobia, or generalised anxiety disorder. Those above average on all sub-scales or only on the panic and subjective sub-scales had agoraphobia and panic with agoraphobia rather than obsessive–compulsive disorder, social phobia, or generalised anxiety disorder.

Koksal, Power, and Sharp (1991) also obtained evidence of symptom specificity. They used the Four Systems Anxiety Questionnaire, which assesses the somatic (physiological), behavioural (especially avoidance), cognitive (especially worry), and feeling (experience of anxiety) components of anxiety. This questionnaire was administered to patients who were diagnosed as suffering from one of the following anxiety disorders on the basis of the DSM-III: social phobia; panic disorder; generalised anxiety disorder; simple phobia; obsessive–compulsive disorder.

The findings of Koksal et al. (1991) are shown in Fig. 4.1. As might be expected, social phobics scored much higher than the other groups on behavioural anxiety, whereas the obsessive–compulsives scored the highest on cognitive anxiety. However, panic disorder patients scored suprisingly low on somatic anxiety, and patients with generalised anxiety disorder scored surprisingly high on somatic anxiety.

Part of what is involved in providing a theoretical account of clinical anxiety is the identification of some of the major precipitating or predisposing factors associated with specific anxiety disorders. This is difficult to do, in part because any anxiety disorder can be produced in a number of different ways. For example, McKeon, Roa, and Mann (1984) considered the number of life events experienced by obsessive–compulsive disorder patients in the year prior to onset of the disorder. Those with a non-anxious premorbid personality experienced three times as many life events as normal controls, whereas those with a highly anxious premorbid personality did not experience a surplus of

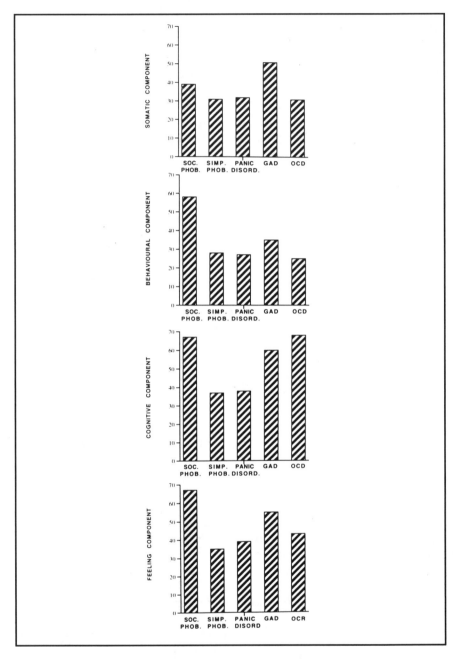

FIG. 4.1. Somatic, behavioural, cognitive, and feeling components of anxiety in social phobia (soc. phob.), simple phobia (simp. phob.), panic disorder (panic disord.), generalised anxiety disorder (GAD), and obsessive–compulsive disorder (OCD). Data from Koksal et al. (1991).

life events on average. Thus, the relative importance of premorbid personality and prevalence of life events in precipitating obsessive–compulsive disorder varies from patient to patient.

In addition to the findings of McKeon et al. (1984), there is reasonable evidence that life events play a role in other anxiety disorders. Barrett (1979) asked anxious patients to complete a 61-item life event inventory for the six months prior to onset of their anxiety disorder. They reported significantly more undesirable events than controls, and this was more so for panic disorder patients than for generalised anxiety disorder patients. Finlay-Jones and Brown (1981) found using an interview approach that anxious and depressed patients were both more likely than normal controls to have experienced at least one severe event in the 12 months prior to onset. They also found that anxious patients tended to have experienced danger events (involving future threats), whereas depressed patients were more likely to report loss events (involving past losses). Andrews (1988) reviewed the relevant studies, and came to the following conclusion: "Four controlled studies supported the clinical wisdom that panic and agoraphobia tend to follow an especially severe period of stress, stress that was more pronounced than that preceding GAD [generalised anxiety disorder] or other neurosis, and much more pronounced than that reported by normal subjects over a comparable period" (p.171).

There is also evidence that genetic factors are of importance. Torgersen (1990) reviewed the relevant literature, and came to the following conclusion: "The family, twin, and linkage studies seem to indicate that anxiety disorders are genetically influenced. When we look at the specific disorders, the best evidence exists for panic disorders. Phobias also seem to be genetically transmitted. With regard to obsessive–compulsive disorder, the evidence is equivocal, but some kind of genetic factors seem to be involved" (p.394).

More recently, Skre, Onstad, Torgersen, Lygren, and Kringlen (1993) carried out a study, in which they compared the prevalence of anxiety disorders in monozygotic and dizygotic co-twins of anxiety disorder probands. They came to the following conclusion: "The results support the hypothesis of a genetic contribution in aetiology of panic disorder, generalised anxiety disorder and post-traumatic stress disorder. The hypothesis that simple and social phobia are mainly caused by environmental experience was also supported" (p.85).

Despite these findings, there are a number of inconsistencies in the literature. McNally (1994) discussed research on genetic factors in panic disorder, and concluded that it had proved difficult to replicate early evidence of the involvement of such factors.

In sum, those who study the anxiety disorders are faced by a number of complexities. These complexities include the large number of different anxiety disorders, widespread comorbidity, a partial lack of symptom specificity from disorder to disorder, and the existence of numerous factors (personality; genetic factors; life events) which seem to be related to anxiety disorders, but not in the same way to all anxiety disorders. Despite these complexities, it will be argued in this chapter that theoretical progress can be made in understanding at least some of the main anxiety disorders. More specifically, a cognitive perspective can usefully be applied to such diverse disorders as generalised anxiety disorder, panic disorder, social phobia, specific phobia, and obsessive–compulsive disorder.

BECK'S SCHEMA THEORY

One of the best-known attempts to provide a coherent theoretical account of the anxiety disorders is that of Beck (e.g., Beck & Emery, 1985; Beck & Clark, 1988). According to Beck, the major features of the anxiety disorders are cognitive in nature, but the cognitive system is not causally involved in the aetiology of clinical anxiety. In the words of Beck and Emery (1985), "We consider that the primary pathology of dysfunction during a depression or an anxiety disorder is in the cognitive apparatus. However, that is quite different from the notion that the cognition *causes* these syndromes—a notion that is just as illogical as an assertion that hallucinations cause schizophrenia" (p.85).

Despite this apparently unequivocal statement, Beck and Emery (1985) included certain kinds of cognitions (e.g., unrealistic goals; unreasonable attitudes) among the factors predisposing to anxiety disorders. Other predisposing factors allegedly include hereditary predisposition, certain physical diseases, developmental traumata, and inadequate personal experiences.

This issue was clarified by Beck and Clark (1988). They focused on schemas, which they defined as "functional structures of relatively enduring representations of prior knowledge and experience" (p.24). According to Beck and Clark (1988), "by possessing latent maladaptive schemas, some individuals evidence a cognitive vulnerability for developing anxiety or depression" (p.24).

The essence of their schema theory approach was expressed succinctly by Beck and Clark (1988): "Cognitive structures [i.e., schemas] guide the screening, encoding, organising, storing and retrieving of information. Stimuli consistent with existing schemas are elaborated and encoded, while inconsistent or irrelevant information is ignored or forgotten ... the maladaptive schemas in the anxious patient involve perceived physical or psychological threat to one's personal domain as well as an exaggerated sense of vulnerability" (pp.24–26). However, patients with different anxiety disorders vary in terms of some of the themes present in their maladaptive schemas. According to Beck and Clark (1988), "With generalised anxiety disorder (GAD) a variety of life situations are viewed as threatening to one's self-concept; in panic disorder (PD) bodily or mental experiences are experienced as catastrophic; with simple phobias danger is attributed to specific avoidable situations; and in agoraphobia panic attacks are associated with external situations" (pp.26–27).

How do schemas influence cognitive functioning? In essence, they serve to direct processing resources to those aspects of the external or internal environment which are congruent with them. In other words, anxious patients will attend to stimuli which present a physical or psychological threat, ambiguous stimuli will be interpreted in a threatening fashion, and threatening information will be retrieved readily from long-term memory.

One of the important consequences of having maladaptive schemas is that anxious patients are subject to a number of cognitive distortions. According to Beck (1976), two cognitive distortions which are of particular importance are attention binding and catastrophising. Attention binding involves a preoccupation with danger and an involuntary focus on concepts related to danger and to threat. Catastrophising involves focusing on the worst possible outcome of any given situation, combined with an over-estimate of the probability of its occurrence.

Evaluation

The notion that maladaptive schemas influence the processing of threat-related information in a top-down or conceptually driven fashion is a valuable one. There is a considerable amount of evidence that anxious patients do often exhibit the schema-congruent processing predicted by Beck's schema theory (see Eysenck, 1992, for a review). In general terms, it seems reasonable to assume that most of the cognitive distortions exhibited by anxious patients depend on information stored in schemas within long-term memory. The notion that maladaptive schemas tend to be latent, mainly influencing thinking and behaviour in times of stress, is also reasonable.

Despite its strengths, the theory has a number of limitations. First, the central theoretical construct of "schema" is amorphous, and often seems to mean little more than "belief". Second, the evidence for the existence of specific schemas is often based on a circular argument.

Behavioural evidence of a cognitive bias in anxious patients is used to infer the presence of a schema, and then that schema is used to "explain" the observed cognitive bias. In other words, there is generally no direct or independent evidence of the existence of a schema. Third, schema-congruent processing in anxious patients is less extensive in scope than is anticipated on Beck's schema theory. For example, as is discussed in detail in Chapter 5, patients suffering from various anxiety disorders fail to exhibit the memory bias favouring threat-related information predicted by Beck and Clark (1988).

THEORETICAL APPROACHES

One way of attempting to develop a theoretical framework of the anxiety disorders is to adopt a bottom-up approach based on the patterns of symptoms exhibited by patients suffering from the various anxiety disorders. An alternative approach is to adopt a top-down approach in which an attempt is made to understand at least some of the anxiety disorders within a pre-existing theoretical framework. The essence of the distinction is as follows: in the bottom-up approach, the anxiety disorders are characterised primarily on the basis of empirical evidence about patterns of similarity and dissimilarity (e.g., in symptom structure); in the top-down approach, the major anxiety disorders are categorised and accounted for on the basis of theoretical considerations. It is possible within a top-down approach for the major anxiety disorders to be "predicted" by some underlying theory.

Foa and Kozak (1985) proposed an essentially bottom-up approach to the seven anxiety disorders listed in DSM-III: simple phobia; panic disorder; social phobia; agoraphobia; post-traumatic stress disorder; generalised anxiety disorder; and obsessive–compulsive disorder. They argued mainly on the basis of the symptoms exhibited by anxious patients that three major axes are of relevance to clinical anxiety: presence versus absence of avoidance behaviour; presence versus absence of external fear cues; and presence versus absence of anticipated harm.

As can be seen in Fig. 4.2, there are substantial differences among anxiety disorders in terms of these axes. Agoraphobics, some specific phobics, and some social phobics have all three factors present, whereas patients with generalised anxiety disorder have none of them. It can also be seen that some anxiety disorders are harder than others to fit into this categorical scheme. For example, patients with obsessive–compulsive disorder vary between having all three factors present to having none of them present.

External cues present	Anticipated harm present	Avoidance responses present	Anxiety disorders
Yes	Yes	Yes	Specific phobias Agoraphobics Some social phobics Some obsessive–compulsives
Yes	Yes	No	Some social phobics
Yes	No	Yes	Specific phobics Some obsessive–compulsives
Yes	No	No	Some post-traumatic stress disorders Some obsessionals
No	Yes	Yes	Obsessive–compulsives with repeating rituals
No	Yes	No	Panic disorders Obsessionals
No	No	Yes	Post-traumatic stress disorder
No	No	No	Post-traumatic stress disorder Generalised anxiety disorder Ruminators

FIG. 4.2. Locations of seven anxiety disorders within a theoretical framework proposed by Foa and Kozak (1985).

Zinbarg and Barlow (1996) proposed a hierarchical model of anxiety and the anxiety disorders also based on a bottom-up approach. Patients suffering from a variety of anxiety disorders or major depression and non-patient controls were administered a semi-structured clinical interview and several self-report questionnaires. There was a general factor of negative affectivity (closely resembling trait anxiety) which distinguished all of the patient groups from the non-patient control subjects. This finding suggests that there is some commonality among the various anxiety disorders and depression. In addition, there were four more specific discriminant functions or factors. These discriminant functions or factors were identified as fear of fear, agoraphobia, social anxiety, and obsessions and compulsions. Fear of fear was most associated with panic disorder and with panic disorder with agoraphobia, agoraphobia was most associated with panic disorder with agoraphobia, social anxiety with social phobia, and obsessions and compulsions with obsessive–compulsive disorder.

Zinbarg and Barlow (1996) argued that the level within the hierarchy which is more important depends on the issue being considered.

According to Zinbarg and Barlow (1996), "when distinguishing anxiety disordered patients and depressed patients from individuals with no mental disorder, the higher order level is more important, and only a single dimension is required. However, when distinguishing one group of anxiety disordered patients from another, a lower order level is most important" (p.191).

The approaches of Foa and Kozak (1985) and of Zinbarg and Barlow (1996) provide valuable insights into the similarities and dissimilarities among the anxiety disorders. However, the fact that there are substantial differences between the two approaches suggests that it is not easy to derive an unequivocal set of dimensions or axes on the basis of anxious patients' symptoms. In addition, it is difficult to think of effective ways of providing empirical tests of the proposed schemes.

Foa and Kozak (1985) and Zinbarg and Barlow (1996) embarked on the task of devising a theoretical framework for the anxiety disorders by considering the symptoms of patients suffering from the various disorders. However, there is an alternative to this bottom-up approach. The approach adopted in this chapter is more top-down in emphasis. It starts with a theory of emotion, and this theory is then used to predict the kinds of symptoms which might be exhibited by clinically anxious patients. Theorising about the anxiety disorders is constrained by the assumptions of the theory of emotion, and so it is not possible to create additional dimensions of symptoms on an *ad hoc* basis. Furthermore, it is hoped that anchoring the approach to the anxiety disorders in a theory of emotion will make the proposed theory more testable than previous bottom-up approaches.

General assumptions

The four-factor theory of clinical anxiety to be presented here is based on the assumption that there are important links between personality in normals in the form of high trait anxiety on the one hand, and the anxiety disorders on the other hand. There is convincing evidence that patients suffering from most of the anxiety disorders have elevated levels of trait anxiety (Clark, Watson, & Mineka, 1994; Mathews & Eysenck, 1987; Watson, Clark, & Carey, 1988; Zinbarg & Barlow, 1996). For example, Watson et al. (1988) found that obsessive–compulsive disorder patients, social phobics, and specific phobics all had high levels of negative affectivity, a personality dimension closely related to trait anxiety.

As Clark et al. (1994) pointed out, the association between trait anxiety or negative affectivity and the anxiety disorders is consistent with various theoretical approaches or models. According to the pathoplasty model, personality modifies the course or expression of a disorder, but is not of direct relevance in terms of aetiology. According to the scar model, the anxiety disorders affect personality. In other words, high levels of anxiety cause personality changes. Two other models (the continuity and vulnerability models) are closely related to each other. It is assumed within the continuity model that high trait anxiety and the anxiety disorders reflect the same underlying processes, with the anxiety disorders representing extreme manifestations of normal personality characteristics. According to the vulnerability model, normal individuals with certain personality or other characteristics (e.g., high trait anxiety) are especially likely to develop anxiety disorders. This vulnerability may be general or relatively specific.

These various models are not mutually exclusive, and it is possible or even likely that they are all partially correct (Clark et al., 1994). However, the four-factor theory proposed here is based on the continuity and vulnerability models rather than on the pathoplasty or scar models. More specifically, what will be proposed is a diathesis–stress model, in which there are predisposing or vulnerability factors, but in addition a relevant stressor is generally also needed to trigger the onset of an anxiety disorder.

Eysenck (1992) proposed a limited version of the theory to be put forward here. Eysenck's (1992) theoretical approach conformed to the diathesis–stress model:

> It is assumed that generalised anxiety disorder occurs mainly (although not exclusively) in those individuals who are semi-permanently vulnerable and who are exposed to stressful life events ... it is assumed that there is a cognitive vulnerability factor, and that this vulnerability factor involves systematic biases in the cognitive system which influence the emotional impact of environmental events ... it is assumed that high levels of trait anxiety predispose to generalised anxiety disorder (p.36).

As we saw in Chapter 3, normal individuals high in trait anxiety tend to possess selective attentional and interpretive biases for four sources of threat-related information: threat-related environmental stimuli; physiological stimuli; stimuli relating to their own behaviour; and thoughts based on information in long-term memory. These biases are more likely to manifest themselves when state anxiety is high than when it is low. In general terms, it is assumed that anxious patients and high trait-anxious normals have similar selective attentional and interpretive biases in their processing of threat-related information.

However, with the exception of generalised anxiety disorder, these biases tend to apply to a more restricted range of stimuli in anxious patients than in high trait-anxious normals. This greater specificity is discussed later in the chapter. Another difference between the cognitive biases (and especially interpretive biases) of anxious patients and of high trait-anxious normals is that the effects of these biases are perceived as less controllable, more disruptive, and more intense in anxious patients.

The theoretical assumptions presented so far are based on the notion that there is continuity between normal and clinical anxiety in terms of cognitive biases. It is also assumed that there is continuity in terms of symptoms. However, it is clear that additional theoretical assumptions are required in order to understand why it is that the anxiety experienced by clinical patients is stronger and much more disruptive of normal functioning than is the anxiety experienced by high trait-anxious normals. More specifically, we need to explain apparent qualitative differences between the two groups (e.g., in terms of uncontrollability of thoughts, behaviour, and so on). These differences can be understood on the assumption that there is a reciprocal relationship between cognitive biases and state anxiety (see Chapter 3). That is to say, cognitive biases applied to the processing of threat-related information increase the level of state anxiety, and elevated state anxiety exaggerates the cognitive biases. This can create a positive feedback loop which eventually creates extremely high levels of uncontrollable experienced anxiety. Anxious patients often have more pronounced cognitive biases than normals high in trait anxiety, and so may be especially likely to become trapped in such positive feedback loops.

The differences between normals high in trait anxiety and anxious patients can also be considered in terms of the distinctions among *actual symptoms*, *perceived symptoms*, and *interpreted symptoms*. We will consider elevated heart rate to illustrate the distinction. The actual symptom is the objectively measurable heart rate in beats per minute. The perceived symptom is the heart rate as perceived by the individual; this may or may not correspond to the actual heart rate, in part because of the operation of selective attentional bias and opposite selective attentional bias. Finally, there is the interpreted symptom, which refers to the significance which the individual attaches to the perceived symptom. For example, elevated heart rate can be interpreted as indicative of a possible heart attack or simply as the result of strenuous physical exercise. Interpreted symptoms depend in part on interpretive bias and opposite interpretive bias.

It is assumed that anxious patients tend to differ from high trait-anxious individuals more with respect to interpreted symptoms than perceived symptoms. More specifically, anxious patients are more likely to interpret their anxiety-related symptoms as indicative of possible catastrophe or complete loss of control than are high trait-anxious normals, presumably because of the positive feedback loop described above.

Dalgleish (1994) has put forward views which overlap in part with those proposed here. According to Dalgleish (1994):

> The basic mechanisms underlying selective attention on the one hand, and the emotional response of anxiety on the other hand, are the same in all individuals. What differentiates those people who are diagnosed as having an anxiety disorder or those who are high in trait anxiety from non-anxious individuals is the type of information which leads to an appraisal of threat. For example, in subjects with GAD [generalised anxiety disorder] a wide range of stimuli are [sic] anxiety provoking; however, many of those stimuli would not be seen as in any way threat-laden by the majority of people and would not cause them to be anxious (pp.162–163).

It is undeniable that anxious patients, and perhaps especially generalised anxiety disorder patients, do experience anxiety in response to many stimuli which do not create anxiety in normals. As Beck and Emery (1985) pointed out on the basis of their experience as therapists, "the range of stimuli that can evoke anxiety in generalised anxiety disorder may increase until almost any stimulus is perceived as a danger" (p.32). However, it is strongly argued here that what most importantly differentiates clinical patients from normals high in trait anxiety is the intensity and uncontrollability of interpreted symptoms rather than the sheer number of different stimuli causing anxiety.

Specific theoretical assumptions

The emphasis so far has been on general theoretical issues such as the continuity between anxiety in high trait-anxious normals and in anxious patients. This general approach clearly offers no explanation of why it is that there are several different anxiety disorders, each with its own pattern of symptoms. In order to provide such an explanation, it is necessary to consider the proposed theory in more detail.

As can be seen in Fig. 4.3, the four-factor theory of clinical anxiety closely resembles the four-factor theory of trait anxiety presented in Chapter 3. Thus, there are four sources of information which can be used to determine the level of state anxiety, and each source can be affected by selective attentional and interpretive bias. These biases are assumed

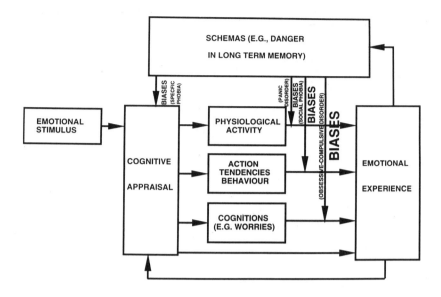

FIG. 4.3. A new four-factor theory of clinical anxiety.

to be determined by processes operating below the level of conscious awareness. As well as cognitive biases affecting the level of state anxiety, it is assumed that the level of state anxiety affects the cognitive biases. In other words, anxious patients when highly anxious should exhibit more pronounced selective attentional and interpretive bias than when relatively non-anxious.

As can also be seen in Fig. 4.3, there is a continuous line running from the conscious experience of anxiety to the cognitive appraisal of the situation, whereas this line is broken in the four-factor theory of trait anxiety. The implication of the continuous line is that the extent to which clinically anxious patients appraise the situation as threatening or dangerous is partly determined by their own emotional reactions. Arntz, Rauner, and van den Hout (1995) refer to this as *ex consequentia* reasoning, which they describe as follows: "The S does not only conclude that danger implies feeling anxious, but also that feeling anxious implies danger" (p.917).

As was mentioned in Chapters 2 and 3, Arntz et al. (1995) tested the view that the experience of anxiety can influence situational appraisal. Spider phobics, panic patients, social phobics, other anxious patients, and normal controls were presented with four scenarios, one of which was spider phobia relevant, one panic disorder relevant, one social phobia relevant, and one was a control scenario. Each scenario was followed by information indicating either that the situation was objectively safe or objectively dangerous. In addition, the scenario also contained an anxious response or a non-anxious response. For example, one scenario concerned being trapped in a lift, and the anxious response was "Suddenly you become very anxious". In contrast, the non-anxious response was "One of the passengers accidentally falls into your arms. You smile. You have been interested in this person for some time and this seems to be a good opportunity". For each scenario, the perceived danger of the event was rated.

The main findings are shown in Fig. 4.4. As can be seen, the ratings of situational danger by all of the anxious patient groups were greater when there was an anxious response than when there was a non-anxious response, but this was not the case for the normal controls. This *ex consequentia* reasoning occurred regardless of the nature of the scenario: "There is no evidence that the effect of anxiety response information on danger ratings is specific. All anxiety disorders showed this phenomenon, regardless of whether the event was specific for their anxiety, or not" (Arntz et al., 1995, p. 922). In contrast, the situational danger ratings of the normal controls were not affected at all by anxiety response information. However, very different findings were obtained by Alison Wheeler and Eysenck (unpubl.).

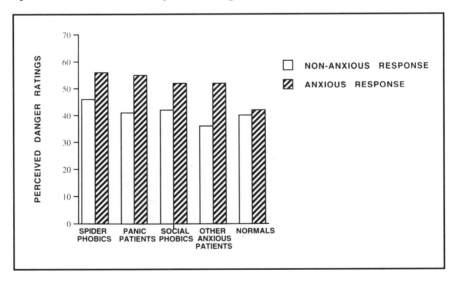

FIG. 4.4. Perceived danger of events as a function of response (anxious vs. non-anxious) in spider phobics, panic patients, social phobics, other anxious patients, and normals. Data from Arntz et al. (1995).

Why does the experience of anxiety seem to influence situational appraisal to a greater extent in anxious patients than in normals? Self-focus tends to be greater in anxious patients than in normals (Ingram, 1990), and this may increase the extent of *ex consequentia* reasoning. However, it is premature to speculate too much in the absence of further research evidence.

It is simplest to apply the four-factor theory of clinical anxiety to patients with generalised anxiety disorder. It is assumed that generalised anxiety disorder generally depends in a fairly direct way on a preceding high level of trait anxiety (Eysenck, 1992; Rapee, 1991). According to Eysenck (1992), normals high in trait anxiety anxiety have a cognitive vulnerability factor for generalised anxiety disorder, which includes hypervigilance as part of it (see also Chapter 1). According to Rapee (1991), generalised anxiety disorder represents "a relatively pure manifestation of high trait anxiety" (p.422). The assumption that there are direct links between high trait anxiety and generalised anxiety disorder leads to the expectation that generalised anxiety disorder patients will tend to have selective attentional and interpretive biases for all four sources of information.

There are two important qualifications which need to be applied to the theoretical assumptions made above. First, even if groups of generalised anxiety disorder patients show significant evidence of selective attentional and interpretive biases for all four sources of information, this does not mean that all of the patients have the biases for every source of information. Indeed, it is probable that generalised anxiety disorder patients form a heterogeneous group, with different patients having cognitive biases for different sources of information.

Second, it is an over-simplification to assume that all high trait-anxious individuals have selective attentional and interpretive biases for all four sources of information. As we saw in Chapter 3, there is good evidence that groups of high trait-anxious individuals possess biases for all four sources of information. However, it is probable that most high trait-anxious individuals have more pronounced cognitive biases for some sources of information than for others. More evidence is needed in order to establish the extent of such specificity of cognitive bias.

Is it justified to assume that there are great similarities between high trait anxiety and generalised anxiety disorder? This assumption is supported by the finding that 80% of generalised anxiety disorder patients cannot recall when or how it started (Rapee, 1991). In addition, many patients report that their generalised anxiety disorder has been lifelong (Rapee, 1991).

Despite the plausibility of assuming that there is a close association between trait anxiety and generalised anxiety disorder, there is one important finding which is apparently inconsistent. Eysenck, Mogg, May, Richards, and Mathews (1991) found that the mean level of trait anxiety in recovered generalised anxiety disorder patients was close to that of a normal control group. Similar findings have been reported in other studies (Ingham, 1966; see Eysenck, 1992). It is not totally clear why recovered patients do not report high levels of trait anxiety. One possibility is that there is a "contrast" effect, with recovered anxious patients under-estimating their level of trait anxiety because they feel relatively less anxious than they did in the clinical state. Another possibility is that trait anxiety is essentially a summary of anxious states over a period of months, with successful treatment producing a consistent reduction in state anxiety over long periods of time (Mogg, pers. comm.). Alternatively, it is possible that their actual level of trait anxiety is lower than it was premorbidly.

Most anxious patients probably exhibit cognitive biases with respect to two or more of the four sources of information determining the experience of anxiety. However, the main focus within the four-factor theory of clinical anxiety is on those patients who display the selective attentional and interpretive biases primarily in connection with only one of the four sources of information. According to this approach, the implication is that there are four basic anxiety disorders, each of which is identified below.

According to the theory, there should be some anxious patients who display the selective attentional and interpretive biases primarily with respect to their own physiological activity and bodily sensations. The diagnostic category which corresponds most closely to this specification is that of panic disorder without agoraphobia.

According to the theory, some anxious patients should display the selective attentional and interpretive biases mainly in connection with their own action tendencies and behaviour. The diagnostic category which corresponds most closely to this specification is that of social phobia, especially generalised social phobia. A crucial ingredient in social phobia is the existence of self-perceived behavioural deficits, some of which relate to social avoidance. Fear of negative evaluation (Watson & Friend, 1969) is undoubtedly of importance in social phobia, and there are probably complex links between self-perceived behavioural deficits and fear of negative evaluation. However, it is assumed that the self-perceived behavioural deficits are of fundamental importance.

According to the theory, some anxious patients should display cognitive biases primarily with respect to their own thoughts or cognitions. The diagnostic category corresponding most closely to this specification is that of obsessive–compulsive disorder. It is assumed that inflated responsibility plays a major role in producing the obsessions and compulsions of obsessive–compulsive disorder patients (Salkovskis, 1985, 1989). As Salkovskis (1991) expressed it, the behaviour patterns of obsessive–compulsive disorder patients "reflect attempts to prevent themselves from being responsible for adverse consequences that might arise from not acting on the content of the thought (prevention of harm through, for example, washing and checking)" (pp.13–14).

How does inflated responsibility produce obsessional thoughts? Eysenck (1992) argued that the frequency with which an individual thinks about a given worry depends on its threat value, and that there are four factors which determine the threat value of a given possible negative event. These factors are its subjective probability, its subjective imminence, its perceived aversiveness, and perceived post-event coping strategies. It is clear that an inflated sense of responsibility could increase the perceived aversiveness of possible negative events (e.g., a burglar gaining entry to one's house because the door was unlocked).

It is less obvious how an inflated sense of responsibility could influence subjective probability. One likely possibility is that the availability heuristic (Tversky & Kahneman, 1973) is involved. According to the availability heuristic, people base their estimates of the future probability of a given class of events on the ease with which instances of such events can be brought to mind. It is assumed that an inflated sense of responsibility for certain events increases anxious mood, that anxious mood then facilitates retrieval of any obsession-related thoughts, and that this increases the subjective probability of the threatening event happening. As a consequence, the individual subsequently spends more time thinking about his or her obsessions.

Tallis (1995) is generally supportive of the notion that an inflated sense of responsibility is important in obsessive–compulsive disorder. However, he did point out that there are some problems with this approach:

> It is unclear why the appraisals and beliefs described in cognitive behavioural models result in the emergence of predominantly washing and checking behaviours. Given the immensity of the human behavioural repertoire, it is remarkable that preventative and reparative behaviours take, in the main, only two forms. Moreover, some affected individuals exhibit glaring inconsistencies in their behaviour. In their efforts to avoid harm coming to others, they cause enormous distress to their own family members. This is often considered acceptable. Finally, it is unclear why

individuals with obsessive–compulsive disorder feel excessively responsible for negative events, but not positive events (p.81).

The main thrust of Tallis's (1995) argument can be expressed as follows: if an inflated sense of personal responsibility were the sole factor involved in obsessive–compulsive disorder, then many more people would suffer from that disorder, and they would exhibit a much wider range of symptoms than is actually observed. Inflated personal responsibility is a key factor in obsessive–compulsive disorder, but we need a more detailed theoretical understanding of the additional factors involved in that disorder.

According to the theory, some anxious patients should display cognitive biases mainly in connection with their cognitive appraisal of certain environmental stimuli. The diagnostic category which corresponds most closely to this specification is that of specific phobia.

Other anxiety disorders

According to DSM-IV, there are 12 different anxiety disorders. However, the four-factor theory of clinical anxiety is directly applicable to only five of them: social phobia; panic disorder; specific phobia; obsessive–compulsive disorder; and generalised anxiety disorder. What about the other seven anxiety disorders? Two of the remaining anxiety disorders (anxiety disorder due to a general medical condition; substance-induced anxiety disorder) are of little or no relevance to a cognitive theory of anxiety. According to DSM-IV, the symptoms of anxiety experienced in both disorders are a direct physiological response to a general medical condition or a drug of abuse, medication, or toxin exposure, respectively. Another anxiety disorder (anxiety disorder not otherwise specified) is a residual and ill-defined category.

One of the four remaining anxiety disorders is agoraphobia without history of panic disorder. This disorder seems to occur very rarely. According to DSM-IV, "In clinical settings, almost all individuals (over 95%) who present with a Agoraphobia also have a current diagnosis (or history) of Panic Disorder" (p.403). This was confirmed by Goisman, Warshaw, Steketee, Fierman, Rogers, Goldenberg, Weinshenker, Vasile, and Keller (1995). They reached the following conclusion:

> Most of the subjects who had agoraphobia without a history of panic disorder and for whom adequate information was available (17 [77%] of 22 subjects) had definite or probable situational panic attacks, and almost as many (15 [68%] of

22) had definite or probable limited symptom attacks, so that their diagnosis would change to panic disorder given a slight difference in symptom patterns or in diagnostic criteria ... it supports a view of agoraphobia without a history of panic disorder as on a continuum with uncomplicated panic disorder and with panic disorder with agoraphobia, rather than as a separate entity (p.1441).

Another anxiety disorder is panic disorder with agoraphobia. It is assumed that this complex disorder typically starts with panic disorder on its own. Concerns about suffering a panic disorder in public places then lead to the development of the symptoms of agoraphobia.

The two final anxiety disorders are post-traumatic stress disorder and acute stress disorder. According to DSM-IV, the latter disorder "is characterised by symptoms similar to those of Post-traumatic Stress Disorder that occur immediately in the aftermath of an extremely traumatic event" (p.393). Both of these anxiety disorders clearly involve systematic effects on the cognitive appraisal of trauma-related events. Thus, they both resemble specific phobia in terms of cognitive biases applied to external stimuli. These cognitive biases can be very extensive and long-lasting in the case of post-traumatic stress disorder.

The main reason why the four-factor theory of clinical anxiety has not been extended to cover post-traumatic stress disorder and acute stress disorder is because there are doubts as to whether these disorders are appropriately classified as anxiety disorders. Several authorities, including Davidson and Foa (1991) and O'Donohue and Elliott (1992), have expressed their doubts on this issue. According to Davidson and Foa (1991):

> Almost any statement about the relation of PTSD to other psychiatric categories can be supported ... data can support the claim that PTSD is a form of anxiety and is properly placed, or on the other hand, PTSD can be shown to be a dissociative or somatoform disorder. Also, because of PTSD's close connection to depression in terms of comorbidity, then it can perhaps be classified as a depressive variant ... If classification is best viewed as a function of aetiology, and if psychiatry is serious in aspiring to take this direction, then PTSD may be considered to represent a new diagnostic category, which may perhaps be called *disorders of psychological trauma* (p.352–353).

According to O'Donohue and Elliott (1992), "PTSD differs from the other anxiety disorders in that anxiety does not have such a clearly predominant role in PTSD ... the anxiety experienced in PTSD is more rational than in the other anxiety disorders" (p.426). They concluded as follows: "If PTSD is to remain a subclassification of mental disorders, we propose that it be removed from the subclassification of anxiety disorders and listed as a separate diagnostic category" (p.433).

Precipitating or predisposing factors

The four-factor theory of clinical anxiety is also of relevance to the issue of precipitating or predisposing factors for the various anxiety disorders. There are numerous predisposing factors for each anxiety disorder, some of which are probably relatively general (e.g., trait anxiety; genetic factors; life events). These general factors can serve to expose any specific vulnerability within the individual. However, the main focus within the theory is on predisposing or precipitating factors which are specific to one anxiety disorder rather than another, and especially on the precipitating and predisposing factors for panic disorder without agoraphobia, social phobia, obsessive–compulsive disorder, and specific phobia.

It is worth considering the relationship between trait anxiety and the anxiety disorders in more detail at this point. There are two main arguments in favour of the notion that individuals high in trait anxiety are more vulnerable than those low in trait anxiety to the various anxiety disorders. First, there are similarities between the cognitive biases shown by high trait-anxious normals and those shown by anxious patients. Second, patients suffering from various anxiety disorders tend to have elevated levels of trait anxiety (e.g., L.A. Clark et al., 1994).

There are reasonably convincing counter-arguments to the above points. First, cognitive biases tend to be more general in normals high in trait anxiety than in anxious patients. Logan and Goetsch (1993) reviewed the literature on selective attentional bias, and came to the following conclusion:

> In 14 studies [of anxiety-disordered subjects] that attempted to determine whether attentional bias was to specific or general threat cues, 11 found attentional biases to specific, personally relevant threat cues ... Four of five studies with nonclinical subjects demonstrated an attentional bias toward threat cues in subjects with high trait anxiety ... Of the four studies that attempted to determine whether attentional bias was more pronounced with specific or general threat cues, three found greater attentional bias toward general threat (p.556).

Second, trait-anxiety levels in anxious patients typically become lower during recovery, suggesting that their premorbid level of trait anxiety was not significantly elevated on average.

An idealised view of the premorbid patterns of cognitive bias producing vulnerability to various anxiety disorders is shown in Fig. 4.5. As can be seen, it is assumed that different specific selective attentional and interpretive biases are associated with specific phobia, social phobia, panic disorder, obsessive–compulsive disorder, and generalised anxiety disorder. Some of the possible reasons for such specificity of cognitive biases are discussed below.

It is assumed that specific precipitating or predisposing factors for panic disorder without agoraphobia will be those factors producing concern about the individual's own physiological system. For example, suppose that someone has suffered from a respiratory disease such as bronchitis. This may lead to the development of selective attentional bias and interpretive bias for internal bodily sensations, which in turn may play a part in producing panic disorder. It has been established that one of the major clusters of symptoms in panic disorder patients relates to shortness of breath and choking (Shiori, Someya, Murashita, & Takahashi, 1996).

McNally and Lorenz (1987) proposed that anxiety sensitivity (involving selective attentional bias and interpretive bias) might be a risk factor for panic disorder. Convincing evidence to support this hypothesis has recently been obtained by Schmidt (unpubl.). He studied recruits to the US Air Force Academy who went through stressful basic training. He controlled for trait anxiety and for previous history of panic. However, he still found that pre-stressor anxiety sensitivity (assessed by the Anxiety Sensitivity Index) predicted the occurrence of spontaneous panic attacks.

Specific precipitating or predisposing factors for social phobia will be those producing concern about the individual's own behaviour in social situations. For example, it is assumed that high levels of introversion can play a part in the development of selective attentional bias and interpretive bias for an individual's own behaviour.

Specific precipitating or predisposing factors for obsessive–compulsive disorder will be those producing concern about the individual's own negative thoughts. It is assumed that situations involving high levels of actual or perceived responsibility can play a role in the development of selective attentional bias and interpretive bias for one's own negative thoughts. However, high levels of perceived responsibility are likely to be much more relevant to the development of checking and repeating behaviour in obsessive–compulsive disorder patients than to washing and ordering rituals (McNally, pers. comm.).

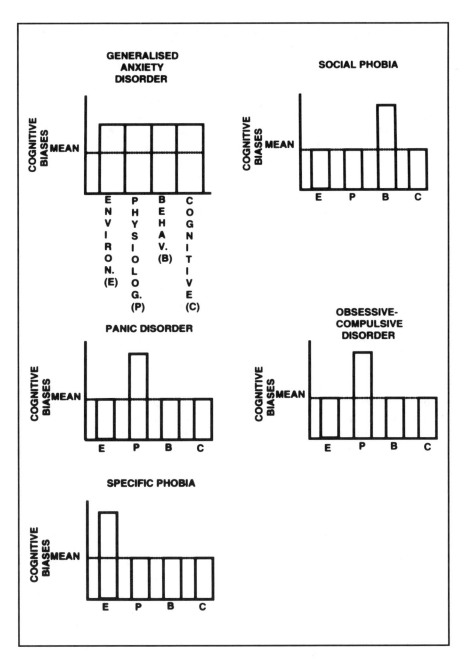

FIG. 4.5. Premorbid patterns of cognitive bias (selective attentional and interpretive biases) associated with specific phobia, social phobia, panic disorder, obsessive–compulsive disorder, and generalised anxiety disorder.

Specific precipitating or predisposing factors for specific phobia will be those producing concern about certain relevant environmental stimuli. For example, observing the fearful reactions of others to phobic stimuli may assist in the development of selective attentional bias and interpretive bias for such stimuli (see Cook & Mineka, 1991). However, specific phobias can develop in other ways (Rachman, 1977). For example, conditioning experiences can contribute to specific phobias (Cook & Mineka, 1991), as can being exposed to information which heightens fear of phobic stimuli (Rachman, 1977). However, there is increasing evidence that specific phobias very often develop in the apparent absence of any relevant observational or vicarious learning experiences (see Menzies & Clarke, 1994, for a review).

Relevance to other approaches
The proposed theory incorporates elements of several previous approaches, and it is not the intention here to discuss each one in detail. What will be done instead is to focus on three approaches which resemble the one proposed here in some of their general characteristics. In particular, we will focus on approaches in which attempts were made to identify some of the major dimensions in terms of which anxiety disorders differ.

The research of Koksal et al. (1991) was discussed earlier in the chapter. In essence, they used their Four Systems Anxiety Questionnaire to compare patients with different anxiety disorders. This questionnaire assesses the behavioural, cognitive, somatic, and feeling components of anxiety. Social phobics were very high on the behavioural component, obsessive–compulsive disorder patients were high on the cognitive component, but panic disorder patients were not especially high on the somatic component.

There is a fair degree of similarity between the general approach of Koksal et al. (1991) and the one adopted here. Three of the sources of information emphasised in the four-factor theory (i.e., behaviour; cognitions; and bodily sensations) have corresponding components in the Four Systems Anxiety Questionnaire. However, the two approaches differ considerably in that Koksal et al. (1991) were mainly concerned with anxious symptoms, whereas the central focus in the four-factor theory of clinical anxiety is on the sources of information and cognitive processes and biases which produce clinical symptoms. As a consequence, cognitive appraisal of the situation is of importance within the four-factor theory, but not within the approach of Koksal et al. (1991). Another important difference is that the feeling component in their approach is not regarded as being directly dependent on the other components. Within the four-factor theory, in contrast, the experience of anxiety depends in part on the previous processing of behavioural, cognitive, and physiological information.

As we saw earlier in the chapter, Zinbarg and Barlow (1996) proposed a hierarchical approach to the anxiety disorders, and the four-factor theory of clinical anxiety can also be regarded as a hierarchical approach. The higher level of their theory consists of negative affectivity or trait anxiety, and the lower level consists of fear of fear, agoraphobia, social anxiety, and obsessions and compulsions. It is assumed within the four-factor theory that high trait anxiety is of some relevance to most anxiety disorders (especially generalised anxiety disorder). There also seem to be links between their fear of fear factor and physiological activity as a source of information, between their social anxiety and one's own behaviour as a source of information, and between their obsessions and compulsions and one's own cognitions as a source of information. However, a major difference is that the emphasis of Zinbarg and Barlow (1996) is on patterns of symptoms, whereas the focus within the four-factor theory is on the underlying processes and sources of information which produce those symptoms.

Wells and Matthews (1994) put forward an interesting theory of anxiety, which they called the Self-Regulatory Executive Function (SREF) model. According to this model, there are three levels of cognition: (1) automatic low-level processing; (2) controlled processing involving conscious appraisal and regulation of action; and (3) self-knowledge and strategies for self-regulation stored in long-term memory. According to Wells and Matthews (1994), "Three types of information can be represented initially at the lower level: (1) external stimulus information; (2) cognitive state information (e.g., errors in cognition; discrete thoughts); and (3) body state information (e.g., heart rate, temperature, pain)" (p.267).

The SREF is the middle level in the system. Its functioning is affected by what happens at the lower level, and also by the self-beliefs and other knowledge stored in long-term memory. The SREF influences the immediate focus of attention, for example, by means of monitoring, "which refers to increased vigilance for self-relevant products of lower-level processing" (Wells & Matthews, 1994, p. 269). Self-relevant knowledge stored in long-term memory "is the primary influence on the processing operations of the SREF" (p.271). Trait anxiety or neuroticism is "directly related to predominantly negative self-knowledge … [and] should lead to a raised probability of dysfunctional SREF activity and pathology, which may in turn feed back into increased negative self-beliefs" (pp.276–277).

There are several similarities between the SREF model and the four-factor theory of clinical anxiety. First, the role of attentional processes in general and self-focused attention in particular is of major importance in both theories. Second, it is assumed within both theories that schematic information stored in long-term memory greatly influences cognitive processing in normals high in trait anxiety or neuroticism and in anxious patients. Third, the sources of information available at the lower level of the model put forward by Wells and Matthews (1994) correspond fairly closely to those identified within the four-factor theory. Fourth, according to Wells and Matthews (1994), "the various disorders share qualitatively similar features, such as excessive self-focus and guidance of attention by maladaptive knowledge structures" (p.319).

In spite of these similarities, there are some important differences between the two approaches. First, Wells and Matthews (1994) concentrate much more on selective attentional biases than on interpretive biases, which is not the case in the four-factor theory of clinical anxiety. The existence of selective attentional biases typically depends on prior interpretive biases. In other words, a mildly threatening stimulus is selectively processed by an anxious individual because it is interpreted as being highly threatening. In view of this dependence of selective attentional bias or interpretative bias, it is not appropriate to place the main emphasis on attentional biases.

Second, Wells and Matthews (1994) do not specify clearly how the various anxiety disorders differ from each other in terms of cognitive processing. For example, Wells and Matthews (1994) argued as follows:

> Studies of the emotional Stroop suggest that interference from words congruent with the patient's disorder is found across a wide range of anxiety-related conditions. The stimulus material generating interference effects is usually quite specific; spider-related words in spider phobics, and so forth. Other tasks provide somewhat mixed results, including some demonstrations of selective attention bias in phobics, obsessive–compulsive patients and panic patients, but such research is too limited for general conclusions to be drawn (pp.78–79).

In similar vein, Wells and Matthews (1994) also stated, "The exact nature of the types of threat to be monitored may vary across different clinical conditions" (p.289). In contrast, it is specifically assumed within the four-factor theory that there are considerable differences in the content of selective attentional and interpretive biases among the anxiety disorders.

Third, although Wells and Matthews (1994) accept that there may be differences in the specific cognitive biases shown by patients with different anxiety disorders, they do not address fully the issue of the origins of these specific biases. In contrast, this issue is considered in some detail within the four-factor theory of clinical anxiety.

Experimental evidence: Continuity assumption

The detailed experimental evidence relevant to the theory is discussed in Chapter 5. However, some of the evidence relating to the fundamental assumption that there is an underlying continuity between normal and clinical anxiety in terms of symptoms will be considered here. We will focus on some of the anxiety disorders with which the theory is primarily involved, namely, panic disorder, social phobia, and obsessive–compulsive disorder. In line with the continuity assumption, it is predicted that anxious normals can display the great majority of symptoms exhibited by clinically anxious patients.

It used to be assumed that normal individuals practically never experience panic attacks. If this assumption were correct, it would pose problems for the notion of continuity between normal and clinical anxiety. However, there is increasing evidence that panic attacks are far more common than used to be thought. Norton, Dorward, and Cox (1986) found that approximately 35% of college students had experienced one or more DSM-III defined panic attacks over the preceding year. Cox, Endler, and Swinson (1991) compared patients suffering from panic disorder with agoraphobia and non-clinical panickers who had had at least one panic attack in the preceding three weeks. The anxious patients reported more severe symptoms, but there was a correlation of +0.62 in the symptom structure of the two groups. As Cox et al. (1991) concluded, "The results support the prediction that clinical and non-clinical panickers experience a qualitatively similar form of anxiety" (p.30).

According to the new theory of clinical anxiety, it would be expected that the patients suffering from panic disorder with agoraphobia studied by Cox et al. (1991) would differ from the non-clinical panickers more with respect to interpreted symptoms than perceived symptoms. Measures of trait anxiety can be regarded as providing an approximate measure of perceived symptoms. In contrast, the Anxiety Sensitivity Index (Peterson & Reiss, 1987) primarily assesses sensitivity to one's own physiological symptoms, and thus is in part a measure of interpreted physiological symptoms. Both groups had comparably high scores on the social evaluation, physical danger, and ambiguous situations dimensions of the Endler Multidimensional Anxiety Scales, which is a measure of trait anxiety. However, the patients having panic disorder with agoraphobia had significantly higher scores than the non-clinical panickers on the Anxiety Sensitivity Index.

We turn now to social phobia. It is assumed that there is much similarity between social phobia and shyness in normal individuals. Social phobia is obviously a more serious condition, and this is reflected in its much lower prevalence rate (approximately 2% vs. 40%, respectively, according to Turner, Beidel, & Townsley, 1990). Turner et al. (1990) reviewed the relevant literature, and came to the following conclusions:

> Although a comparison of the somatic responses of shy and socially phobic populations has yet to be conducted, somatic responses in both children and adults appear to be a significant aspect of each. Based on currently available data, shy individuals and diagnosed social phobics share similar somatic responses in social situations ... The consistency of the research and clinical descriptions for both conditions supports fear of negative evaluation as the primary cognitive component for both conditions (p.499).

The only significant difference between social phobia and shyness identified by Turner et al. (1990) concerned behavioural avoidance: "The degree to which shyness and social phobia share the same behavioural characteristics is unclear. But the weight of the evidence at this time seems to suggest that those who are socially phobic are much more likely to avoid social settings than those who are shy" (p.501). There are various ways of interpreting this difference, but it seems likely that avoidance behaviour by social phobics mainly reflects the greater intensity of anxiety experienced by them in social situations.

It used to be thought that very few normal individuals experienced the obsessions and compulsions of obsessive–compulsive disorder patients. However, Rachman and de Silva (1978) discovered that approximately 80% of normals reported obsessional thoughts and impulses. Among them, 32% had only obsessional thoughts, 14% had only impulses, and 54% had both obsessional thoughts and impulses. In order to ascertain the degree of similarity between the obsessions of obsessive–compulsive disorder patients and normals, clinically trained experts tried to distinguish between the two sets of obsessions. According to Rachman and de Silva (1978), "The judges were not able to identify the clinical obsessions too well, but on the other hand they were moderately good at identifying non-clinical obsessions" (p.239). Rachman and de Silva (1978) came to the following conclusion: "Broadly speaking, normal and abnormal obsessions are similar in form and content, but differ in frequency, intensity, and in their consequences" (p.247).

Potential problems

A possible objection to the proposed theory is that it is excessively top-down in emphasis. More specifically, the simple and clear-cut assumptions of the theory appear to be at variance with the complex and messy state of affairs actually found when anxious patients are diagnosed and tested experimentally. However, there is plentiful evidence that it is generally easier to obtain a theoretical understanding of any disorder by focusing on relatively "pure" cases rather than by focusing on patients possessing symptoms irrelevant to the disorder in question. For example, cognitive neuropsychologists typically study patients with very specific damage and cognitive impairment in order to understand cognitive functioning (Ellis & Young, 1988). This is done even though many brain-damaged patients have relatively widespread cognitive impairments.

There are various reasons for assuming that the specificity of cognitive biases assumed by the theory would not be found. First, there is comorbidity, which is likely to blur any differences in cognitive functioning between patients with different anxiety disorders. Second, we saw in Chapter 3 that normal individuals high in trait anxiety display cognitive biases with respect to all four sources of information underlying emotional experience. It has been found that most groups of anxiety disorder patients, with the exception of simple phobics, have relatively high levels of trait anxiety (see L.A. Clark et al., 1994, for a review). It follows that patients with different anxiety disorders may show cognitive biases to most or all of the four sources of information.

Third, even if clinically anxious patients initially have cognitive biases that are directed to only one source of information, the range of cognitive biases will often increase over time. For example, the cognitive biases of panic disorder patients may initially relate primarily to their own physiological activity. However, the resulting symptoms of panic can cause considerable social embarrassment. This may in turn lead to panic disorder with agoraphobia, with cognitive biases being applied to more sources of information.

It is undeniable that there are several factors (such as those identified above) which militate against the cognitive biases of anxious patients being specific to one source of information. However, despite these factors, there is still concrete evidence of specificity when different anxiety disorders are compared. For example, Logan and Goetsch (1993) in their review of the literature on selective attentional bias, concluded that this bias is generally specific to certain kinds of threat-related stimuli in different anxiety disorders.

It could be argued that the existence of extensive comorbidity suggests that there would be very little evidence of specific precipitating or predisposing factors for any given anxiety disorder. However, the strength of that argument depends in part on the reasons why comorbidity exists in the first place. There are several possible reasons for the high level of comorbidity reported by Barlow et al. (1986); Goisman, Goldenberg et al. (1995b), and others. As was pointed out by Hunt and Andrews (1995), "Comorbidity may be (1) due to the independent occurrence of disorders (this would be consistent with the lifetime risks for each disorder); (2) due to the experience of one disorder acting as a stressor that predisposed to, or somehow caused, the secondary disorder; or (3) due to disorders not being independent, influenced by underlying predisposing or causal factors (in which case the increased risks would be general and proportionate to the vulnerability factors)" (p.467).

Hunt and Andrews (1995) focused on the second mechanism, namely, the extent to which one anxiety disorder plays a role in producing a different anxiety disorder. This was explored by using the Composite International Diagnostic Interview (CIDI) to obtain detailed information about the onset, peaks, and sequences of symptoms and diagnoses, and their relationship to other variables. This was followed by the life-chart method, in which information from the CIDI was used to plot the patient's illness history and other significant events on a longitudinal chart. The key findings related to patients who had suffered from more than one anxiety disorder. Of these patients, 68% seemed to have one primary disorder and one or more secondary disorders, with the rest having two or more independent disorders.

The findings of Hunt and Andrews (1995) suggest strongly that clinical anxiety typically starts with a single anxiety disorder, and that subsequent anxiety disorders are generally produced to some extent as a consequence of the original anxiety disorder. If this is so, then it seems reasonable that specific precipitating or predisposing factors could be important in producing the original disorder.

In sum, the fact that there is widespread comorbidity among the anxiety disorders causes problems for theory and research. However, some of these problems can be alleviated by focusing on relative "pure" cases. In addition, the findings of Hunt and Andrews (1995) offer hope that the existence of comorbidity will not necessarily prevent the discovery of precipitating and predisposing factors for the various anxiety disorders.

There is another issue which needs to be addressed. It is assumed within the four-factor theory of clinical anxiety that specific phobics, social phobics, obsessional–compulsive disorder patients, and panic disorder patients have cognitive biases primarily with respect to one source of information, whereas the cognitive biases of generalised anxiety disorder patients can apply to any of the four sources of information. However, there seem to be significant differences between generalised anxiety disorder and the other anxiety disorders in the ways in which the cognitive biases operate on some sources of information. For example, obsessive–compulsive disorder patients and generalised anxiety disorder patients have interpretive biases with respect to their own thoughts based on information stored in long-term memory. However, there seem to be important differences between the obsessive thoughts of obsessive–compulsive disorder patients and the unrealistic worries of generalised anxiety disorder patients. Turner, Beidel, and Stanley (1992) pointed out that worries usually related to everyday experiences, whereas obsessions are concerned with dirt, contamination, and so on. In addition, worries are perceived as less intrusive and more acceptable than obsessions. As yet, the four-factor theory of clinical anxiety has not been developed to account for such complexities.

SUMMARY AND CONCLUSIONS

The theoretical approach adopted in this chapter is based on the assumption that there are important continuities between normals high in trait anxiety and clinically anxious patients in terms of symptoms and the presence of cognitive biases. This continuity assumption is incorporated into a diathesis–stress model in which there is a cognitive vulnerability factor in the form of selective attentional and interpretive biases. Clinical anxiety develops when there is a positive feedback loop between these biases and state anxiety, in which high levels of anxiety exaggerate the biases, and the exaggerated biases increase state anxiety.

According to the theory, clinically relevant cognitive biases can develop with respect to any of the following: the cognitive appraisal of the situation; the interpretation of one's own action tendencies and behaviour; the interpretation of one's own physiological activitiy; and the interpretation of one's own thoughts based on information in long-term memory. It is assumed that patients with generalised anxiety disorder can possess cognitive biases with respect to all four sources of information, but most of them probably have a more circumscribed range of biases. Patients suffering from panic disorder without agoraphobia have selective attentional and interpretive biases primarily with respect to their own physiological activity and bodily sensations. Of particular importance are respiratory symptoms. Social phobics have cognitive biases mainly in connection with their own action tendencies and behaviour, whereas obsessive–compulsive patients have cognitive biases mainly with respect to their own thoughts or cognitions. Specific phobics have cognitive biases with respect to their cognitive appraisal of phobia-relevant environmental stimuli.

Specific precipitating or predisposing factors with respect to some of the anxiety disorders are as follows: a previous history of respiratory disease is of relevance to the development of panic disorder; a very low level of extraversion relates to the development of social phobia; a high level of actual or perceived responsibility can lead to obsessive–compulsive disorder, and observational learning or conditioning can lead to specific phobia.

CHAPTER FIVE

Clinical experimental evidence

INTRODUCTION

This chapter is devoted to a review of the research evidence relevant to the four-factor theory of clinical anxiety proposed in Chapter 4. Before proceeding to that review, it is important to consider some important general issues. A key research issue was analysed in detail by MacLeod (1993). He pointed out that there are substantial differences between the cognitive approach as practised by cognitive psychologists and the cognitive approach within clinical psychology. The latter approach has a serious limitation which is not found in the former approach. According to Macleod (1993), clinical researchers "saw the adoption of cognitivism as a means of legitimatising the study and analysis of self-report data yielded by the introspective appraisal of mental events ... the enhancement of the self-report data, yielded by introspection, as an acceptable source of information concerning mental processes, must place our discipline clearly outwith the boundaries of legitimate science" (p.170).

MacLeod (1993) obtained supporting evidence by considering the issues of *Cognitive Psychology* and *Cognitive Therapy and Research* for 1991. Of the experiments reported in *Cognitive Psychology*, a central journal in cognitive psychology, 100% had the measurement of overt responses as the key dependent variable or variables. In contrast, only 28% of the experiments in *Cognitive Therapy and Research* relied mainly on explicit performance measures. This is a matter for concern, since there is powerful evidence for the fallibility of introspective evidence. For example, there is implicit learning, which was defined by Seger (1994) as "learning complex information without complete verbalisable knowledge of what is learned" (p.163). Berry and Broadbent (1984) found that subjects mastered a complex task involving maintaining a specified level of output in a sugar-production factory, but most of them could not describe the principles underlying their performance.

Research on subliminal perception also undermines reliance on introspective reports. There is considerable evidence that stimuli of which the individual is unaware often have effects on behaviour and on experience (see Eysenck and Keane, 1995, for a review). As Macleod (1993) pointed out, "if stimuli that a subject cannot even report being present can systematically influence ... a wide variety of judgements, behaviours, and experiences, there is little prospect that the cognitive mechanisms mediating these psychological phenomena can be apprehended through the use of introspection" (p.177).

Some of MacLeod's (1993) analysis of the limitations of much clinical research adopting a cognitive approach is convincing. However, even if self-report data are uninformative about underlying cognitive processes, such data still have a valid role to play in clinical research in at least two ways. First, the assessment of symptom severity or of changes in symptom severity seems inevitably to depend on self-report evidence. Second, in order to test the four-factor theory of clinical anxiety put forward in Chapter 4, it is necessary to consider discrepancies between self-report evidence and more objective forms of evidence. Such discrepancies are of central importance within cognitive therapy (see Chapter 6), and can only be investigated in the laboratory by including self-report measures among the dependent variables. In sum, self-report data are of potential importance, but they need to be interpreted with care and compared against other kinds of evidence.

In fact, much of the research which is relevant to the theory put forward in Chapter 4 has avoided an undue reliance on self-report measures. The central focus of the theory is on the selective attentional and interpretive biases, and there are various tasks available which provide overt performance measures of these biases. There is no doubt that such measures are preferable to a sole reliance on self-report measures.

Behavioural measures of cognitive biases are limited in some ways. If subjects show an attentional bias for physical threat words (e.g., paralysed; blood), it is often assumed that this indicates an attentional bias for internal bodily sensations. In similar fashion, it is assumed that interpretive bias for certain ambiguous sentences (e.g., "You feel your heart racing for no apparent reason") reflects interpretive bias for actual bodily symptoms. McNally (1995) has criticised this approach very effectively:

> Most cognitive bias research has involved the processing of visual and auditory verbal stimuli, and is therefore somewhat artificial in that verbal cues act as proxies for the genuine threat stimuli that anxious patients presumably selectively process in ordinary life. Thus, for example, researchers have assumed that the biased attentional mechanisms that figure in panic patients' exhibiting Stroop interference for the word *heartbeat* are the same as those that figure in enhanced interoceptive acuity for actual heartbeats … Needless to say, this assumption warrants further justification (p.750).

The theory of clinical anxiety which was put forward in Chapter 4 is primarily concerned with only five out of the various anxiety disorders: generalised anxiety disorder; panic disorder; social phobia; obsessive–compulsive disorder; and specific phobia. As was pointed out in Chapter 4, the theory could be applied at least to some extent to other anxiety disorders. However, working out the details of such applications is a task for the future, and is not attempted in this book. Accordingly, nearly all of the experimental evidence discussed in this chapter is of direct relevance only to generalised anxiety disorder, panic disorder, social phobia, obsessive–compulsive disorder, and specific phobia.

GENERALISED ANXIETY DISORDER

Much of the evidence relevant to the theoretical predictions of the four-factor theory of clinical anxiety for generalised anxiety disorder was discussed at length in Eysenck (1992). Accordingly, only a relatively brief discussion of some of the key studies will be included here.

Selective attentional bias
MacLeod, Mathews, and Tata (1986) used the dot-probe task to assess selective attentional bias. Patients with generalised anxiety disorder showed selective attentional bias for threat-related words (both social and physical threats), whereas the normal controls had a non-significant tendency to allocate attention away from threat. Similar findings were reported by Bradley, Mogg, Millar, and White (1995a); Mathews, Mogg, Kentish, and Eysenck (1995); Mogg, Bradley, Millar,

and White (1995); and by Mogg, Bradley, Williams, and Mathews (1993). In these studies, interference effects on the modified Stroop task were obtained from generalised anxiety disorder patients with both subliminal and supraliminal presentation of threat-related words. Evidence that the bias with subliminal threat-related stimuli is specific to anxiety rather than depression was obtained in two of these studies (Bradley et al., 1995; Mogg et al., 1993).

Further evidence for a selective attentional bias in patients with generalised anxiety disorder was obtained from the dot-probe task by Mogg, Bradley, and Williams (1995): "Anxious individuals showed an attentional bias towards the spatial location of negative stimuli in both supraliminal and subliminal conditions relative to normal controls" (p.29).

According to the four-factor theory of clinical anxiety, selective attentional bias in generalised anxiety disorder patients should depend on processes operating below the level of conscious awareness. There is convincing converging evidence from different experimental tasks for this prediction in the frequent finding that this bias can be found even with subliminal presentation of threat-related stimuli.

It is predicted by the four-factor theory that generalised anxiety disorder patients should have selective attentional bias for a wider range of stimuli than social phobics, specific phobics, obsessive–compulsive disorder patients, and panic disorder patients. Some support for that prediction emerges from a review of the literature on selective attentional bias by Logan and Goetsch (1993). The great majority of studies on anxiety disorders other than generalised anxiety disorder have reported that the selective attentional bias is specific to a certain type of stimulus. In contrast, selective attentional bias has usually been relatively general in generalised anxiety disorder patients. However, it is noteworthy that the bias tends to be relatively general with subliminal presentation of the stimuli (e.g., Bradley et al., 1995a; Mogg et al., 1993), but is often more specific with supraliminal presentation (e.g., Mathews & MacLeod, 1985; Mogg, Mathews, & Eysenck, 1992; Mogg, Mathews, & Weinman, 1989). For example, Mogg et al. (1992) found that the attentional bias for social threat words was associated with the extent of the patients' social concerns. As Mogg (pers. comm.) pointed out, the findings can be interpreted by assuming that there is a relatively crude semantic analysis prior to conscious awareness, followed by more detailed processing thereafter.

Mogg, Bradley, and Millar (1995) found that the attentional bias for subliminal threat had disappeared following treatment. They also found that the reduction in preconscious bias in generalised anxiety disorder patients during cognitive-behaviour therapy significantly predicted the extent of the reduction in their self-reported worries. It is thus possible that the preconscious bias for threat involves the same cognitive mechanism as the one responsible for the extensive worrying found in generalised anxiety disorder patients.

Interpretive bias

Mathews, Richards, and Eysenck (1989) used three groups of subjects: patients with a diagnosis of generalised anxiety disorder, a recovered group of patients who had had generalised anxiety disorder, and normal controls. The generalised anxiety disorder patients produced significantly more threatening interpretations of homophones than did the normal controls, indicating the existence of an interpretive bias. The recovered anxious group was intermediate between the other two groups.

Eysenck et al. (1991) presented a mixture of ambiguous and neutral sentences to patients with generalised anxiety disorder, recovered generalised anxiety disorder patients, and normal controls in their first experiment. These sentences were followed by an unexpected test of recognition memory, in which the subjects had to decide whether each sentence corresponded in meaning to one of the sentences presented previously. The generalised anxiety disorder patients recognised more of the threatening interpretations and fewer of the neutral interpretations than did the other two groups, indicating the existence of an interpretive bias. There was very little difference between the recovered anxious and normal control groups.

In their second experiment, Eysenck et al. (1991) used a very similar task, but used signal-detection analyses to distinguish between sensitivity and response-bias effects. Generalised anxiety disorder patients differed from normal controls in their recognition-memory performance in terms of sensitivity but not response bias. These findings indicate that the interpretive bias shown by generalised anxiety disorder patients does not simply reflect response bias.

Other cognitive factors

The possibility that generalised anxiety disorder patients have an explicit memory bias (often called negative memory bias) for threat-related material has been investigated in various studies. Mogg et al. (1987) found on tests of both recall and recognition that generalised anxiety disorder patients had poorer retention of threat-related words than did normal controls. In other words, there was no evidence at all of a negative memory bias in the patients.

Mogg (1988) reported five additional experiments in which the retention of threatening and neutral stimulus material was considered.

The typical finding was a complete absence of a negative memory bias in the generalised anxiety disorder patients, a finding which was obtained in four separate experiments using recall as the measure of retention. In the remaining experiment, anxious patients showed a negative memory bias with recall, but failed to do so with recognition memory. Mathews, Mogg, May, and Eysenck (1989) also failed to find evidence for a negative memory bias in generalised anxiety disorder patients.

In some ways, the failure to find a negative memory bias in generalised anxiety disorder patients is puzzling and contrary to the prediction of the four-factor theory of clinical anxiety. According to the theory, such patients should have facilitated access to negative information stored in long-term memory. The failure to find a negative memory bias in generalised anxiety disorder patients may depend in part on cognitive avoidance (Williams et al., 1988). However, it cannot be argued that generalised anxiety disorder patients are characteristically successful at avoiding focusing on negative information in long-term memory. For example, chronic unrealistic worry is a central feature of generalised anxiety disorder in DSM-III-R and DSM-IV, and generalised anxiety disorder patients score even higher than other groups of anxiety disorder patients on the Penn State Worry Questionnaire (Molina & Borkovec, 1994).

It is not altogether clear why generalised anxiety disorder patients seem to have facilitated access to negative information in long-term memory in their everyday lives but not when specifically instructed to retrieve such information in the laboratory. One possibility is that such facilitated access applies to information which is of direct personal relevance to the patient's life, but does not apply to threat-related information generally. However, similar threat-related information has been used with other tasks, and has been associated with selective attentional bias in generalised anxiety disorder patients (e.g., MacLeod, Mathews, & Tata 1986). Another possibility was suggested by Williams et al. (1997). They argued that generalised anxiety disorder patients tend to engage in non-memorial elaboration of threat-related material, and this can disrupt subsequent long-term memory for such material.

Mathews, Mogg et al. (1989) found an implicit memory bias in generalised anxiety disorder patients using a word-completion task. MacLeod and McLaughlin (1995) obtained evidence of an implicit memory bias in generalised anxiety disorder patients using tachistoscopic identification as the measure of implicit memory. However, the existence of an implicit memory bias in generalised anxiety disorder patients was not replicated by Mathews et al. (1995) or by Bradley, Mogg, and Williams (1995b). One reason for the inconsistent findings with implict memory bias may be because there are various different types of implicit memory. For example, Tulving and Schachter (1990) distinguished between perceptual and conceptual implicit memory tests, with perceptual attributes of stimuli being important to the former and stimulus meaning to the latter. There is no good reason to predict that generalised anxiety disorder patients should show an implicit memory bias for perceptual (e.g., orthographic) attributes of threat-related stimuli (McNally, pers. comm.).

Precipitating and predisposing factors

According to Eysenck (1992) and the four-factor theory of clinical anxiety presented in Chapter 4, those high in trait anxiety are more vulnerable to the development of generalised anxiety disorder than are those low in trait anxiety. More specifically, there is a cognitive vulnerability factor for generalised anxiety disorder. Hypervigilance forms an important part of this vulnerability factor, which includes cognitive biases such as selective attentional bias and interpretive bias.

One approach to testing this part of the theory is to compare cognitive functioning in normals high in trait anxiety and in patients with generalised anxiety disorder. This approach was combined by Eysenck (1992) with an attempt to decide among three possible reasons why generalised anxiety disorder patients have various cognitive biases:

1. the biases are a secondary consequence of clinical levels of anxiety;
2. the biases form part of a manifest vulnerability factor, so that they will be found in vulnerable individuals whether or not they are currently highly anxious;
3. the bias form part of a latent vulnerability factor, so that they will be found in vulnerable individuals mainly when they are highly anxious.

Eysenck (1992) discussed relevant findings obtained from normals high in trait anxiety in conditions of either high or low state anxiety, from generalised anxiety disorder patients, and from patients who have recovered from generalised anxiety disorder. The overall picture as it existed in 1992 is shown in Fig. 5.1. Those cases in which there was little or no relevant evidence are indicated by a ?. There have been relatively few changes to this picture in the last few years. However, it now seems less likely that there is an implicit memory bias in generalised anxiety disorder patients (Bradley et al., 1995b; Mathews et al., 1995), and the same is true of normals high in trait anxiety (Eysenck, submitted; Nugent & Mineka, 1994).

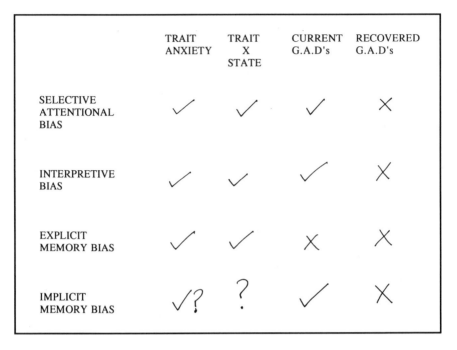

	TRAIT ANXIETY	TRAIT X STATE	CURRENT G.A.D's	RECOVERED G.A.D's
SELECTIVE ATTENTIONAL BIAS	✓	✓	✓	✗
INTERPRETIVE BIAS	✓	✓	✓	✗
EXPLICIT MEMORY BIAS	✓	✓	✗	✗
IMPLICIT MEMORY BIAS	✓?	?	✓	✗

FIG. 5.1. Cognitive effects in various normal and generalised anxiety disorder groups. Based on Eysenck (1992).

What conclusions can be drawn from the pattern of findings shown in Fig. 5.1? First, the fact that normals high in trait anxiety show all, or nearly all, of the biases is difficult to account for if clinically anxious mood state is required to produce each of the biases. Therefore, it must be concluded that the various cognitive biases are probably not merely a secondary consequence of being clinically anxious. Secondly, much of the evidence is inconsistent with the notion that there is a manifest vulnerability factor. Of particular importance, recovered generalised anxiety disorder patients have practically no cognitive biases, which is totally at variance with what would be expected if there were a manifest vulnerability factor.

Third, most of the evidence is consistent with the notion that there is a latent vulnerability factor. As Eysenck (1992) concluded:

> The fact that recovered anxious patients do not display cognitive biases can be accounted for on the grounds that they are not stressed or high in state anxiety. However, the main support for a latent vulnerability factor comes from the interactions between trait anxiety and state anxiety or

stress which have been found with four of the cognitive biases. In other words, it appears that cognitive biases in information processing can be obtained most readily in individuals who possess a cognitive vulnerability factor and who are also in stressed conditions or high in state anxiety (p.155).

PANIC DISORDER

Selective attentional bias

Most of the researchers who have investigated selective attentional bias in panic patients have found evidence for such a bias, and have also found that it applies primarily to panic-relevant threatening stimuli. Ehlers, Margraf, Davies, and Roth (1988) found on the modified Stroop that patients with panic disorder and non-clinical subjects with panic attacks showed greater interference for physical threat words than did control subjects, However, the groups did not differ in the extent of interference with colour words.

McNally, Riemann, and Kim (1990) used the modified Stroop with catastrophe, bodily sensation, fear, and neutral words. Patients with panic disorder exhibited greater interference for all categories of threat words than did normal controls, and this was especially the case for catastrophe words. Hope, Rapee, Heimberg, and Dombeck (1990) also used the modified Stroop task. They found that patients with panic disorder showed more interference to physical threat words than to social threat words. McNally, Riemann, Louro, Lukach, and Kim (1992) found that panic disorder patients showed more interference on the modified Stroop in naming positive, fear, bodily sensation, and catastrophe words than meaningless neutral stimuli. However, obsessive–compulsive patients showed the same pattern of interference, and the only difference between the panic patients and normal controls was that the former group showed more interference for catastrophe words than for fear and positive words.

An alternative approach to selective attentional bias involves using the mental-tracking task described in Chapter 3. In essence, subjects simply attempt to count their heartbeats, and their estimate of the number of heartbeats over a period of time is compared against the actual number. Errors on this task are nearly always in the form of under-estimates, suggesting that failures of attention are mainly responsible for poor performance.

Ehlers and Breuer (1992) compared performance on the mental-tracking task of panic disorder patients, simple phobia patients, and normal controls. The mean error rate for the panic patients (22%) was significantly less than the error rate for the simple phobics (36%) or the controls (31%). In a second experiment, patients suffering from panic disorder, generalised anxiety disorder, and depression were compared on the mental-tracking task. All of the groups had very similar actual heart rates. The panic patients had a much lower error rate than the depressed patients (23% vs. 43%, respectively), but did not differ from the generalised anxiety disorder patients (21% error rate). These findings suggest that the panic patients attend more closely to their own physiological activity than simple phobics and normal controls, but no more so than generalised anxiety disorder patients.

Ehlers (1995) carried out a one-year prospective study of panic attacks. She assessed performance on the mental-tracking task at the outset for panic disorder patients who were being treated, and for panic disorder patients who were in remission. As can be seen in Fig. 5.2, mental-tracking performance was a good predictor of whether patients being treated would retain their panic disorder status. It also predicted

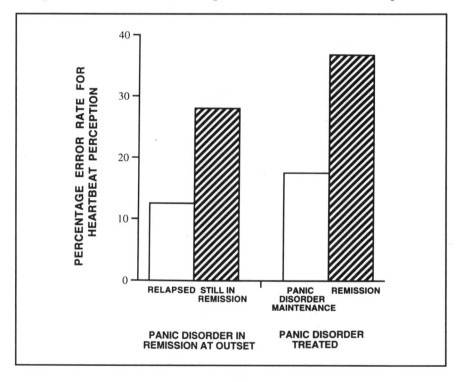

FIG. 5.2. Remission of panic disorder and relapse of recovery from panic disorder predicted by previous error rate in heartbeat perception. Data from Ehlers (1995).

whether patients in remission would relapse. These findings indicate that the amount of attention devoted to one's own bodily sensations may influence the likelihood of subsequent panic attacks.

Despite the impressive findings of Ehlers and Breuer (1992) and of Ehlers (1995), it has not always been found that patients with panic disorder perform especially well on the mental-tracking task. Antony, Brown, Craske, Barlow, Mitchell, and Meadows (1995) used the mental-tracking task with panic disorder patients, social phobia patients, and normal controls, and discovered that the three groups did not differ in the accuracy of their heartbeat estimates. However, anxiety over cardiac sensations was related to accurate heartbeat perception.

Interpretive bias

Clark, Salkovskis, Gelder, Koehler, Martin, Anastasiades, Hackmann, Middleton, and Jeavons (1988) assessed interpretive bias in panic disorder patients on the basis of the interpretations of a wide range of ambiguous events. The panic disorder patients showed an interpretive bias for bodily sensations, but not for social, general, or hypochondriacal events. They also found that panic disorder patients were faster at naming a word which completed a sentence if the sentence formed a negative interpretation of a bodily sensation than if it formed a neutral one. This finding also suggests that panic patients have an interpretive bias for bodily sensations.

Stoler and McNally (1991) obtained findings resembling those of Clark et al. (1988), in that they discovered that panic disorder patients had an interpretive bias more or less restricted to ambiguous internal events or bodily sensations. Similar findings were reported by Westling and Ost (1995). They administered the Bodily Sensations Interpretation Questionnaire to panic disordered patients and normal controls, and found that the patients interpreted internal bodily sensations in a much more threatening fashion than the controls. However, the two groups did not differ in their interpretation of external events. An interesting additional finding was that the interpretive bias shown by panic patients disappeared after treatment.

A more wide-ranging interpretive bias in panic disorder patients was reported by McNally and Foa (1987) and by Harvey, Richards, Dziadosz, and Swindell (1993). In both studies, panic disorder patients demonstrated an interpretive bias for both internal and external ambiguous events. It is not clear why this difference in results occurred. However, it is possible that panic disorder patients with agoraphobia are more likely than panic disorder patients without agoraphobia to have an interpretive bias for external events.

There have been several studies of interpretive bias in panic disorder patients based on biological challenges such as lactate infusion or inhalation of a mixture of carbon dioxide and oxygen. In essence, what is typically found is that panic disorder patients exhibit panic attacks or numerous symptoms of panic under biological challenge, but normal controls do not (e.g., Gaffney, Fenton, Lane, & Lake, 1988; Yeragani, Balon, & Pohl, 1989). Such findings have generally been explained by assuming that patients with panic disorder are inclined to produce catastrophic misinterpretations of their bodily sensations (Clark, 1986; McNally, 1990).

In order to demonstrate that the findings with panic patients are due to interpretive bias, it is necessary to show that there are small or non-existent differences between panic patients and normal controls in their actual physiological activity in response to challenge. This is true of most of the studies. Panic disorder patients have been found to respond comparably to non-clinical control subjects to biological challenge on measures of heart rate, respiratory rate, forearm muscle tension, and blood pressure (Gaffney et al., 1988; Rainey, Frohman, Freedman, Pohl, Ettedgui, & Williams, 1984; Rapee, Brown, Antony, & Barlow, 1992; Woods, Charney, Goodman, & Heninger, 1988). However, Charney, Heninger, and Breier (1984) obtained a significant difference in the sitting systolic blood pressure response to yohimbine, but not on other measures of blood pressure or pulse rate. Nutt, Glue, Lawson, and Wilson (1990) found that panic disorder patients responded more than normal controls to flumazenil infusions on measures of heart rate, but not on measures of systolic or diastolic blood pressure. The pattern of the findings indicates that panic patients differ from normal controls in terms of their interpreted bodily symptoms rather than in terms of actual physiological responsiveness to biological challenge.

There is additional convincing evidence for the importance of cognitive factors. Rapee, Mattick, and Murrell (1986) found that panic patients had far fewer catastrophic cognitions and panic symptoms when they were provided with detailed advance information about the effects of the biological challenge.

There have been various attempts to specify more precisely the nature of the interpretive bias in panic patients. In an especially interesting study, Sanderson, Rapee, and Barlow (1989) used inhalations of carbon dioxide in air. Some panic disorder patients were given potential control over the concentration of carbon dioxide, whereas others were not. Despite the fact that none of the patients used the control they had been given, the patients with control had less subjective anxiety, fewer panic symptoms, and less intense symptoms than those without control. They were also far less likely to experience a panic attack, 20% versus 80%, respectively. These findings indicate that perceived uncontrollability plays an important part in determining the response to biological challenge.

According to the four-factor theory of clinical anxiety, panic disorder patients should have a greater interpretive bias when high in state anxiety than when low. Some support for this prediction was reported by Zoellner, Craske, and Rapee (1996). They asked panic patients to indicate the strength of their conviction that their catastrophic thoughts would actually happen while in the midst of a panic attack and at other times. The patients reported much higher belief that their catastrophic thoughts would happen when they were in the midst of a panic attack than at other times.

Other anxiety disorders

In terms of the theory presented in Chapter 4, it would be predicted that panic disorder patients would exhibit a greater interpretive bias for their own physiological activity than would patients with other anxiety disorders. There is empirical support for this prediction. Perna, Bertani, Arancio, Ronchi, and Bellodi (1995) compared the response to carbon dioxide challenge in panic patients and obsessive–compulsive disorder patients. They found that 52% of the panic patients had a panic attack, compared to only 4% of the obsessive–compulsive disorder patients. In addition, the patients with panic disorder had a much greater increase than the obsessive–compulsives in subjective disturbance. As Perna et al. (1995) concluded, "These results confirm that obsessive–compulsive disorder and panic disorder are two distinct syndromes and that patients with these disorders have different sensitivity to CO_2 inhalation" (p.85).

Verburg, Griez, Meijer, and Pols (1995b) compared patients with panic disorder and those with generalised anxiety disorder as they underwent 35% carbon dioxide challenge. Both groups had equivalent increases in panic symptoms based on the 13 DSM-III-R panic symptoms. However, the panic patients had a considerably greater increase in subjective anxiety than did the patients with generalised anxiety disorder. These findings are consistent with the view that the two groups of patients differ more with respect to interpreted bodily symptoms than with respect to perceived bodily symptoms.

The prediction that interpretive bias for one's own physiological symptoms (i.e., interpreted symptoms) is greater in panic disorder patients than in other anxiety disorder groups can also be tested by means of the Anxiety Sensitivity Index (Peterson & Reiss, 1987). Various views have been expressed about what it is measuring, with some researchers arguing that it contains four factors (e.g., Telch, Shermis,

& Lucas, 1989; Cox, Parker, & Swinson, 1996). For example, Cox et al. (1996) identified these factors: fear of cognitive symptoms; fear of symptoms in public; fear of cardiorespiratory and gastrointestinal sensations; and fear of trembling and fainting. However, most of the evidence indicates that it measures mainly a "specific tendency to react anxiously to one's own anxiety and anxiety-related sensations" (Lilienfeld, Turner, & Jacob, 1993). If that is the case, then the Anxiety Sensitivity Index provides an approximate measure of interpreted symptoms relating to physiological activity.

In an important study, Taylor, Koch, and McNally (1992) compared the Anxiety Sensitivity Index scores of patients suffering from panic disorder, post-traumatic stress disorder, generalised anxiety disorder, obsessive–compulsive disorder, social phobia, and simple phobia. The panic disorder group had highly significant greater Anxiety Sensitivity Index scores than every other group except the post-traumatic stress disorder group, for which the group difference was marginally significant.

Additional evidence that panic disorder patients have a greater interpretive bias for their own physiological symptoms than do other anxiety disorder patients was reported by Taylor, Koch, and Crockett (1991). They found that the Anxiety Sensitivity Index items which best discriminated panic disorder from other anxiety disorders were those directly assessing fears of anxiety-related bodily sensations.

Other cognitive factors

According to the theory presented in Chapter 4, it is not specifically predicted that panic disorder patients should have facilitated access to threat-related information stored in long-term memory. However, it follows from schema theories (e.g., Beck & Emery, 1985; Beck & Clark, 1988) that patients suffering from any of the anxiety disorders should exhibit a negative memory bias. Some of the evidence points to the existence of a memory bias in panic patients. McNally, Foa, and Donnell (1989) found that anxiety-related words were recalled better than non-threatening words by panic patients but not by normals. This memory bias was not specific to words referring to physical symptoms. Cloitre and Liebowitz (1991) found that panic disorder patients had a negative memory bias for physical threat. Cloitre, Shear, Cancienne, and Zeitlin (1994) found that panic patients showed negative memory bias in cued recall for catastrophic associations to bodily sensation words.

Despite these findings, it has proved difficult to obtain evidence for a negative memory bias in panic disorder patients in some recent studies. Beck, Stanley, Averill, Baldwin, and Deagle (1992) failed to find a memory bias for somatic sensation and physical threat information in panic disorder patients. Part of the reason for this failure may be their use of recognition memory, which tends to be insensitive. Rapee (1994) studied memory for physical and social threat words in panic disorder patients in explicit memory (free recall) and implicit memory (word completion). The patients did not exhibit a memory bias on either memory test. As Rapee (1994) concluded, "A specific memory bias for threat in the anxiety disorders is predicted by both schema theories (Beck & Emery, 1985) and semantic network theories (Lang, 1985). The fact that this phenomenon has proved so difficult to demonstrate is a problem for such theories" (p.298).

Implicit memory bias was also investigated by Cloitre et al. (1994); Becker, Rinck, and Margraf (1994); Amir, McNally, Riemann, and Clements (1996). Cloitre et al. (1994) found that panic patients had a memory bias on an implicit memory task (word completion) for catastrophic associations to bodily sensation words. Becker et al. (1994) found that there was a greater memory bias on an explicit memory task than on an implicit memory task. Amir et al. (1996) used a different paradigm to assess implicit memory. The subjects heard a set of neutral and panic-related sentences. After that, they heard a mixture of new and old sentences, and rated the volume of the white noise accompanying each sentence. Implicit memory in this paradigm is revealed by rating the white noise for old sentences as less loud than that for new sentences. Panic patients had an implicit memory bias for panic-related sentences, whereas controls did not.

Precipitating and predisposing factors

According to the theoretical framework, those precipitating or predisposing factors of greatest relevance to panic disorder rather than to other anxiety disorders are those which produce concern about one's own physiological system. Promising findings were reported by Zanbergen, Bright, Pols, Fernandez, De Loof, and Griez (1991). They compared the prevalence of respiratory diseases in panic disorder patients, obsessive–compulsive disorder patients, and eating disorder patients. The panic disorder patients had a significantly higher lifetime prevalence than did either of the other two groups. However, the three groups did not differ in terms of current respiratory diseases.

These findings were replicated and extended by Verburg, Griez, Meijer, and Pols (1995a). They discovered that 43% of their panic disorder patients had suffered from at least one respiratory disease during their lives, which was considerably higher than the 16% of all other anxiety disorder patients. However, there was no difference between panic disorder patients and other anxiety disorder patients in the incidence of diseases other than respiratory ones. This suggests that the panic disorder patients did not tend to over-report their previous diseases.

Findings that are superficially inconsistent in with those of Zanbergen et al. (1991) and Verburg et al. (1995a) were reported by Ben-Amnon, Fux, Maoz, and Benjamin (1995). They compared patients with panic disorder with or without agoraphobia against patients with other anxiety disorders. More of the panic disorder patients reported respiratory symptoms, but there was a non-significant difference between the two groups on that measure. Ben-Amnon et al. (1995) also reviewed other studies, most of which had produced only modest evidence that panic disorder patients have more respiratory symptoms than patients with other anxiety disorders.

The available evidence indicates that panic disorder patients are much more likely than patients with other anxiety disorders to have had a respiratory disease in the past. However, they are only slightly more likely to have current respiratory symptoms. This pattern of findings is entirely consistent with the notion that respiratory diseases are precipitating or predisposing factors in panic disorder. Respiratory diseases may tend to produce greater attentional focus on the respiratory system specifically and on the physiological system in general, and may also tend to produce an interpretive bias for physical symptoms, especially those connected with the respiratory system. In addition, respiratory diseases may cause derangement of the respiratory receptor set-point in the brain-stem (cf. Klein, 1993).

Respiratory diseases may be a precipitating or predisposing factor for panic disorder, but there must be other relevant factors as well. Most people who suffer from a respiratory disease do not subsequently develop panic disorder, and most patients with panic disorder have not previously suffered from a respiratory disease.

SOCIAL PHOBIA

According to the theory put forward in Chapter 4, social phobics should selectively attend to their own behaviour, and they should also misinterpret their own behaviour in a negative fashion. In view of the social concerns of social phobics, it might be imagined that social phobics would focus mainly on the perceived reactions of other people. However, the theory predicts that their main focus should be on their own behaviour rather than on the reactions of others, and that they should interpret their own behaviour in a negative fashion.

Selective attentional bias

Relevant evidence relating to selective attentional bias was reported by Stopa and Clark (1993). They asked social phobics, other clinically anxious patients, and normal controls to speak out loud the thoughts they had had during a previous social interaction. For all three groups, very low percentages of their thoughts involved possible negative evaluation by the person with whom they interacted, and there were no significant group differences. In contrast, there were substantial differences among groups in the percentage of their thoughts devoted to negative evaluations of themselves and of their own behaviour. Among the social phobics, 39.4% of their thoughts fell into this category, compared to only 9.1% of the thoughts of other clinically anxious individuals, and 6.5% of the thoughts of the normal controls. Thus, these findings provide support for the notion that social phobics selectively attend to their own behaviour to a greater extent than do other anxious patients.

Additional evidence that social phobics attend to their own behaviour was obtained by Makris and Heimberg (1995). They used the Scale of Maladaptive Self-Consciousness, and found that social phobics scored much higher than normal controls. This scale assesses the degree of self-consciousness experienced in 24 social situations, and so the finding suggests that social phobics are acutely aware of their own behaviour in social settings.

Further evidence of selective attentional bias in social phobics was reported by Hope et al. (1990) and by Mattia, Heimberg, and Hope (1993). Hope et al. (1990) used the modified Stroop task with social and physical threat words, and found that social phobics showed selective attentional bias for social threat only. Mattia et al. (1993) also used the modified Stroop task, and replicated the findings of Hope et al. (1990). They also found that this selective bias was eliminated in social phobics who responded to treatment.

Asmundson and Stein (1994) used the dot-probe task to assess selective attentional bias. Social and physical threat words were both used, but the social phobics selectively attended to social threat only: "The results of the present investigation suggest that patients suffering from SP [social phobia] (generalised type) are characterised by a specific attentional bias that favours the processing of social-evaluative threat cues" (p.115).

There is a significant limitation in all of the studies of selective attentional bias which have been discussed so far in this section. These studies demonstrate the existence of a selective attentional bias in social phobics, but they do not demonstrate that this bias affects emotional experience and behaviour. In order to do that, it is necessary to manipulate experimentally the level of self-attention or self-focus. This was done by Woody (1996). In her crucial condition, social phobics stood passively while someone standing nearby described either the speaker's behavioural symptoms or those of the patient in front of other people. There was evidence that the patients engaged in more self-attention or self-focus when their own symptoms were being discussed. Self-reported and rated behavioural anxiety among social phobics were both higher in the self-focus condition than in the control condition.

Interpretive bias

Stopa and Clark (1993), in a study already discussed, reported relevant data with respect to the prediction that social phobics have an interpretive bias for their own behaviour. The subjects and observers assessed the extent to which the subjects manifested various negative and positive forms of behaviour. The social phobics perceived their own behaviour to be significantly more negative and significantly less positive than did an observer. In contrast, other clinically anxious patients perceived their own behaviour to be less negative than did an observer, and they did not differ from an observer in their assessment of their own positive behaviour. The normal control subjects did not differ from the observer in their assessment of their own negative or positive forms of behaviour.

Rapee and Lim (1992) also obtained evidence on interpretive bias for their own behaviour from social phobics. They found that social phobics and normal controls did not differ in observers' ratings of their behaviour while delivering a public talk, but the social phobics rated their own behaviour as significantly worse than did the control subjects (see Fig. 5.3). Of particular importance, interpretive bias in terms of worse self-reported than rated behaviour was significantly greater in the social phobics than in the normal controls.

Additional evidence of interpretive bias for their own behaviour in social phobics was reported by Alden and Wallace (1995). The social phobics and the normal controls both assessed their own non-verbal behaviour as being more negative than did observers, but the discrepancy (or interpretive bias) was significantly greater for social phobics than for the control subjects.

Other cognitive factors

The emphasis so far has been on those cognitive processes assumed theoretically to be of relevance to social phobia. However, it is obviously possible that other cognitive factors might be involved. The notion that social phobics have facilitated access from long-term memory for threat-related information was investigated by Rapee, McCallum,

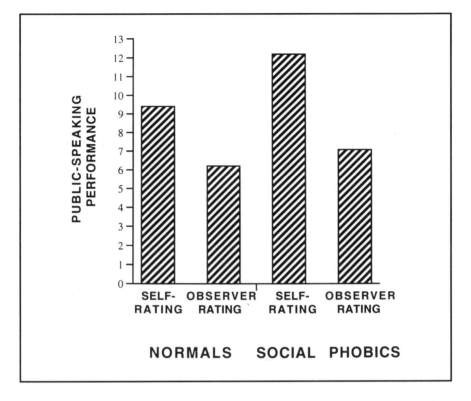

FIG. 5.3. Public-speaking performance of normal controls and social phobics, based on self-ratings and observer ratings (high scores indicate poor performance). Data from Rapee and Lim (1992).

Melville, Ravenscraft, and Rodney (1994) in a series of four studies. In the first study, social and physical threat words were presented as well as neutral words, followed by free recall and a test of recognition memory. There was no evidence of a negative memory bias in the performance of social phobics.

In their second study, Rapee et al. (1994) considered the memory performance of social phobics and normals high and low on the Fear of Negative Evaluation Scale. There was a test of explicit memory (cued recall) and a test of implicit memory (word completion). None of the groups displayed any evidence of negative memory bias for social threat words on either test. In their third study, Rapee et al. (1994) gave their subjects feedback from an imaginary judge following a hypothetical speech given by the experimenter or by the subject. The feedback was directed either at the experimenter or at the subject, and the comments in the feedback divided up equally between positive and negative. On a test of free recall, the social phobics failed to show any evidence of a negative memory bias. In the fourth study, subjects thought of memories about themselves, a sibling, or a close friend in response to stimulus words. The social phobics did not remember more negative memories than normal controls.

This thorough programme of research by Rapee et al. (1994) makes it unlikely that social phobics have facilitated access to threat-related information in long-term memory. As Rapee et al. (1994) concluded, "The four studies consistently failed to demonstrate a memory bias for social threat information in social phobics. This was the case whether memory was assessed using direct tasks or an indirect task, and whether the information was presented in the form of individual words, in a hypothetical context, or in the form of real-life experiences" (p.98).

Cloitre, Cancienne, Heimberg, Holt, and Liebowitz (1995) also investigated negative memory bias in social phobics. Memory for social threat words was tested by free recall and by high-speed recognition, but there was no evidence of negative memory bias.

There is one important limitation in the research carried out to date. Social phobics may be more sensitive to threatening or angry faces than to threat-related words, and so it might be possible to obtain evidence for a negative memory bias with such stimuli. There is already evidence that conditioning can be established to subliminally presented angry faces but not to happy faces (Esteves, Dimberg, Parra, & Ohman, 1994). This suggests that angry faces may have special significance, and it seems reasonable that this would be particularly so for social phobics.

Precipitating and predisposing factors

According to the theoretical framework, those precipitating or predisposing factors of greatest relevance to social phobia rather than to other anxiety disorders are those which produce concern about the adequacy of one's own behaviour in social situations. A potentially fruitful starting point for an investigation of such factors for social phobia is the research of Turner, Beidel, and Townsley (1990). They compared the symptoms of social phobia and of shyness in normals, and discovered that there was a high degree of similarity. This suggests that shyness or social inhibition might be a predisposing factor for social phobia.

Normals high in shyness tend to be high in neuroticism and low in extraversion (Crozier, 1979). Accordingly, it might be predicted that social phobics would have a childhood history of shyness and would tend to be low in extraversion and high in neuroticism. These predictions were tested by Stemberger, Turner, and Beidel (1995), who distinguished between generalised social phobia and specific social phobia. They found that childhood shyness was significantly more prevalent in those with generalised social phobia than in normal controls. In addition, the three groups (generalised social phobia; specific social phobia; and normal control) differed at $p < 0.0001$ on extraversion and on neuroticism. The generalised social phobics were significantly lower on extraversion and higher on neuroticism than either of the other two groups. Enright and Beech (1990) found that other groups of anxiety disorder patients were somewhat introverted. However, as can be seen in Fig. 5.4, none of these groups was nearly as introverted as social phobics were in the study by Stemberger et al. (1995).

Further evidence of the strong link between introversion and socially avoidant behaviour was reported by Lehrer and Woolfolk (1982). They devised a self-report questionnaire that contained separate somatic, behavioural, and cognitive factors of anxiety. Introversion correlated much higher with the behavioural or social avoidance factor than with either of the other two factors.

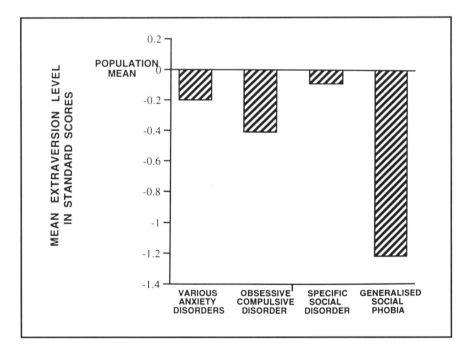

FIG. 5.4. Mean extraversion scores in other anxious patients and obsessive–compulsive disorder patients (data from Enright & Beech, 1990), and in specific social phobia and generalised social phobia (data from Stemberger et al., 1995).

Another related line of research has involved behavioural inhibition in children. Behavioural inhibition consists of social inhibition, discomfort with novelty, and heightened physiological arousal, and so probably combines elements of introversion and of anxiety. Behavioural inhibition typically has an early onset. Biederman, Rosenbaum, Hirshfeld, Faraone, Balduc, Gersten, Meminger, Kagan, Snidman, and Reznick (1990) found that the most common anxiety disorders in behaviourally inhibited children were social and over-anxious disorder. In other research (Rosenbaum, Biederman, Hirshfeld, Balduc, Faraone, Kagan, Snidman, & Reznick, 1991), the parents of behaviourally inhibited children were found to have a much higher incidence of social phobia than the parents of behaviourally uninhibited children. However, there were small, and non-significant differences between the two sets of parents for agoraphobia and for simple phobia.

Parental rearing styles may have an important impact on introversion or behavioural inhibition. Gerslman, Emmelkamp, and Arrindell (1990) carried out a meta-analysis of the literature on parental rearing practices in depressed and anxious patients, focusing on the dimensions of affection and control or over-protection. Patients with obsessive–compulsive disorder did not differ from controls with respect to either of these dimensions. However, phobics (including social phobics) were significantly lower than control subjects on parental affection and significantly higher on parental control or over-protection. It seems reasonable to assume that high parental control and low affection could increase a child's tendency towards introversion and behavioural inhibition.

The evidence suggests that introversion or behavioural inhibition is probably a predisposing factor for social phobia. Introversion is probably of more specific relevance, because it is relatively unrelated to trait anxiety or neuroticism (H. J. Eysenck, 1967), whereas this is unlikely to be the case with behavioural inhibition. Ohman, Dimberg, and Ost (1985) argued that social phobia develops as a result of social conflict. More specifically, dominance hierarchies form in adolescence, and individuals of low status with a given hierarchy are more likely to develop social phobia. It is probable that introversion and behavioural inhibition both contribute towards low status in social hierarchies.

There are at least two reasons for continuing the search for other predisposing factors. First, there are many more individuals who are very high in introversion or in behavioural inhibition than there are social phobics, so that social phobica may depend on introversion or behavioural inhibition in combination with other factors. Second, there are issues about the direction of causality. For example, the strong association that Stemberger et al. (1995) found between generalised social phobia and introversion may have arise at least in part because suffering from generalised social phobia increases the level of introversion.

OBSESSIVE–COMPULSIVE DISORDER

Selective attentional bias

Foa and McNally (1986) carried out the first study on selective attentional bias in obsessive–compulsive disorder patients. They used a dichotic listening task, and instructed their patients to detect idiosyncratically fear-relevant targets and neutral targets presented on either the attended or the unattended channel. The detection rate on the unattended channel was greater for fear-relevant than for neutral targets. Di Benedetto and Evans (1989) used the modified Stroop task with contamination, checking, general threat, and neutral words. Obsessive–compulsive disorder patients with fear of contamination had significantly slower colour naming than normal controls with contamination words, but the groups did not differ with the other category of words.

Foa, Ilai, McCarthy, Shoyer, and Murdock (1993) also used the modified Stroop task. Obsessive–compulsive disorder patients who were washers showed interference to contamination words. However, obsessive–compulsive disorder patients who were checkers did not.

Lavy, van Oppen, and van den Hout (1994) also used the modified Stroop task. Obsessive–compulsive disorder patients who were either checkers or washers showed interference for their dominant threat, but neither group showed interference for general threat words. After these patients had received treatment, there were no interference effects on the modified Stroop task. McNally, Amir, Louro, Lukach, Riemann, and Calamari (1994) also used the modified Stroop task. Obsessive–compulsive disorder patients, panic disorder patients, and normals were presented with panic-related, general threat, and neutral words. The obsessive–compulsive disorder patients did not show greater interference for panic-related than for neutral words.

Finally, Tata, Leibowitz, Prunty, Cameron, and Pickering (1996) used the dot-probe task with obsessive–compulsive disorder patients with contamination fears, as well as with normals high or low in trait anxiety. The obsessive–compulsive patients showed greater selective attentional bias for contamination-threat words than for social-threat words, whereas high trait-anxious normals showed the opposite pattern.

According to the four-factor theory of clinical anxiety, obsessive–compulsive disorder patients should have facilitated access to threat-related information in long-term memory. An interesting study on this issue was reported by Wilhelm, McNally, Baer, and Florin (1996). Obsessive–compulsive disorder patients and normal controls were presented with a range of negative, positive, and neutral words, and instructed either to remember or to forget them. All of the subjects were then instructed to remember all of the words, regardless of whether they had previously been told to remember or to forget them. The obsessive–compulsive disorder patients differed mainly from the controls in that they remembered more of the negative words they had been told to forget. According to Wilhelm et al. (1996), "Obsessive–compulsive disorder patients rate forget-words that they remember as having greater personal, negative emotional significance than forget-words that they forgot" (p.639). Their inability to forget personally threatening information may be of importance in the development and maintenance of obsessive–compulsive disorder.

Interpretive bias

It is known that normals and obsessive–compulsive disorder patients report similar obsessions, but that patients regard these obsessions as more intense, uncontrollable, and more generally threatening (e.g., Rachman & de Silva, 1978). Such findings suggest strongly that obsessive–compulsive disorder patients have an interpretive bias for at least some of their own negative thoughts. However, it has not proved possible to find any laboratory studies specifically investigating interpretive bias in obsessive–compulsive disorder patients.

Other cognitive factors

Other cognitive accounts of obsessive–compulsive disorder than the one favoured here could potentially explain many of the relevant phenomena. For example, obsessive–compulsive disorder patients might have very poor memory for their own actions, or they might find it unusually difficult to distinguish between what they have experienced and what they have imagined. As Tallis (1995) pointed out, there is some inconsistent evidence suggesting that some obsessive–compulsive disorder patients have minor memory problems, but it is improbable that such problems provide an adequate explanation for their symptoms.

One of the more convincing refutations of the notion that the memory abilities of obsessive–compulsive disorder patients are substantially worse than those of normals was provided by Brown, Kosslyn, Besiter, Baer, and Jenike (1994). They used a recognition-memory test on which the subjects had to discriminate between words they had seen and words they had imagined previously. The obsessive–compulsive disorder patients had significantly better memory discrimination than normal controls, but further analysis indicated that this was due to the performance of cleaners but not checkers. Subsequent unpublished research by Brown and her colleagues found that there was no difference between obsessive–compulsive disorder patients and normals on a similar task.

Similar findings were reported by Constans, Foa, Franklin, and Mathews (1995). They pointed out that the tasks used in previous studies of memory in obsessive–compulsive disorder patients were irrelevant to their concerns, and this might explain the failure to find evidence of large memory impairments. Accordingly, they asked obsessive–compulsive patients with checking compulsions to engage in real and imagined actions, some of which were related to the patients' fears. The obsessive–compulsive patients were more accurate than controls in remembering whether anxiety-related actions had actually been carried out or not. As Constans et al. (1995) concluded, "Our results … strongly suggest that checking is not motivated by deficits in reality-monitoring" (p.670).

Precipitating and predisposing factors

Probably the dominant view of obsessive–compulsive disorder is that an inflated sense of responsibility is of central importance (Salkovskis, 1985, 1989). In the words of Salkovskis (1989), "Clinical obsessions are intrusive cognitions, the occurrence and content of which patients interpret as an indication that they might be responsible for harm to themselves or others unless they take action to prevent it" (p.678). Dysfunctional beliefs such as "Having a thought about an action is like performing the action" and "Failing to prevent harm to self or others is the same as having caused the harm in the first place" make obsessive–compulsive disorder patients extremely anxious about their obsessional thoughts.

Ladouceur, Rheaume, Freeston, Aublet, Jean, Lachance, Langlois, and Pokomandy-Morin (1995) manipulated responsibility in a study in which the subjects had to classify pills as rapidly and as accurately as possible. In the high-responsibility condition, they were told that they could influence the manufacture of a medication, whereas in the low-responsibility condition they were told that the experimenter was interested in the perception of colours. There was twice as much checking and nearly twice as many hesitations in the high-responsibility condition. High responsibility also increased preoccupation with errors and increased the level of anxiety.

Lopatka and Rachman (1995) also manipulated perceived responsibility. They wanted to observe its effects on obsessive–

compulsive disorder patients who were primarily checkers. The patients were asked to imagine themselves with high or low responsibility in situations in which they generally engaged in checking behaviour. Decreasing their perceived responsibility led to a significant decrease in the urge to check, reduced discomfort, reduced probability of anticipated harm, reduced severity of anticipated harm, and reduced severity of anticipated criticism. There was an interesting bias towards confounding responsibility with the probability of anticipated harm: "If I am only minimally or not at all responsible for ensuring safety, then the probability of a misfortune will decline" (p.683).

In Chapter 4, it was suggested that inflated responsibility might affect the subjective probability of negative future events in obsessive–compulsive patients via the availability heuristic. According to this heuristic, the subjective probability of events is based on the accessibility of instances of such events. MacLeod and Campbell (1992) provided evidence for the availability heuristic. The relative accessibility of memories of positive and negative events was manipulated using mood induction (positive or negative). The subjects were presented with a short description of an event or situation, and instructed to recall a time when they had a similar experience. After that, they rated the probability that they would experience that situation or event in the next six months. The average correlation across subjects between recall latencies and subjective probability judgements was –0.50. In line with the availability heuristic, reductions in recall latencies produced by the mood manipulation were related to increases in perceived subjective probability, and vice versa.

An implication of these theoretical ideas and evidence is that some of the predisposing or precipitating factors for obsessive–compulsive disorder are likely to involve circumstances in which there is a substantial increase in responsibility. Very relevant evidence was reported by Buttolph and Holland (1990). They reported that 69% of female obsessive–compulsive disorder patients linked the onset or the worsening of their symptoms to pregnancy and childbirth. This is explicable if we assume that most women regard having a child as a major source of increased responsibility.

Khanna, Rajendra, and Channabasavanna (1988) reported that patients with obsessive–compulsive disorder had suffered a significant excess of life events in the six months prior to onset of the disorder. Most of these events were undesirable and uncontrolled events in the areas of health and bereavement. From the theoretical perspective adopted here, it is important to distinguish between the direct emotional effects of bereavement in terms of mourning and depression and the indirect effects in terms of increased personal responsibility. It is assumed that the latter effects may be more important than the former ones in the onset of obsessive–compulsive disorder.

SPECIFIC PHOBIA

According to the theory of clinical anxiety put forward in Chapter 2, specific phobics should attend selectively to phobia-relevant stimuli, and they should also have an interpretive bias for such stimuli.

Selective attentional bias

In an early study on selective attentional bias in phobics, Streblow, Hoffmann, and Kasielke (1985) carried out a study in which the subjects had to decide whether each in a set of neutral pictures was a household object or not. Animal phobics had significantly slower response times when the peripheral picture was a fear-relevant animal than when it was not. Lavy, van den Hout, and Arntz (1993b) used a similar task. Three pictures were presented together, and the subjects had to decide whether a statement was true of the central one (e.g., "It is a spider"). Spider phobics responded faster than controls when the central picture was of a spider and the two peripheral pictures were neutral, which could be taken as evidence for attentional bias. It was predicted that spider phobics would respond slower than controls when the central picture was neutral and the two flankers were phobia-relevant, but this prediction was not supported. Lavy et al. (1993b) suggested that the fact that the flankers were at some distance from the central picture may have meant that the spider phobics simply ignored them.

Watts, Trezise, and Sharrock (1986) found that spider phobics showed significant interference effects on a modified Stroop task with spider-related words. After treatment, this interference effect disappeared. In a similar study, Lavy, van den Haut, and Arntz (1993a) also found evidence that spider phobics have interference for spider-related words on the modified Stroop task. They also replicated Watts et al.'s (1986) finding that this effect was no longer present after treatment.

More recent evidence is less supportive of the view that specific phobics have an attentional bias for phobia-relevant stimuli. Merckelbach, Kenemans, Dijkstra, and Schouten (1993) required their subjects to decide as rapidly as possible whether horizontal or vertical bars had been presented, with a spider or a flower picture being presented at the same time. The spider phobics responded more slowly than the control subjects, but this effect did not depend at all on the nature of the distracting picture. The fact that there was greater spatial separation between the threat-related stimulus and the task stimulus in this study than in studies of the modified Stroop task suggests that selective attentional bias may be limited to situations in which the threatening stimulus is very close to the task stimulus. Merckelbach et al. (1993) obtained a significant interaction between groups and trials, with the greater slowness of the spider phobics being more pronounced over trials. This may have been due to increasing anxious arousal or cognitive avoidance.

Harris and Menzies (unpubl.) found that spider phobics showed more interference than non-phobics on the modified Stroop task with spider-related words. However, they failed to obtain any evidence for selective attentional bias in spider phobics on the dot-probe task, which provides a more direct assessment of the allocation of attention.

Interpretive bias

It has often been assumed that specific phobics realise at the cognitive level that phobia-relevant stimuli are harmless. In the words of Matchett and Davey (1991), "people regularly exhibit fear reactions to animals that they admit are harmless" (p.93). Evidence inconsistent with that viewpoint was reported by Arntz, Lavy, van den Berg, and van Rijsoort (1993). They argued that specific phobics are most likely to endorse irrational beliefs when in the presence of phobia-relevant stimuli. They asked spider phobics to indicate their irrational spider beliefs when confronted by a spider. Of the sample, 84% believed spiders may jump onto them, 61% that spiders can scent that they are anxious, and 35% that spiders tease them. When confronted by a spider, 89% of the spider phobics were concerned about losing control, 91% of panic and not knowing what they were doing, 91% of becoming crazy because of anxiety, and 64% that they might die because of fear. As Arntz et al. (1993) concluded, "Irrational ideas about the person's own reactions to an encounter with a spider appeared to be dominated by ideas that strongly resemble those held by panic patients" (p.265).

Similar evidence for extensive interpretive bias in specific phobics was reported by Thorpe and Salkovskis (1995). They asked spider phobics, non-spider phobics, and controls to rate statements on the Phobic Beliefs Questionnaire while imagining that their phobic object was in the room with them. Large numbers of the spider phobics (percentages are in brackets) had more than a 40% belief that they would experience the following thoughts if confronted by a spider: I would make a fool of myself (62%); I would go mad (56%); I would be hysterical (68%); I would be paralysed (50%). In contrast, very few of the non-spider phobics indicated that they would have any of these irrational thoughts. Thorpe and Salkovskis (1995) concluded that the beliefs of phobics "are to do with the amount of perceived harm emanating from the phobic object itself (possible physical harm or contamination), the amount of harm experienced by the phobic (going mad, having hysteria, paralysis, syncope) combined with a feeling of helplessness (not being able to cope, feeling trapped, unable to escape)" (p.815).

The studies by Arntz et al. (1993) and by Thorpe and Salkovskis (1995) demonstrate very clearly that specific phobics subscribe to a wide range of irrational beliefs when confronted by the phobic object. Some of these irrational beliefs relate to the phobic object itself, whereas others are self-related beliefs. In the terminology we have been using, specific phobics have extensive interpretive biases.

Predisposing and precipitating factors
According to the theory proposed here, those predisposing factors of greatest relevance to specific phobia rather than to other anxiety disorders should involve negative experiences relating to the phobic object or objects. This is only superficially similar to the behaviourist position (e.g. H. J. Eysenck, 1979; Watson & Rayner, 1920). According to this position, the development of a specific phobia involves classical conditioning, with the conditioned stimulus being the phobic object and the unconditioned stimulus being some aversive event. The key difference is that it is only the behaviourist account that requires a very precise temporal relationship between two stimuli, one of which is neutral and one of which is aversive.

It has been known for many years that there are significant problems with the conditioning account of the origins of phobias. For example, Keuthen (1980) reported that half of all phobics were unable to remember any highly unpleasant experiences relating to the phobic object. Menzies and Clarke (1994) discussed several problems with the way in which the method of retrospective reporting is usually used. The criteria for counting a memory as revealing classical conditioning are often too broad, and alternative possibilities (e.g., vicarious learning) are sometimes ignored. Furthermore, a control group has been used relatively infrequently. It is important to include a control group, in order to demonstrate that conditioning experiences are more prevalent among phobics than among non-phobics. In one study in which this was done (Jones & Menzies, 1995), it was found that significantly more non-phobic subjects than spider phobics had experienced conditioning events.

Those who favour a conditioning account of the origins of phobias can always argue that phobics often forget conditioning experiences when the retrospective method is used. In order to reduce this problem,

Menzies and Clarke (1993) made use of child subjects suffering from water phobia. Only 2% of the subjects reported a direct conditioning experience involving water, and 56% said that they had always been frightened of water, even on their first encounter with it.

Other factors leading to the development of specific phobias have been identified. There is good evidence from other species that observational learning can produce specific phobias (Cook & Mineka, 1991). However, observational learning seems to be of less importance in producing specific phobias in humans (see Menzies and Clarke, 1994). There is also evidence that exposure to threat-related information about phobic stimuli can contribute to the development of specific phobias (see Rachman, 1977). Once again, there is relatively little evidence that this is an important factor (Menzies & Clarke, 1994).

SUMMARY AND CONCLUSIONS

The four-factor theory of clinical anxiety put forward in Chapter 4 makes a series of predictions about the kinds and degree of specificity of cognitive biases which should be associated with various anxiety disorders. Five anxiety disorders were considered in detail: generalised anxiety disorder; panic disorder; social phobia; obsessive–compulsive disorder; and specific phobia. As far as possible, the focus was on studies in which cognitive functioning was assessed by relatively objective behavioural measures rather than by self-report measures.

In general terms, there is reasonably good evidence that anxious patients possess the predicted selective attentional and interpretive biases. In addition, it appears that these biases are usually relatively specific to the source of information of most concern to each group of patients. There is also evidence that the precipitating and predisposing factors identified as important within the four-factor theory of clinical anxiety play a role in the development of each of the five anxiety disorders considered in detail. However, it is clear that there are several other precipitating and predisposing factors. Future research will need to explore these factors in more detail.

CHAPTER SIX

Cognitive-behaviour therapy

INTRODUCTION

As Brewin (1996) pointed out, cognitive-behaviour therapy involves an extremely heterogeneous set of techniques and procedures. However, he argued persuasively that some theoretical coherence can be imposed on cognitive-behaviour therapy by drawing a distinction between interventions designed to modify conscious beliefs and representations and those designed to modify unconscious representations in memory. More specifically, Brewin (1996) concluded as follows:

> The basis of behaviour therapy was the assumption that actions and emotions are under the control of learned associations represented in a consciously inaccessible form. Hence its techniques attempt to alter situationally accessible knowledge by changing behaviour. In contrast, cognitive therapists accepted that conscious cognitions such as beliefs, plans, and goals also influence behaviour and emotions. In addition to trying to change situationally accessible knowledge, they also developed techniques to boost compensatory strategies and to rectify misconceptions in verbally accessible knowledge (p.53).

Brewin's (1996) distinction between situationally accessible knowledge and verbally accessible knowledge resembles to some extent that between procedural and declarative knowledge. Cohen (1984) claimed that procedural knowledge is involved when "experience serves to influence the organisation of processes that guide performance without access to the knowledge that underlies the performance" (p.96). In contrast, declarative knowledge is represented "in a system...in which information is...first processed or encoded, then stored in some explicitly accessible form for later use, and then ultimately retrieved upon demand" (p.96).

There are some differences between procedural knowledge and situationally accessible knowledge. Several theorists (e.g., Anderson, 1983) have argued that procedural learning typically depends on extensive over-learning, and develops out of earlier declarative learning. It has also been assumed that procedural learning mainly involves the acquisition of motor responses. In contrast, situationally accessible knowledge can often be acquired with limited opportunities for learning, and such knowledge is not limited to motor responses.

Brewin (1996) also drew a distinction between circumscribed disorders and generalised problems. In essence, circumscribed disorders (e.g., panic disorder) can be traced to specific faulty beliefs, whereas generalised problems (e.g., generalised anxiety disorder; depression) involve "complex sets of negative beliefs about the self or the external world that are activated in a variety of situations" (p.40).

In terms of Brewin's (1996) two-dimensional framework, the central focus of this chapter is clearly on interventions designed to modify conscious beliefs in patients suffering from circumscribed disorders. The theory of clinical anxiety proposed in Chapter 4 was explicitly designed to be mainly applicable to the less complex or more circumscribed disorders, and this theoretical emphasis is reflected in the coverage of therapy in this chapter. It is accepted that it is important to alter consciously inaccessible knowledge in the treatment of many anxiety disorders. However, most of the implications for therapy will emphasise the value of altering conscious beliefs.

Brewin (1996) identified exposure therapy as one of the main ways in which new situationally accessible knowledge can be acquired by anxious patients. Exposure therapy has proved successful in the treatment of several anxiety disorders, and so it is important to try to establish how it works. Foa and Kozak (1986, 1991) put forward a theoretical account offering a potential explanation for the effectiveness of exposure therapy. According to Foa and Kozak (1991), two conditions are required for fear reduction: "First, fear-relevant information must be made available in a manner that will activate the fear memory...Next, information made available must include elements that are incompatible with some of those that exist in the fear structure, so that a new memory can be formed. This new information, which is at once cognitive and affective, has to be integrated into the evoked information structure for an emotional change to occur" (p.29).

Brewin (1996) pointed out that the evidence from the memory literature is more consistent with the notion that memories are overwritten by new memories rather than that they are actually changed. The assumption that exposure therapy produces new memories makes it easy to understand how relapse can occur: "relapse may occur when the patient encounters a new situation more similar to the original fear memory than to the new memory created in therapy" (Brewin, 1996, p. 43). In contrast, accounting for relapse is more problematical if the old fear memories have been altered. Foa (e.g., Foa & McNally, 1996) has now accepted that new associations are formed rather than pre-existing associations being altered.

From the present perspective, it is assumed that exposure therapy often has relatively large effects on cognitive processes, biases, and beliefs. For example, phobic patients may have beliefs concerning the uncontrollability of their physiological responses and their behaviour in the presence of phobic stimuli, and such beliefs may be modified as a consequence of exposure therapy. Of particular importance is the assumption contained within the four-factor theory of clinical anxiety that the cognitive biases of anxious patients tend to be greater when they are highly anxious than when they are not. It is more valuable to demonstrate the inaccuracy of cognitive biases in situations in which such biases are strongly present (e.g., *in vivo* exposure) than in situations in which they are only weakly present.

It is unfortunate that relatively little is known in detail of the processes underlying the success of exposure therapy. An indication of the kind of information that would be useful was reported by Hope, Heimberg, and Bruch (1995), in a study comparing the effectiveness of cognitive-behaviour therapy and exposure therapy in the treatment of social phobia. They obtained self-ratings of performance quality in a social setting from the patients, and ratings of performance quality from judges. As can be seen in Fig. 6.1, patients receiving both forms of treatment showed increased self-ratings after treatment. However, it was only those receiving cognitive-behaviour therapy who eliminated the interpretive bias of perceiving the quality of their performance to be lower than it appeared to judges.

In recent years, there has been a tremendous growth in the use of cognitive therapy for patients suffering from the various anxiety disorders. In general, the various forms of cognitive therapy have proved either moderately or very successful in the treatment of clinical anxiety. It is notoriously dangerous to use therapeutic success as proof of the

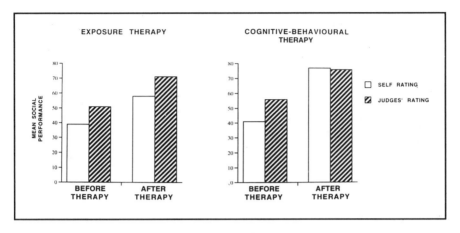

FIG. 6.1. Mean self-reported and rated social performance in social phobics before and after cognitive-behavioural therapy or exposure therapy. Data from Hope et al. (1995).

correctness of the theoretical underpinnings of therapy. For example, giving flowers to someone who is anxious about a forthcoming examination may prove useful because it distracts them from thinking about the examination. However, this does not demonstrate that a lack of flowers was the source of the original anxiety! In spite of such considerations, the many successes of cognitive therapy do provide some reassurance that we are developing a good understanding of the cognitive processes and structures involved in the anxiety disorders.

There are indications that cognitive therapy has proved more effective with some disorders than with others. According to Rachman (1993), "As far as anxiety disorders are concerned, the greatest theoretical and clinical progress has been made in applying cognitive-behaviour therapy (CBT) to the explanation and treatment of panic" (p.274). One of the most impressive features of cognitive therapy as applied to panic disorder, according to Rachman (1993), is that it "is legitimately deduced from the theory, and the theory itself is gaining some support...This cohesiveness of the theory and therapy is an added source of strength" (p.275).

Why has the cognitive approach proved especially successful with panic disorder? Probably, the major reason is because cognitive therapy generally focuses on the central symptom of panic disorder, namely, the catastrophic misinterpretation of the patient's bodily sensations. There are often numerous other symptoms present in panic disorder patients, but these other symptoms receive less attention from the therapist. Why is this advantageous? According to the four-factor theory of clinical anxiety, what differentiates clinical anxiety most clearly from anxiety in normals is that anxious patients are much more likely to perceive aspects of the external or internal environment as uncontrollable. For patients with panic disorder, it is typically their bodily sensations that are perceived as uncontrollable, and thus cause them the greatest anxiety. As a consequence, the most rapid way of reducing their anxiety below the clinical level is by focusing on their misinterpretation of bodily sensations.

This line of argument can be developed further. It is assumed within the theory (as was argued by Clark, 1986) that panic patients become extremely anxious when a vicious circle develops: misinterpretation of their bodily sensations increases their level of anxiety, which increases the extent of the misinterpretation, and so on. Such vicious circles leading to perceived uncontrollability are much more likely to occur in panic patients with respect to symptoms relating to perceived bodily sensations than to their other symptoms. It is assumed that it is of particular importance in therapy to address key symptoms associated with such vicious circles and perceived uncontrollability before considering other, less anxiety-generating, symptoms.

It could be argued with some reason that this approach harks back to the older versions of behaviour therapy, which were frequently criticised for concentrating on symptoms rather than causes. However, it is important to note that it is not being suggested that cognitive therapists should focus only on the central symptom or symptoms. Rather, it is being argued that a crucial early stage in therapy should involve trying to eliminate vicious circles and perceptions of uncontrollability. When that has been accomplished, therapy should then focus on the patient's other symptoms and concerns. The clinical theory put forward in Chapter 4 was in part an attempt to identify the major uncontrollable symptoms associated with different anxiety disorders, and to place them into a theoretical context.

The evidence discussed in Chapter 5 indicates that patients with various anxiety disorders possess a range of selective attentional and interpretive biases. However, the main focus in this chapter is on changing interpretive biases rather than selective attentional biases. Why is this so? In general terms, it is assumed that selective attentional biases typically develop as a consequence of some pre-existing interpretive bias. In other words, the main reason why anxious patients (but not normal controls) selectively attend to certain types of stimuli is because they interpret those stimuli as being more threatening than do normal controls. As a result, it is a reasonable assumption that elimination of the interpretive bias will tend to lead to removal of the selective attentional bias.

The success of the type of approach to therapy outlined above will obviously depend on various factors. The focus within the clinical theory put forward in Chapter 4 was on only five anxiety disorders: specific phobia; panic disorder without agoraphobia; obsessive–compulsive disorder; social phobia; and generalised anxiety disorder. The focus in what follows is on the first four of those anxiety disorders, followed by some consideration of generalised anxiety disorder. It is accepted that more complex forms of therapy may be needed for other anxiety disorders, but this issue is not pursued in this book.

One final issue needs to be considered before we move on to the various forms of cognitive therapy appropriate to the various anxiety disorders. According to the four-factor theory of clinical anxiety proposed in Chapter 4, clinically anxious patients are characterised by strong interpretive biases for different sources of information. How do these biases persist in the face of real-world evidence that they are inaccurate? Salkovskis, Clark, and Gelder (1996) have proposed a plausible answer to this question. According to Salkovskis et al. (1996), "People who believe they that they are in danger usually act in a way that they expect to make them safer. Such behaviour is a highly adaptive response to real threat. If the perception of danger is based on a misinterpretation then the safety seeking behaviour not only reduces anxiety at the time but also prevents the person from discovering that their fears are groundless" (p.453).

Salkovskis et al. (1996) obtained evidence of safety-seeking behaviours from panic disorder patients. They found that patients with panic disorder reported holding on to objects and people to prevent fainting, sat down and kept still to prevent heart attacks, and asked for help and focused attention on the body to prevent choking to death. They argued that exposure is most likely to be effective when patients manage to avoid making use of safety-seeking behaviours. This should maximise the probability that the patient will be able to disconfirm the misinterpretations which are maintaining the anxiety disorder.

PANIC DISORDER

It is generally accepted that the central feature of panic disorder without agoraphobia is the perceived uncontrollability of bodily sensations produced by catastrophic misinterpretations of those sensations (e.g., Clark, 1986). Many forms of cognitive therapy for panic disorder are based squarely on this theoretical account. For example, Clark and Salkovskis (1986) proposed a cognitive treatment for panic disorder in which the central focus was on challenging dysfunctional thoughts (e.g., catastrophic interpretations of bodily sensations) and on replacing them with rational thoughts. The possible role of hyperventilation as a link between somatic symptoms and anxiety was discussed, and patients monitored the automatic thoughts preceding or accompanying panic attacks.

The notion that hyperventilation plays an important causal role in panic attacks was assessed in a direct fashion by Garssen, Buikhuisen, and van Dyck (1996). They took ambulatory measures of the symptoms of hyperventilation in panic disorder patients as they exposed themselves to fear-provoking situations. There was evidence of hyperventilation in only 4% of the resultant panic attacks. This led Garssen et al. (1996) to conclude as follows: "The hypothesis that hyperventilation is an important symptom-producing mechanism in panic may be dismissed" (p.513).

That form of cognitive therapy, and slightly modified versions of it, have proved very successful. Gould, Otto, and Pollack (1995) carried out a meta-analysis of treatment outcome based on 43 controlled studies with pharmacological, cognitive-behavioural, and combined pharmacological and cognitive-behavioural treatments. They concluded as follows: "Our analysis has provided ample support for the conclusion that CBT [cognitive-behaviour therapy] is at least as effective as pharmacological treatments and offers powerful effects on measures of panic frequency as well as overall measures of outcome. In addition, CBT [cognitive-behaviour therapy] relative to pharmacologic treatment is associated with lower rates of attrition, and appears to confer a very promising long-term term outcome, with less slippage of treatment over time" (p.840).

Arntz and van den Hout (1996) came to a similar conclusion: "Despite some differences between the various cognitive treatments, results appear to be remarkably similar: percentages of panic-free patients after treatment varied from 75 to 90%; CT [cognitive therapy] appeared to be clearly superior to waiting-list or psychological placebo treatments (like supportive therapy or progressive relaxation); and CT appeared to be at least as effective as pharmacological treatment" (p.113).

Arntz and van den Hout (1996) carried out their own controlled study, in which they compared cognitive therapy based on Clark and Salkovskis (1986) with applied relaxation, based on techniques developed by Ost. Applied relaxation involved teaching the patients relaxation skills, which they were taught to apply as rapidly as possible at the early signs of panic. Towards the end of treatment with applied relaxation, the patients were given graduated exposure *in vivo* to feared situations so that they could practise their relaxation skills. Cognitive therapy was significantly more effective than applied relaxation in reducing the incidence of panic attacks. At the end of treatment, 78% of the panic patients who had received cognitive therapy were panic-free, compared to only 50% of those who had received applied relaxation. Precisely the same percentages were free of panic at the six-month follow-up. These percentages are very similar to those reported by Clark, Salkovskis, Hackmann, Middleton, Anastasiades, and Gelder (1994) in their study of the effects of cognitive therapy and applied relaxation.

It seems reasonable to assume that the very specific focus of cognitive therapy on panic symptoms means that it is more likely to reduce the incidence of panic attacks than to have other beneficial effects. In this connection, it is important to note that the patients in the study by Arntz and van den Hout (1996) had no or mild agoraphobia. In a previous study, van den Hout, Arntz, and Hoekstra (1994) investigated the effectiveness of cognitive therapy and exposure on panic patients with agoraphobia. Cognitive therapy reduced the incidence of panic, but had little or no effect on agoraphobic avoidance. In contrast, exposure *in vivo* reduced agoraphobic avoidance, but did not reduce panic attacks.

Additional evidence that panic disorder with agoraphobia is more difficult to treat than panic disorder without agoraphobia was reported by Williams and Falbo (1996). They considered the effectiveness of cognitive therapy, exposure therapy, and combined therapy. They found that 94% of the low agoraphobia patients were free of panic after treatment compared to only 52% of the high agoraphobia patients. Williams and Falbo (1996) concluded: "One can get a misleading picture of treatment effectiveness by selecting for psychiatric diagnosis (in this case, for 'pure' panic disorder) rather than for the target psychological phenomenon of interest (panic attacks). If one wants to know in general how panic treatments affect panic attacks, it is best to select for the presence of panic attacks, and not for the absence of other problems" (p.263).

It follows from the four-factor theory of clinical anxiety presented in Chapter 4 that it might be possible to reduce the symptoms of panic disorder patients by reducing their selective attentional bias for their own bodily sensations. Wells (1990) reported a case study in which a patient with panic disordere received therapy based on learning how to direct attention to external stimuli rather than to internal ones. This proved markedly more successful than relaxation therapy.

In sum, cognitive therapy focused very largely on the misinterpretation of bodily sensations by panic patients has proved to be extremely successful. Such cognitive therapy is most likely to succeed if panic disorder patients try to avoid using safety-seeking behaviours (Salkovskis et al., 1996). As might be expected, however, such cognitive therapy is more effective in panic patients without agoraphobia than in panic patients with agoraphobia (van den Hout et al., 1994). Such evidence is consistent with the notion that it is easier to gain a theoretical understanding of, and to develop effective cognitive therapy for, relatively circumscribed anxiety disorders.

OBSESSIVE–COMPULSIVE DISORDER

For obsessive–compulsive disorder patients, perceived uncontrollability of symptoms applies primarily to their own obsessional thoughts. Before considering possible implications of the clinical theory for the treatment of obsessive–compulsive disorder, it is worth reminding ourselves of the key factors claimed to underlie obsessional thoughts. First, there is often an inflated sense of personal responsibility, which greatly increases the perceived aversiveness of threatening outcomes. Second, there is the tendency of patients with obsessive–compulsive disorder to exaggerate greatly the probability of such threatening outcomes. Thoughts are most likely to become obsessional when the subjective probability of a negative outcome and the aversiveness of that outcome are both high. In approximate terms, there is a multiplicative relationship between subjective probability and outcome aversiveness in determining how troubling obsessional thoughts are likely to be.

Salkovskis (1985, 1989, 1996) has claimed that an inflated sense of personal responsibility is of central importance in most cases of obsessive–compulsive disorder. For example, according to Salkovskis (1996), "OCD [obsessive–compulsive disorder] patients show a number of characteristic thinking errors linked to their obsessional difficulties. Probably the most typical and important is the idea that 'Any influence over outcome = responsibility for outcome' " (p.121). However, as was pointed out in Chapter 4, it is probable that a high level of perceived responsibility is far more relevant to some of the symptoms of obsessive–compulsive disorder than to others. More specifically, the notion of responsibility is applicable to actions (or lack of actions) that may cause harm to others (e.g., checking), but is much less less so to actions (or lack of actions) that may cause harm only to the patient (e.g., washing).

Van Oppen and Arntz (1994) discussed a form of cognitive therapy for obsessive–compulsive disorder which focuses directly on these factors. As they pointed out, "It may be useful for the patient and therapist to investigate collaboratively two aspects of the danger as perceived by the patient: (i) whether the patient overestimates the chance of danger; and (ii) whether the patient overestimates the extent or the consequences of the danger" (p.82). One way of examining the subjective probability of danger is to invite the patient to think of the various events that would need to happen in order for the threatening outcome to materialise. The cumulative probability of these events is usually considerably lower than the patient's original estimated probability. For example, a patient thought that there was a 0.2 probability that her house would burn down if she did not put out her cigarette. She accepted that this could only happen if a spark fell on the carpet, the carpet caught fire, she failed to notice this, and she finally noticed the fire too late to stop the house burning down. On her own estimates, the probability of all these events occurring was 0.0000001.

Perceived responsibility can be examined by means of the pie technique. With this technique, the patient indicates the degree of responsibility that various people would have if the threatening outcome happened. Finally, the patient's degree of responsibility is given by the amount of "pie" not accounted for by others' responsibility. This is typically much less than the patient's perception of the extent of his or her responsibility. For example, a patient believed that he would be 100% responsible if there were a bad car crash after his bicycle fell down in the street. On detailed questioning, he admitted that the car driver would be 45% responsible, the weather 25%, the approaching car 20%, and the car mechanic 5%. This left the patient with only a 5% responsibility for the car crash.

Two other approaches to altering a patient's level of perceived responsibility were discussed by van Oppen and Arntz (1994). One approach is the "double standard" technique. The patient is asked whether he or she would find someone else responsible and guilty if the threatening outcome or event happened to them. Typically, the patient would not hold the other person responsible for the event. The major discrepancy between that view and the very high level of responsibility which the patient feels for his or her thoughts and behaviour is pointed out to the patient.

The other approach is to use behavioural experiments to test empirically whether the patient needs to feel a high level of responsibility. It is shown to the patient that omitting compulsive behaviour (e.g., cleaning; checking) does not in fact lead to dire consequences, and so there is no need for him or her to have an overwhelming sense of responsibility. For example, a patient who was concerned that he would lose money if he filled in a bank transfer form incorrectly was encouraged to do precisely that with a small sum of money. This demonstrated to him that the bank would credit the money to him in spite of his incorrect completion of a form.

Van Oppen, de Haan, van Balkom, Spinhoven, Hoogduin, and van Dyck (1995) carried out a controlled study to consider the effectiveness of cognitive therapy based in large measure on the approach advocated by van Oppen and Arntz (1994). It was compared against self-controlled exposure *in vivo* with response prevention in the treatment of patients with obsessive–compulsive disorder. As van Oppen et al. (1995) concluded, "Cognitive therapy as well as exposure in vivo led to statistically significant improvement. Multivariate significant differences suggested a superior efficacy of cognitive therapy in comparison to exposure *in vivo* on the obsessive–compulsive measures and on the measures for associated psychopathology" (p.379). Three measures of recovery were used (Padua Inventory–Revised; Yale Brown Obsessive Compulsive Scale; and Anxiety Discomfort Scale). Of the patients receiving cognitive therapy 39% recovered on all three measures, compared to only 17% receiving exposure *in vivo*.

Freeston, Rheaume, and Ladouceur (1996) provided some interesting suggestions for the treatment of obsessive–compulsive disorder patients, based on an approach resembling that of van Oppen and Arntz (1994). Some of their suggestions will be mentioned here. Patients often over-estimate the importance of their obsessional thoughts, based on the following illogical belief: "It must be important because I think about it, and I think about it because it is important" (p.437). One way of challenging this belief is to ask patients to record their thoughts to demonstrate that many unimportant thoughts occur every day. Another method is to ask patients to attend closely to something obviously unimportant (e.g., the tip of their nose). This demonstrates that it is entirely possible to spend as much time thinking about matters which possess very little importance.

Freeston et al. (1996) also challenged the belief of some obsessive–compulsive disorder patients that thoughts can increase the probability of an event. This can be done by asking the patient to buy a lottery ticket, and to spend 30 minutes a day thinking repetitively about winning the jackpot. Another method is for the patient to identify a household appliance which is known to be in good working order. The patient is told to think 100 times a day that the appliance will break down within the next week.

Freeston et al. (1996) also tried to change the excessive responsibility which is often experienced by obsessive–compulsive disorder patients. Patients' experiences of guilt or feeling uncomfortable are used to identify situations in which excessive responsibility is perceived. One method of treatment is to ask the patient to predict his or her reactions if responsibility were transferred to someone else who was paid a large amount of money to take care of the situation. Patients usually indicate that they would be much less anxious and concerned in those circumstances. Another method is to challenge responsibility appraisals by asking the patient to act as prosecution lawyer and as defence lawyer to argue the merits of the patient's appraisals. The patient is then asked to consider the large differences between the two arguments, and this is used to demonstrate the modifiable nature of responsibility appraisals.

In sum, cognitive therapy for obsessive–compulsive disorder focusing specifically on the key factors making obsessional thoughts uncontrollable has proved to be very effective. This is no mean achievement. In 1986, Davison and Neale concluded as follows: "Obessive–compulsive disorder is overall one of the most difficult psychological problems to treat" (p.138). However, there can be practical difficulties in applying the form of cognitive therapy advocated by van Oppen and Arntz (1994). Some patients do not report dysfunctional thoughts about the subjective probability or the consequences of the aversive event happening. Another problem in some cases is that the aversive consequences which the patient expects to follow from his or her involvement in a behavioural experiment can only be shown not to occur over a very long time period.

At the theoretical level, van Oppen and Arntz (1994) concluded that there is an important unresolved matter: "As a consequence of the cognitive formulation of obsessive–compulsive disorder which differentiates between the perception of danger and the perception of responsibility, further research is needed to compare the effect of addressing these issues separately. This may indicate which is the essential one in the treatment of obsessive–compulsive disorder" (p.86). According to the theory put forward in Chapter 4, the perception of danger and of responsibility are linked together. It would thus be predicted that cognitive therapy needs to focus on both the perception of danger and the perception of responsibility if it is to be maximally effective.

SOCIAL PHOBIA

According to the four-factor theory put forward in Chapter 4, a central problem in social phobia is that social phobics misinterpret their own behaviour as being considerably more anxious and lacking in social skill than is actually the case (e.g., Rapee & Lim, 1992; Stopa & Clark, 1993). This problem is exacerbated by the tendency of social phobics to attend excessively to their own behaviour in social situations. It is assumed that the attentional bias to their own behaviour is generally a consequence of the interpretive bias. In other words, the main reason why social phobics attend excessively to their own behaviour is because they have already misinterpreted it as being wholly inadequate.

It would be quite wrong to assume that the only problems possessed by social phobics relate to their cognitive biases for their own behaviour. As Stopa and Clark (1993) found, the actual social performance of social phobics was significantly worse than that of other groups. This indicates the potential importance of using social skills training and other techniques designed to improve the actual social behaviour of social phobics, in addition to techniques focusing on cognitive biases.

According to the above view of social phobia, it is of importance in therapy to convince patients that their interpretations of their own social behaviour are unduly negative. If the interpretive bias can be reduced, this should produce a reduction in the attentional bias towards their own behaviour. How might this interpretive bias be reduced? In the study by Hope et al. (1995), mentioned earlier in the chapter, attempts were made to challenge the dysfunctional thoughts of social phobics, and to provide them with feedback from others on their social performance. This cognitive-behaviour therapy was much more effective than exposure therapy in reducing the patients' interpretive bias for their own behaviour.

According to the theory put forward in Chapter 4, any interpretive bias is likely to be more pronounced when the patient is currently highly anxious. This suggests the value of instructing social phobics to interpret the adequacy of their social behaviour when they are *not* anxious. They could be done by taking video recordings of social phobics in social situations, and then asking them to rate the adequacy of their social performance some time thereafter in a non-social situation. Those ratings could then be compared with ratings obtained in the social situations themselves. It would be predicted that social phobics would rate their social performance as significantly better when viewing the video recordings in a non-social situation. This demonstration that their social performance is less inadequate than they had believed might then lead to reduced interpretive bias for their own behaviour in subsequent social situations.

There do not seem to be any published accounts of thorough clinical trials of this approach. However, Rapee and Hayman (1996) reported some relevant evidence from high-anxious and low-anxious normals. Both groups provided self-ratings of their social performance at the time and after looking at a video of their performance. The self-ratings of their performance based on the video were significantly more favourable than those obtained in the social situation. As Rapee and Hayman (1996) concluded, "In the case of socially anxious individuals, the input from current symptoms and long-term memory may considerably outweigh any external feedback, thereby providing an inaccurate appraisal of their own performance" (p.321).

Several different forms of cognitive therapy have been used in the treatment of social phobia (see Feske and Chambless, 1995, for a review). Some approaches rely on distraction or self-statement training. Heimberg (1991) devised a form of cognitive-behaviour group therapy involving graduated role-played exposures to feared situations conducted within group sessions. There is also identification, analysis, and disputation of irrational thoughts, with the irrational thoughts of social phobics being challenged by behavioural evidence within the group. However, it seems likely that it would be more difficult to reduce social phobics' interpretive bias for the adequacy of their own behaviour on the basis of other people's assessment than on the basis of self-assessment from video recordings. One reason is that social phobics may be inclined to disbelieve the assessments of others, for example, because they are perceived as wanting to avoid hurting the patients' feelings.

Feske and Chambless (1995) carried out a meta-analysis of 15 studies comparing cognitive-behaviour therapy and exposure treatment for social phobia. Feske and Chambless (1995) came to the following definite conclusion: "The results of this meta-analysis indicate that exposure with and without cognitive modifications are equally effective in the treatment of social phobia. In none of the comparisons did the effects of CBT (exposure with cognitive modification) tend to exceed those of exposure alone" (p.712). This negative conclusion is supported by a study not included in the meta-analysis. Mersch (1995) compared an integrated treatment (rational emotive therapy, social skills training, and exposure *in vivo*) against exposure *in vivo* alone. The integrated treatment was not superior to exposure on its own.

It follows from the four-factor theory that exposure therapy should be effective to the extent that it promotes elimination or reduction of the interpretive biases of social phobics. The general expectation is that interpretive biases should be reduced more successfully by cognitive therapy than by exposure therapy (see Hope et al., 1995). Wells, Clark, Salkovskis, Ludgate, Hackmann, and Gelder (1995) argued that interpretive biases are less likely to be reduced if social phobics use safety-seeking behaviours (e.g., avoid eye contact; talk less; avoid talking about self) in the exposure situation than if they do not. The reason is that patients who use safety-seeking behaviours tend to attribute the non-occurrence of feared catastrophes to the use of these behaviours. As predicted, Wells et al. (1995) found that within-situation anxiety and belief in the feared catastrophe were reduced to a significantly greater extent during exposure when patients were instructed to avoid safety-seeking behaviours.

According to the four-factor theory of clinical anxiety, social phobics have an interpretive bias for their behaviour in social situations. Many of the safety-seeking behaviours discussed by Wells et al. (1995) represent an attempt on the part of social phobics to minimise the evidence indicating that their behaviour is inadequate. This can either take the form of minimal behavioural involvement in a social situation (e.g., becoming uncommunicative) or refusing to take account of feedback from others (e.g., by avoiding eye contact).

It is worth emphasising at this point that cognitive therapy for social phobia has proved successful, even though it has not been demonstrated to be more successful than exposure. There are various possible reasons why cognitive therapy has so far proved no better than exposure. Two reasons were offered by Feske and Chambless (1995): "Training therapists to do good CBT [cognitive-behaviour therapy] may be more difficult and time-consuming than training therapists to do good exposure ... In the majority of studies, CBT was applied in group settings with five or more clients per group, perhaps providing insufficient time for the intensive therapist–client dialogue needed to achieve optimal cognitive change" (p.714).

There may be important theoretical reasons as well why cognitive therapy has not been superior to exposure on its own. It follows from the theory presented in Chapter 4 that the most significant focus in therapy should be to reduce, or eliminate, social phobics' interpretive bias for the adequacy of their own behaviour. This can perhaps best be done by a variety of techniques. First, as was discussed earlier, patients can assess their own social performance in tranquillity from video recordings. Second, other people can provide their assessments of the social performance of social phobics. Third, the above approaches should be adopted across a range of social situations varying in their stressfulness. If that is not done, there is a real danger that social phobics will develop a belief along the lines of, "My social performance is adequate in the treatment group, but it is still very inadequate in most other social situations."

SPECIFIC PHOBIA

According to the theory put forward in Chapter 4, a central feature in specific phobia is a systematic interpretive bias relating to the threateningness of the phobic stimuli. However, cognitive-behaviour treatment for specific phobia has typically not involved direct attempts to modify such biases and other dysfunctional beliefs.

In vivo exposure has been the most common form of treatment for specific phobia for many years. It has generally been found to be effective. For example, Ost (1989) reported a very high level of success with his one-session treatment of specific phobias based on *in vivo* exposure. This differed from the traditional treatment in that the patient was presented with the whole hierarchy of feared stimuli within a single session, and modelling was used if required. Ost (1989) evaluated the success of this form of treatment as follows: "Altogether 90% of the patients obtained a clinically significant improvement ... which was maintained at the follow-up after an average of 4 yr. This result is as good as, or better than, what has been reported for regular behavioural treatment across multiple sessions" (p.6).

As was discussed in Chapter 5, there is evidence that specific phobics demonstrate a range of interpretive biases in the presence of their phobic stimuli (e.g., Arntz et al., 1993; Thorpe & Salkovskis, 1995). In view of these findings, it would be of interest to investigate the impact that *in vivo* exposure has on such cognitive biases. At the very least, this might increase our theoretical understanding of the mechanisms and processes underlying the success of exposure therapy in the treatment of specific phobics.

GENERALISED ANXIETY DISORDER

According to the four-factor theory presented in Chapter 4, patients with generalised anxiety disorder have a wide range of interpretive biases closely resembling those shown by normals high in trait anxiety. It follows that successful cognitive therapy for generalised anxiety disorder needs to be more extensive than in the case of the more specific anxiety disorders discussed so far. More specifically, it is assumed by the four-factor theory of clinical anxiety presented in Chapter 4 that patients with generalised anxiety disorder may possess interpretive biases with respect to more than one (or even all) of the four sources of information producing anxiety. As a consequence, cognitive therapy might benefit from addressing each of these sources of information in turn.

There have been a number of recent attempts to compare the success of cognitive therapy in treating generalised anxiety disorder against other forms of therapy. Cognitive therapy or cognitive-behaviour therapy has mostly involved procedures resembling those advocated by Beck and Emery (1985). The rationale for these procedures was described in the following terms by Butler, Fennell, Robson, and Gelder (1991): "anxiety is maintained by anxious thoughts (e.g., about symptoms and about situations that provoke anxiety) and by lack of self-confidence defined as reduced belief in the ability to carry out activities successfully ... anxiety can be controlled by learning to recognise anxious thoughts, to seek more realistic and helpful alternatives, and to take action to test these in practice" (p.169).

Durham and Allan (1993) compared cognitive therapy against biofeedback, behaviour therapy, relaxation training, and non-directive psychotherapy. They concluded as follows: "On balance, the best results are likely to be obtained by cognitive therapy, although the few comparative studies suggest that non-specific factors are important" (p.25).

Butler et al. (1991) compared the effectiveness of cognitive-behaviour therapy modelled on the procedures of Beck and Emery (1985) with behaviour therapy based on relaxation, graded exposure, and re-engagement in pleasurable and rewarding activities. Butler et al. (1991) concluded that, "results show a clear advantage for CBT [cognitive-behaviour therapy] over BT [behaviour therapy]. A consistent pattern of change favouring BT was evident in measures of anxiety, depression, and cognition" (p.167). Of particular relevance to the approach adopted in this book, the most significant differences between the two forms of therapy were in the reduction in the perceived likelihood of unpleasant threatening events, and in the reduction in the tendency to interpret ambiguous material in a threatening way. Both of these measures showed greater reduction with cognitive-behaviour therapy than with behaviour therapy. These findings are consistent with the notion following from the four-factor theory that the effectiveness of cognitive therapy in treating generalised anxiety disorder depends crucially on reducing or eliminating the interpretive biases of generalised anxiety disorder patients.

Durham, Murphy, Allan, Richard, Treliving, and Fenton (in press) compared cognitive therapy based on Beck and Emery (1985) with analytic psychotherapy based on psychoanalysis. At the six-month follow-up, nearly twice as many generalised anxiety disorder patients who had received cognitive therapy rated themselves as at least moderately improved. At that time, about 60% of patients who had been given cognitive therapy were in the normal range of functioning, against only about 20% who had received analytic psychotherapy.

SUMMARY AND CONCLUSIONS

Therapists need to be aware of the fact that successful treatment often involves the patients' acquiring new situationally accessible knowledge as well as verbally accessible knowledge. Behaviour therapy has traditionally focused on situationally accessible knowledge, whereas cognitive therapy has concentrated more on verbally accessible knowledge. There are advantages in focusing on a key interpretive bias in therapy; this interpretive bias will often relate directly to one of the four sources of information determining experienced anxiety. If interpretive biases can be reduced or eliminated, this will typically reduce any associated selective attentional biases. The key interpretive bias will tend to be associated with perceived uncontrollability, and may form part of a vicious circle in which the bias increases anxiety and increased anxiety increases the bias. Safety-seeking behaviours may serve to maintain anxious patients' interpretive biases, and it is important for treatment that patients endeavour to avoid such behaviours.

Cognitive therapy for panic disorder based largely on reducing the key interpretive bias (i.e., catastrophic misinterpretations of bodily sensations) has proved very successful provided that there is little or no agoraphobia. Obsessive–compulsive disorder patients often have as their key interpretive biases inflated subjective probabilities of aversive outcomes combined with inflated perceived aversiveness of those outcomes due to an inflated sense of personal responsibility. In those cases, cognitive therapy should focus on those interpretive biases.

The key interpretive bias in social phobia often involves an exaggerated perception of the patient's behavioural anxiety and behavioural inadequacy. Cognitive therapy should focus on reducing the discrepancy between the patient's actual behaviour and his or her perception of that behaviour. This can be done by means of the patient viewing videotapes of his or her social performance some time afterwards, combined with feedback provided by other participants in social situations. The key interpretive bias in specific phobia involves an exaggerated perception of threateningness of the phobic stimuli. In principle, cognitive therapy could focus on this key interpretive bias.

Generalised anxiety disorder differs from the other anxiety disorders considered in this chapter in that it does not have a central symptom associated with it. The focus within cognitive therapy has been on attempting to correct the unrealistic worries and interpretive biases possessed by generalised anxiety disorder patients. According to the four-factor theory of clinic anxiety, it would be predicted that cognitive therapists might find it useful to focus on interpretive biases with respect to some, or even all, of the four sources of information producing anxiety. The available evidence suggests that the cognitive approach is somewhat more successful than other therapeutic approaches in the treatment of generalised anxiety disorder.

References

Ainsworth, M.D.S., & Bell, S.M. (1970). Attachment, exploration, and separation: Illustrated by the behaviour of one-year-olds in a strange situation. *Child Development, 41*, 49–67.

Albersnagel, F.A. (1988). Velten and musical mood induction procedures: A comparison with accessibility of thought associations. *Behaviour Research and Therapy, 26*, 79–96.

Alden, L.E., & Wallace, S.T. (1995). Social phobia and social appraisal in successful and unsuccessful social interactions. *Behaviour Research and Therapy, 33*, 497–505.

Amir, N., McNally, R.J., Riemann, B.C., & Clements, C. (1996). Implicit memory bias for threat in panic disorder: Application of the "white noise" paradigm. *Behaviour Research and Therapy, 34*, 157–162.

Anderson, J.R. (1983). *The architecture of cognition.* Harvard: Harvard University Press.

Andrews, G. (1988). Stressful life events and anxiety. In R. Noyes, M. Roth, & G.D. Burrows (Eds.), *Handbook of anxiety* (Vol. 2). Amsterdam: Elsevier.

Antony, M.M., Brown, T.A., Craske, M.G., Barlow, D.H., Mitchell, W.B., & Meadows, E.A. (1995). Accuracy of heartbeat perception in panic disorder, social phobia, and nonanxious subjects. *Journal of Anxiety Disorders, 9*, 355–371.

Arntz, A., Dreessen, L., & Merckelbach, H. (1991). Attention, not anxiety, influences pain. *Behaviour Research and Therapy, 29*, 41–50.

Arntz, A., Lavy, E., van den Berg, G., & van Rijsoort, S. (1993). Negative beliefs of spider phobics: A psychometric evaluation of the Spider Phobia Beliefs Questionnaire. *Advances in Behavioural Research and Therapy, 15*, 257–277.

Arntz, A., Rauner, M., & van den Haut, M. (1995). "If I feel anxious, there must be danger": Ex-consequentia reasoning in inferring danger in anxiety disorders. *Behaviour Research and Therapy, 33*, 917–925.

Arntz, A., & Schmidt, A.J.M. (1989). Perceived control and the experience of pain. In A. Steptoe & A. Appels (Eds.), *Stress, personal control, and health*. Chichester: Wiley.

Arntz, A., & van den Hout, M. (1996). Psychological treatments of panic disorder without agoraphobia: Cognitive therapy versus applied relaxation. *Behaviour Research and Therapy, 34*, 113–121.

Asendorpf, J.B. (1987). Videotape reconstruction of emotions and cognitions related to shyness. *Journal of Personality and Social Psychology, 53*, 542–549.

Asmundson, G.J.G., & Stein, M.B. (1994). Selective processing of social threat in patients and generalised social phobia: Evaluation using a dot-probe paradigm. *Journal of Anxiety Disorders, 8*, 107–117.

Bandler, R.J., Madaras, G.R., & Bem, D.J. (1968). Self-observation as a source of pain perception. *Journal of Personality and Social Psychology, 9*, 205–209.

Bargh, J.A. (1989). Conditional automaticity: Varieties of automatic influence in social perception and cognition. In J. S. Uleman & J. A. Bargh (Eds.), *Unintended thought*. New York: Guilford Press.

Barlow, D.H., Di Nardo, P.A., Vermilyea, J.A., & Blanchard, E.B. (1986). Comorbidity and depression among the anxiety disorders: Issues in diagnosis and classification. *Journal of Nervous and Mental Disease, 174*, 63–72.

Barrett, J.E. (1979). The relationship of life events to the onset of neurotic disorders. In J.E. Barrett (Ed.), *Stress and mental disorder*. New York: Raven Press.

Beck, A.T. (1976). *Cognitive therapy and the emotional disorders*. New York: International Universities Press.

Beck, A.T., & Clark, D.A. (1988). Anxiety and depression: An information processing perspective. *Anxiety Research, 1*, 23–36.

Beck, A.T., & Emery, G. (1985). *Anxiety disorders and phobias: A cognitive perspective*. New York: Basic Books.

Beck, A.T., Stanley, M.A., Averill, P.M., Baldwin, L.E., & Deagle, E.A. (1992). Attention and memory for threat in panic disorder. *Behaviour Research and Therapy, 30*, 619–629.

Beck, A.T., Steer, R.A., & Beck, J.S. (1993). Types of self-reported anxiety in outpatients with DSM-III-R anxiety disorders. *Anxiety, Stress, and Coping, 6*, 43–55.

Becker, E., Rinck, M., & Margraf, J. (1994). Memory bias in panic disorder. *Journal of Abnormal Psychology, 103*, 396–399.

Beers, T.M., & Karoly, P. (1979). Cognitive strategies, expectancy, and coping style in the control of pain. *Journal of Consulting and Clinical Psychology, 47*, 179–180.

Beidel, D.C., Turner, S.M., & Dancu, C.V. (1985). Physiological, cognitive and behavioural aspects of social anxiety. *Behaviour Research and Therapy, 23*, 109–117.

Ben-Amnon, Y., Fux, M., Maoz, B., & Benjamin, J. (1995). Respiratory and other symptoms in panic disorder versus other anxiety disorders. *Israeli Journal of Psychiatry and Relative Science, 32*, 38–43.

Bermond, B., Nieuwenhuyse, B., Fasotti, L., & Schwerman, J. (1991). Spinal cord lesions, peripheral feedback, and intensities of emotional feelings. *Cognition and Emotion, 5*, 201–220.

Berry, D.C., & Broadbent, D.E. (1984). On the relationship between task performance and associated verbalisable knowledge. *Quarterly Journal of Experimental Psychology, 36A*, 209–231.

Biederman, J., Rosenbaum, J.F., Hirshfeld, D.R., Faraone, S.V., Bolduc, E.A., Gersten, M., Meminger, S.R., Kagan, J., Snidman, N., & Reznick, J.S. (1990). Psychiatric correlates of behavioural inhibition in young children of parents with and without psychiatric disorders. *Archives of General Psychiatry, 47*, 21–26.

Blaney, P.H. (1986). Affect and memory: A review. *Psychological Bulletin, 99*, 229–246.

Block, J. (1995). A contrarian view of the five-factor approach to personality description. *Psychological Bulletin, 117*, 187–215.

Bonanno, G.A., Davis, P. J., Singer, J.L., & Schwartz, G.E. (1991). The repressor personality and avoidant information processing: A dichotic listening study. *Journal of Research in Personality, 25*, 386–401.

Borkovec, T.D., & Inz, J. (1990). The nature of worry in generalised anxiety disorder: A predominance of thought activity. *Behaviour Research and Therapy, 28*, 153–158.

Borkovec, T.D., Robinson, E., Pruzinsky, T., & DePree, J.A. (1983). Preliminary exploration of worry: Some characteristics and processes. *Behaviour Research and Therapy, 21*, 9–16.

Borkovec, T.D., Wall, R.L., & Stone, N.M. (1974). False physiological feedback and the maintenance of speech anxiety. *Journal of Abnormal Psychology, 83*, 164–168.

Bradley, B.P., & Mogg, K. (1994). Mood and personality in recall of positive and negative information. *Behaviour Research and Therapy, 32*, 137–141.

Bradley, B.P., Mogg, K., Galbraith, M., & Perrett, A. (1993). Negative recall bias in neuroticism: State versus trait effects. *Behaviour Research and Therapy, 31*, 125–127.

Bradley, B.P., Mogg, K., Millar, N., & White, J. (1995a). Selective processing of negative information: Effects of clinical anxiety, concurrent depression, and awareness. *Journal of Abnormal Psychology, 104*, 532–536.

Bradley, B.P., Mogg, K., & Williams, R. (1995b). Implicit and explicit memory for emotion-congruent information in clinical depression and anxiety. *Behaviour Research and Therapy, 33*, 755–770.

Breck, B.E., & Smith, S.H. (1983). Selective recall of self-descriptive traits by socially anxious and nonanxious females. *Social Behavior and Personality, 11*, 71–76.

Brewin, C.R. (1996). Theoretical foundations of cognitive-behaviour therapy for anxiety and depression. *Annual Review of Psychology, 47*, 33–57.

Broadbent, D.E., & Broadbent, M. (1988). Anxiety and attentional bias: State and trait. *Cognition and Emotion, 2*, 165–183.

Brody, N. (1988). *Personality: In search of individuality*. New York: Academic Press.

Brown, H.D., Kosslyn, S. M., Besiter, H.C., Baer, L., & Jenike, M.A. (1994). Can patients with obsessive–compulsive disorder discriminate between percepts and mental images? A signal detection analysis. *Journal of Abnormal Psychology, 103*, 445–454.

Brown, L.L., Tomarken, A.J., Orth, D.N., Loosen, P.T., Kalin, N.H., & Davidson, R.J. (1996). Individual differences in repressive-defensiveness predict basal salivary cortisol levels. *Journal of Personality and Social Psychology, 70*, 362–371.

Butler, G., Fennell, M., Robson, P., & Gelder, M. (1991). Comparison of behaviour therapy and cognitive behaviour therapy in the treatment of generalized anxiety disorder. *Journal of Consulting and Clinical Psychology, 59*, 167–175.

Butler, G., & Mathews, A. (1987). Anticipatory anxiety and risk perception. *Cognitive Therapy and Research, 11*, 551–555.

Buttolph, L., & Holland, A. (1990). Obsessive compulsive disorder in pregnancy and childbirth. In M.A. Jenike, L. Baer, & W. Minichello (Eds.), *Obsessive-compulsive disorders: Theory and management*. Boston, MA: Year Book Medical Publishers.

Byrne, A., & Eysenck, M.W. (1993). Individual differences in positive and negative interpretive biases. *Personality and Individual Differences, 14*, 849–851.

Calvo, M., & Castillo, M.D. (in press). Mood-congruent bias in interpretation of ambiguity: Strategic processes and temporary activation. *Quarterly Journal of Experimental Psychology*.

Calvo, M.G., & Eysenck, M.W. (1995). Sesgo interpretativo en la ansiedad de evalucacion. *Ansiedad y Estres, 1*, 5–20.

Calvo, M., & Eysenck, M.W. (submitted). Cognitive bias to internal sources of information.

Calvo, M., Eysenck, M.W., & Castillo, M.D. (in press). Interpretation bias in test anxiety: The time course of predictive inferences. *Cognition and Emotion*.

Calvo, M., Eysenck, M.W., & Esterey, A. (1994). Ego-threat interpretive bias in test anxiety: On-line inferences. *Cognition and Emotion, 8*, 127–146.

Cattell, R.B., Eber, H.W., & Tatsouka, M.W. (1970). *Handbook for the Sixteen Personality Factor Questionnaire (16PF)*. Champaign, IL: Institute for Personality and Ability Testing.

Charney, D.S., Heninger, G.R., & Breier, A. (1984). Noradrenergic function in panic anxiety: Effects of yohimbine in healthy subjects and patients with agoraphobia and panic disorder. *Archives of General Psychiatry, 41*, 751–763.

Claeys, W. (1989). Social anxiety, evaluative threat and incidental recall of trait words. *Anxiety Research, 2*, 27–43.

Clark, D.M. (1986). A cognitive approach to panic. *Behaviour Research and Therapy, 24*, 461–470.

Clark, D.M., & Hemsley, D. (1982). Effects of hyperventilation: Individual variability and its relation to personality. *Journal of Behaviour Therapy and Experimental Psychiatry, 13*, 41–47.

Clark, D.M., & Salkovskis, P.M. (1986). *Cognitive treatment of panic: Therapist's manual*. Oxford: Department of Psychiatry, University of Oxford.

Clark, D.M., Salkovskis, P.M., Gelder, M., Koehler, K., Martin, M., Anastasiades, P., Hackmann, A., Middleton, H., & Jeavons, A. (1988). Tests of a cognitive theory of panic. In I. Hand & H.-U. Wittchen (Eds.), *Panic and phobias* (Vol. 2). Berlin: Springer.

Clark, D.M., Salkovskis, P.M., Hackmann, A., Middleton, H., Anastasiades, P., & Gelder, M. (1994). A comparison of cognitive therapy, applied relaxation and imipramine in the treatment of panic disorder. *British Journal of Psychiatry, 164*, 759–769.

Clark, D.M., Salkovskis, P.M., Ost, L.-G., Breitholz, E., Koehler, K.A., Westling, B.E., Jeavons, A., & Gelder, M. (in press). Misinterpretation of body sensations in panic disorder. *Journal of Consulting and Clinical Psychology*.

Clark, J.V., & Arkowitz, H. (1975). Social anxiety and self-evaluation of interpersonal performance. *Psychological Reports, 36*, 211–221.

Clark, L.A., & Watson, D. (1991). Tripartite model of anxiety and depression: Psychometric evidence and taxonomic implications. *Journal of Abnormal Psychology, 100*, 316–336.

Clark, L.A., Watson, D., & Mineka, S. (1994). Temperament, personality, and the mood and anxiety disorders. *Journal of Abnormal Psychology, 103,* 103–116.

Cloitre, M., Cancienne, J., Heimberg, R.G., Holt, C.S., & Liebowitz, M. (1995). Memory bias does not generalise across anxiety disorders. *Behaviour Research and Therapy, 33,* 305–308.

Cloitre, M., & Liebowitz, M.R. (1991). Memory bias in panic disorder: An investigation of the cognitive avoidance hypothesis. *Cognitive Therapy and Research, 15,* 371–386.

Cloitre, M., Shear, M.K., Cancienne, J., & Zeitlin, S.B. (1994). Implicit and explicit memory for catastrophic associations to bodily sensation words in panic disorder. *Cognitive Therapy and Research, 18,* 225–240.

Cohen, N.J. (1984). Preserved learning capacity in amnesia: Evidence for multiple memory systems. In L.R. Squire & N. Butters (Eds.), *Neuropsychology of memory.* New York: Guilford Press.

Conley, J.J. (1984). The hierarchy of consistency: A review and model of longitudinal findings on adult individual differences in intelligence, personality and self-opinion. *Personality and Individual Differences, 5,* 11–25.

Constans, J.I., Foa, E.B., Franklin, M.E., & Mathews, A. (1995). Memory for actual and imagined events in OC checkers. *Behaviour Research and Therapy, 33,* 665–671.

Cook, M., & Mineka, S. (1991). Selective associations in the origins of phobic fears and their implications for behaviour therapy. In P.R. Martin (Ed.), *Handbook of behaviour therapy and psychological science.* New York: Pergamon.

Cornwall, A., & Donderi, D.C. (1988). The effect of experimentally induced anxiety on the experience of pressure pain. *Journal of Abnormal Psychology, 88,* 137–144.

Costa, P.T., & McCrae, R.R. (1985). Comparison of EPI and psychoticism scales with measures of the five-factor model of personality. *Personality and Individual Differences, 6,* 587–597.

Cox, B.J., Endler, N.S., & Swinson, R.P. (1991). Clinical and nonclinical panic attacks: An empirical test of a panic-anxiety continuum. *Journal of Anxiety Disorders, 5,* 21–34.

Cox, B.J., Parker, J.D.A., & Swinson, R.P. (1996). Anxiety sensitivity: Confirmatory evidence for a multidimensional construct. *Behaviour Research and Therapy, 34,* 591–598.

Craske, M.G., & Craig, K.D. (1984). Musical performance anxiety: The three-systems model and self-efficacy theory. *Behaviour Research and Therapy, 22,* 267–280.

Crowne, D.P., & Marlowe, D. (1964). *The approval motive.* New York: Wiley.

Crozier, W.R. (1979). Shyness as a dimension of personality. *British Journal of Social and Clinical Psychology, 18,* 121–128.

Dalgleish, T. (1994). The appraisal of threat and the process of selective attention in clinical and sub-clinical anxiety states: I. Theoretical issues. *Clinical Psychology and Psychotherapy, 1,* 153–164.

Daly, J.A., Vangelisti, A.L., & Lawrence, S.G. (1989). Self-focused attention and public speaking anxiety. *Personality and Individual Differences, 10,* 903–913.

Davidson, J.R., & Foa, E.B. (1991). Diagnostic issues in posttraumatic stress disorder: Considerations for the DSM-IV. *Journal of Abnormal Psychology, 100,* 346–355.

Davis, P.J. (1987). Repression and the inaccessibility of affective memories. *Journal of Personality and Social Psychology, 53*, 585–593.

Davis, P.J. (1990). Repression and the inaccessibility of affective memories. In J.L. Singer (Ed.), *Repression and dissociation: Implications for personality theory, psychopathology, and health.* Chicago: University of Chicago Press.

Davison, G.C., & Neale, J.M. (1986). *Abnormal psychology* (4th ed.). New York: Wiley.

Dawkins, K., & Furnham, A. (1989). The colour naming of emotional words. *British Journal of Psychology, 80*, 383–389.

Derakshan, N., & Eysenck, M.W. (in press). Interpretive biases for one's own behaviour and physiology in high trait-anxious individuals and repressors. *Journal of Personality and Social Psychology.*

Derakshan, N., & Eysenck, M.W. (submitted a). *Heartbeat perception in repressors and high-anxious individuals.*

Derakshan, N., & Eysenck, M.W. (submitted b). *Effects of hyperventilation on bodily symptoms in high-anxious and repressor groups.*

Derakshan, N., & Eysenck, M.W. (submitted c). *Misinterpretation of body sensations in repressors and high-anxious individuals.*

Derakshan, N., & Eysenck, M.W. (submitted d). *Return of the repressed.*

De Ruiter, C., & Brosschot, J. F. (1994). The emotional Stroop interference effect in anxiety: Attentional bias or cognitive avoidance? *Behaviour Research and Therapy, 32*, 315–319.

Di Benedetto, A.M., & Evans, I. (1989). *Selective processing in obsessive–compulsive disorder as measured by a modified Stroop colour word task.* Poster presented at the 23rd annual convention of the Association for Advancement of Behaviour Therapy, Washington, DC.

Digman, J.M. (1990). Personality structure: Emergence of the five-factor model. *Annual Review of Psychology, 41*, 417–440.

Donat, D.C. (1983). Predicting state anxiety: A comparison of multidimensional and unidimensional trait approaches. *Journal of Research in Personality, 17*, 256–262.

Dougher, M.J., Goldstein, D., & Leight, K.A. (1987). Induced anxiety and pain. *Journal of Anxiety Disorders, 1*, 259–264.

Dozier, M., & Kobak, R.R. (1992). Psychophysiology in attachment interviews: Converging evidence for deactivating strategies. *Child Development, 63*, 1473–1480.

Durham, R.C., & Allan, T. (1993). Psychological treatment of generalized anxiety disorder: A review of the clinical significance of results in outcome studies since 1980. *British Journal of Psychiatry, 163*, 19–26.

Durham, R.C., Murphy, T., Allan, T., Richard, K., Treliving, L.R., & Fenton, G.W. (in press). A comparison of cognitive therapy, analytic psychotherapy and anxiety management training in the treatment of generalized anxiety disorder. *British Journal of Psychiatry.*

East, M.P., & Watts, F.N. (1994). Worry and the suppression of imagery. *Behaviour Research and Therapy, 32*, 851–855.

Ehlers, A. (1995). A 1-year prospective study of panic attacks: Clinical course and factors associated with maintenance. *Journal of Abnormal Psychology, 104*, 164–172.

Ehlers, A., & Breuer, P. (1992). Increased cardiac awareness in panic disorder. Journal of Abnormal Psychology, 101, 371–382.

Ehlers, A., & Breuer, P. (1995). Selective attention to physical threat in subjects with panic attacks and specific phobias. *Journal of Anxiety Disorders, 9*, 11–31.

Ehlers, A., Margraf, J., Davies, S., & Roth, W.T. (1988). Selective processing of threat cues in subjects with panic attacks. *Cognition and Emotion, 2*, 201–219.

Eke, M., & McNally, R.J. (1996). Anxiety sensitivity, suffocation fear, trait anxiety, and breath-holding duration as predictors of response to carbon dioxide challenge. *Behaviour Research and Therapy, 34*, 603–608.

Ekman, P., Levenson, R.W., & Friesen, W.V. (1983). Autonomic nervous system activity distinguishes among emotions. *Science, 221*, 1208–1210.

Ellis, A.W., & Young, A.W. (1988). *Human cognitive neuropsychology.* Hove, UK: Lawrence Erlbaum Associates Ltd.

Endler, N.S. (1983). Interactionism: A personality model, but not yet a theory. In M. M. Page (Ed.), *Nebraska symposium on motivation: Personality — Current theory and research.* Lincoln, NE: University of Nebraska Press.

Endler, N.S., Magnusson, D., Ekehammar, B., & Okada, M. (1976). The multi-dimensionality of state and trait anxiety. *Scandinavian Journal of Psychology, 17*, 81–96.

Enright, S.J., & Beech, A.R. (1990). Obsessional states: Anxiety disorders or schizotypes? An information processing and personality assessment. *Psychological Medicine, 20*, 621–627.

Esteves, F., Dimberg, U., Parra, C., & Ohman, A. (1994). Nonconscious associative learning: Pavlovian conditioning of skin conductance responses to masked fear-relevant facial stimuli. *Psychophysiology, 31*, 375–385.

Eysenck, H.J. (1967). *The biological basis of personality.* Springfield, IL: C. C. Thomas.

Eysenck, H.J. (1979). The conditioning model of neurosis. *Behavioural and Brain Sciences, 2*, 155–166.

Eysenck, H.J. (1982). Development of a theory. In C. D. Spielberger (Ed.), *Personality, genetics, and behaviour.* New York: Praeger.

Eysenck, H.J., & Prell, D.B. (1951). The inheritance of neuroticism. *Journal of Mental Science, 97*, 441–465.

Eysenck, M.W. (1991a). Trait anxiety and cognition. In C.D. Spielberger, I.G. Sarason, Z. Kulczar, & J. Van Heck (Eds.), *Stress and emotion* (Vol. 14). Hemisphere.

Eysenck, M.W. (1991b). Cognitive factors in clinical psychology: Potential relevance to therapy. In M. Briley & S.E. File (Eds.), *New concepts in anxiety.* London: Macmillan.

Eysenck, M.W. (1992). *Anxiety: The cognitive perspective.* London: Lawrence Erlbaum Associates Ltd.

Eysenck, M.W. (submitted). *Implicit memory for threat-related material in high-anxious individuals and repressors.*

Eysenck, M.W., & Byrne, A. (1994). Implicit memory bias, explicit memory bias, and anxiety. *Cognition and Emotion, 8*, 415–431.

Eysenck, M.W., & Derakshan, N. (in press). Cognitive biases for future negative events as a function of trait anxiety and social desirability. *Personality and Individual Differences.*

Eysenck, M.W., & Derakshan, N. (submitted a). *Factors influencing the relationship between self-reported and other-rated trait anxiety.*

Eysenck, M.W., & Derakshan, N. (submitted b). *Cognitive approaches to trait anxiety.*

Eysenck, M.W., & Keane, M.T. (1995). *Cognitive psychology: A handbook of cognitive psychology* (3rd ed.). Hove, UK: Lawrence Erlbaum Associates Ltd.

Eysenck, M.W., MacLeod, C., & Mathews, A. (1987). Cognitive functioning and anxiety. *Psychological Research, 49*, 189–195.

Eysenck, M.W., Mogg, K., May, J., Richards, A., & Mathews, A. (1991). Bias in interpretation of ambiguous sentences related to threat in anxiety. *Journal of Abnormal Psychology, 100*, 144–150.

Eysenck, M.W., & van Berkum, J. (1992). Trait anxiety, defensiveness, and the structure of worry. *Personality and Individual Differences, 13*, 1285–1290.

Fahrenberg, J. (1992). Psychophysiology of neuroticism and emotionality. In A. Gale & M.W. Eysenck (Eds.), *Handbook of individual differences: Biological perspectives*. Chichester: Wiley.

Fenigstein, A., Scheier, M. F., & Buss, A.H. (1975). Public and private self-consciousness: Assessment and theory. *Journal of Consulting and Clinical Psychology, 43*, 522–527.

Feske, U., & Chambless, D. L. (1995). Cognitive behavioural versus exposure only treatment for social phobia: A meta-analysis. *Behavior Therapy, 26*, 695–720.

Finlay-Jones, R.A., & Brown, G.W. (1981). Types of stressful life events and the onset of anxiety and depressive disorders. *Psychological Medicine, 11*, 803–815.

Floderus-Myrhed, B., Pedersen, N., & Rasmusson, S. (1980). Assessment of heritability for personality based on a short form of the Eysenck Personality Inventory. *Behavior Genetics, 10*, 153–162.

Foa, E.B., Ilai, D., McCarthy, P.R., Shoyer, B., & Murdock, T. (1993). Information processing in obsessive–compulsive disorder. *Cognitive Therapy and Research, 17*, 173–189.

Foa, E.B., & Kozak, M.J. (1985). Treatment of anxiety disorders: Implications for psychopathology. In A.H. Tuma & J.D. Maser (Eds.), *Anxiety and the anxiety disorders*. Hillsdale, NJ: Lawrence Erlbaum Associates Inc.

Foa, E.G., & Kozak, M.J. (1986). Emotional processing of fear: Exposure to corrective information. *Psychological Bulletin, 99*, 20–35.

Foa, E.B., & Kozak, M.J. (1991). Emotional processing: Theory, research, and clinical implications for anxiety disorders. In J.D. Safran & L.S. Greenberg (Eds.), *Emotion, psychotherapy, and change*. New York: Guilford Press.

Foa, E.B., & McNally, R.J. (1986). Sensitivity to feared stimuli in obsessive-compulsives: A dichotic listening analysis. *Cognitive Therapy and Research, 10*, 477–485.

Foa, E.B., & McNally, R.J. (1996). Mechanisms of change in exposure therapy. In R.M. Rapee (Ed.), *Current controversies in the anxiety disorders*. New York: Guilford Press.

Fox, E. (1993). Allocation of visual attention and anxiety. *Cognition and Emotion, 7*, 207–215.

Fox, E. (1996). Selective processing of threatening words in anxiety: The role of awareness. *Cognition and Emotion, 10*, 449–480.

Freeston, M.H., Rheaume, J., & Ladouceur, R. (1996). Correcting faulty appraisals of obsessional thoughts. *Behaviour Research and Therapy, 34*, 433–446.

Gaffney, F.A., Fenton, B.J., Lane, L.D., & Lake, C.R. (1988). Hemodynamic, ventilatory, and biochemical responses of panic patients and normal controls with sodium lactate infusion and spontaneous panic attacks. *Archives of General Psychiatry, 45*, 53–60.

Garssen, B., Buikhuisen, M., & van Dyck, R. (1996). Hyperventilation and panic attacks. *American Journal of Psychiatry, 153*, 513–518.

Gerdes, E.P. (1979). Autonomic arousal as a cognitive cue in stressful situations. *Journal of Personality, 47*, 677–711.

Gerlsman C., Emmelkamp, P.M.G., & Arrindell, W.A. (1990). Anxiety, depression, and perception of early parenting: A meta-analysis. *Clinical Psychology Review, 10*, 251–277.

Goisman, R.M., Goldenberg, I., Vasile, R.G., & Keller, M.B. (1995a). Comorbidity of anxiety disorders in a multi-centre anxiety study. *Comprehensive Psychiatry, 36*, 303–311.

Goisman, R.M., Warshaw, M.G., Steketee, G.S., Fierman, E.J., Rogers, M.P., Goldenberg, I., Weinshenker, N.J., Vasile, R.G., & Keller, M.B. (1995b). DSM-IV and the disappearance of agoraphobia without a history of panic disorder: New data on a controversial diagnosis. *American Journal of Psychiatry, 152*, 1438–1443.

Gould, R.A., Otto, M.W., & Pollack, M.H. (1995). A meta-analysis of treatment outcome for panic disorder. *Clinical Psychology Review, 15*, 819–844.

Gray, J.A. (1982). *The neuropsychology of anxiety*. Oxford: Clarendon.

Gudjonsson, G.H. (1981). Self-reported emotional disturbance and its relation to electrodermal reactivity, defensiveness and trait anxiety. *Personality and Individual Differences, 2*, 47–52.

Harrigan, J.A., Harrigan, K.M., Sale, B.A., & Rosenthal, R. (submitted). *Detecting anxiety and defensiveness from visual and auditory cues.*

Harrigan, J.A., Suarez, I., & Hartman, J.S. (1994). Effect of speech errors on observers' judgements of anxious and defensive individuals. *Journal of Research in Personality, 28*, 505–529.

Harris, L.M., & Menzies, R.G. (unpubl.). *Treating attentional bias: Can it reduce phobic anxiety?*

Harvey, J.M., Richards, J.C., Dziadosz, T., & Swindell, A. (1993). Misinterpretation of ambiguous stimuli in panic disorder. *Cognitive Therapy and Research, 17*, 235–248.

Haslam, D.R. (1966). The effect of threatened shock upon pain threshold. *Psychonomic Science, 6*, 309–310.

Heimberg, R.G. (1991). *A manual for conducting Cognitive-Behavioural Group Therapy for social phobia* (2nd ed.). Albany, NY: Center for Stress and Anxiety Disorders.

Hohmann, G.W. (1966). Some effects of spinal cord lesions on experienced emotional feelings. *Psychophysiology, 3*, 143–156.

Holloway, W., & McNally, R.J. (1987). Effects of anxiety sensitivity on the response to hyperventilation. *Journal of Abnormal Psychology, 96*, 330–334.

Holmes, D.S., & Houston, B.K. (1974). Effectiveness of situation redefinition and affective isolation in coping with stress. *Journal of Personality and Social Psychology, 29*, 212–218.

Hope, D.A., Heimberg, R.G., & Bruch, M.A. (1995). Dismantling cognitive-behavioural group therapy for social phobia. *Behaviour Research and Therapy, 33*, 637–650.

Hope, D.A., Rapee, R.M., Heimberg, R.G., & Dombeck, M. (1990). Representations of the self in social phobia: Vulnerability to social threat. *Cognitive Therapy and Research, 14*, 177–189.

Hunt, C., & Andrews, G. (1995). Comorbidity in the anxiety disorders: The use of a life-chart approach. *Journal of Psychiatric Research, 29*, 467–480.

Ingham, J.G. (1966). Changes in MPI scores in neurotic patients: A three-year follow-up. *British Journal of Psychiatry, 112*, 931–939.

Ingram, R.E. (1990). Self-focused attention in clinical disorders: Review and a conceptual model. *Psychological Bulletin, 107*, 156–176.

Jacobson, L.I., & Ford, L.H. (1966). Need for approval, defensive denial, and sensitivity to cultural stereotypes. *Journal of Personality, 34*, 596–609.

James, W. (1898). *The principles of psychology* (Vol. 2). London: Macmillan.

Johnson, M.K., & Hirst, W. (1993). MEM: Memory subsystems as processes. In A.F. Collins, S.E. Gathercole, M.A. Conway, & P.E. Morris (Eds.), *Theories of memory*. Hove, UK: Lawrence Erlbaum Associates Ltd.

Johnson, M.K., & Multhaup, K.S. (1992). Emotion and MEM. In S.-A. Christianson (Ed.), *The handbook of emotion and memory: Current research and theory*. Hillsdale, NJ: Lawrence Erlbaum Associates Inc.

Jones, M.K., & Menzies, R.G. (1995). The aetiology of fear of spiders. *Anxiety, Stress, and Coping, 8*, 227–234.

Kendall, P.C. (1978). Anxiety: States, traits, or situations? *Journal of Consulting and Clinical Psychology, 46*, 280–287.

Kennedy, R.E., & Craighead, W.E. (1988). Differential effects of depression and anxiety on recall of feedback in a learning task. *Behaviour Therapy, 19*, 437–454.

Keuthen, N. (1980). *Subjective probability estimation and somatic structures in phobic individuals*. Unpublished manuscript, State University of New York at Stony Brook.

Khanna, S., Rajendra, P.N., & Channabasavanna, S.M. (1988). Life events and onset of obsessive–compulsive disorder. *International Journal of Social Psychiatry, 34*, 305–309.

Klein, D.F. (1993). False suffocation alarms, spontaneous panics, and related conditions. *Archives of General Psychiatry, 50*, 306–317.

Kohlmann, C.-W. (1993). Development of the repression-sensitization construct: With special reference to the discrepancy between subjective and physiological stress reactions. In U. Hentschel, G. Smith, W. Ehlers, & J.G. Draguns (Eds.), *The concept of defence mechanisms in contemporary psychology: Theoretical, research, and clinical perspectives*. New York: Springer.

Koksal, F., Power, K.G., & Sharp, D.M. (1991). Profiles of DSM-III anxiety disorders on the somatic, cognitive, behavioural and feeling components of the Four Systems Anxiety Questionnaire. *Personality and Individual Differences, 12*, 643–651.

Koriat, A., Melkman, R., Averill, J.R., & Lazarus, R.S. (1972). The self- control of emotional reactions to a stressful film. *Journal of Personality, 40*, 601–619.

Ladouceur, R., Rheaume, J., Freeston, M.H., Aublet, F., Jean, K., Lachance, S., Langlois, F., & Pokomandy-Morin, K. (1995). Experimental manipulations of responsibility: An analogue test for models of obsessive–compulsive disorder. *Behaviour Research and Therapy, 33*, 937–946.

Laird, J.D., & Bresler, C. (1992). The process of emotional experience: A self-perception theory. In M.S. Clark (Ed.), *Review of personality and social psychology* (Vol. 13). New York: Sage.

Lamb, D. (1978). Use of behavioural measures in anxiety research. *Psychological Reports, 43*, 1079–1085.

Lang, P.J. (1971). The application of psychophysiological methods to the study of psychotherapy and behaviour modification. In A. Bergin & S. Garfield (Eds.), *Handbook of psychotherapy and behaviour change*. Chichester: Wiley.

Lang, P.J. (1985). The cognitive psychophysiology of emotion: Fear and anxiety. In A.H. Tuma & J. Maser (Eds.), *Anxiety and the anxiety disorders*. Hillsdale, NJ: Lawrence Erlbaum Associates Inc.

Larsen, R.J., Kasimatis, M., & Frey, K. (1990). *Facilitating the furrowed brow: An unobtrusive test of the facial feedback hypothesis applied to negative affect.* Unpublished manuscript.

Lavy, E., van den Hout, M., & Arntz, A. (1993a). Attentional bias and spider phobia: Conceptual and clinical issues. *Behaviour Research and Therapy, 31*, 17–24.

Lavy, E., van den Hout, M., & Arntz, A. (1993b). Attentional bias and facilitated escape: A pictorial test. *Advances in Behaviour Research and Therapy, 15*, 279–289.

Lavy, E., van Oppen, P., & van den Hout, M. (1994). Selective processing of emotional information in obsessive–compulsive disorder. *Behaviour Research and Therapy, 32*, 243–246.

Lazarus, R.S. (1966). *Psychological stress and the coping process.* New York: McGraw-Hill.

Lazarus, R.S. (1982). Thoughts on the relations between emotion and cognition. *American Psychologist, 37*, 1019–1024.

Lazarus, R.S. (1991). *Emotion and adaptation.* Oxford: Oxford University Press.

Lazarus, R.S., & Folkman, S. (1984). *Stress, appraisal and coping.* New York: Springer.

Le Doux, J.E. (1990). Information flow from sensation to emotion: Plasticity in the neural computation of stimulus value. In M. Gabriel & J. Moore (Eds.), *Learning and computational neuroscience: Foundations of adaptive networks.* Cambridge, MA: MIT Press.

Lehrer, P.M., & Woolfolk, R.L. (1982). Self-report assessment of anxiety: Somatic, cognitive, and behavioural modalities. *Behavioral Assessment, 4*, 167–177.

Lennox, R.D., & Wolfe, R.N. (1984). Revision of the Self-Monitoring Scale. *Journal of Personality and Social Psychology, 46*, 1349–1364.

Lilienfeld, S.O., Jacob, R.G., & Turner, S.M. (1989). Comment on Holloway and McNally's (1987) "Effects of anxiety sensitivity on the response to hyperventilation." *Journal of Abnormal Psychology, 98*, 100–102.

Lilienfeld, S.O., Turner, S.M., & Jacob, R.G. (1993). Anxiety sensitivity: An examination of theoretical and methodological issues. *Advances in Behaviour Research and Therapy, 15*, 147–183.

Logan, A.C., & Goetsch, V.L. (1993). Attention to external threat cues in anxiety states. *Clinical Psychology Review, 13*, 541–559.

Lopatka, C, & Rachman, S. (1995). Perceived responsibility and compulsive checking: An experimental analysis. *Behaviour Research and Therapy, 33*, 673–684.

MacLeod, C. (1990). Mood disorders and cognition. In M.W. Eysenck (Ed.), *Cognitive psychology: An international review.* Chichester: Wiley.

MacLeod, C. (1993). Cognition in clinical psychology: Measures, methods or models? *Behaviour Change, 10*, 169–195.

MacLeod, C., & Campbell, L. (1992). Memory accessibility and probability judgements: An experimental evaluation of the availability heuristic. *Journal of Personality and Social Psychology, 63*, 890–902.

MacLeod, C., & Cohen, I.L. (1993). Anxiety and the interpretation of ambiguity: A text comprehension study. *Journal of Abnormal Psychology, 102*, 238–247.

MacLeod, C., & Hagan, R. (1992). Individual differences in the selective processing of threatening information, and emotional responses to a stressful life event. *Behaviour Research and Therapy, 30*, 151–161.

MacLeod, C., & Mathews, A. (1988). Anxiety and the allocation of attention to threat. *Quarterly Journal of Experimental Psychology, 38A*, 659–670.

MacLeod, C., Mathews, A., & Tata, P. (1986). Attentional bias in emotional disorders. *Journal of Abnormal Psychology, 95*, 15–20.

MacLeod, C., & McLaughlin, K. (1995). Implicit and explicit memory bias in anxiety: A conceptual replication. *Behaviour Research and Therapy, 33*, 1–14.

MacLeod, C., & Rutherford, E.M. (1992). Anxiety and the selective processing of emotional information: Mediating roles of awareness, trait and state variables, and personal relevance of stimulus materials. *Behaviour Research and Therapy, 30*, 479–491.

Makris, G.S., & Heimberg, R.G. (1995). The Scale of Maladaptive Self-Consciousness: A valid and useful measure in the study of social phobia. *Personality and Individual Differences, 19*, 731–740.

Maranon, G. (1924). Contribution a l'étude de l'action émotive de l'adrénaline. *Revue Française d'Endocrinologie, 2*, 301–325.

Marshall, G.D., & Zimbardo, P.G. (1979). Affective consequences of inadequately explained physiological arousal. *Journal of Personality and Social Psychology, 37*, 970–988.

Martin, M., Ward, J.C., & Clark, D.M. (1983). Neuroticism and the recall of positive and negative personality information. *Behaviour Research and Therapy, 21*, 495–503.

Maslach, C. (1979). Negative emotional biasing and unexplained arousal. *Journal of Personality and Social Psychology, 37*, 953–969.

Matchett, G., & Davey, G.C. (1991). A test of a disease-avoidance model of animal phobias. *Behaviour Research and Therapy, 29*, 91–94.

Mathews, A., & Eysenck, M.W. (1987). Clinical anxiety and cognition. In H.J. Eysenck & I. Martin (Eds.), *Theoretical foundations of behaviour therapy*. New York: Plenum.

Mathews, A., & Macleod, C. (1985). Selective processing of threat cues in anxiety states. *Behaviour Research and Therapy, 23*, 563–569.

Mathews, A., Mogg, K., Kentish, J., & Eysenck, M.W. (1995). Effect of psychological treatment on cognitive bias in GAD. *Behaviour Research and Therapy, 33*, 293–303.

Mathews, A., Mogg, K, May, J., & Eysenck, M.W. (1989). Implicit and explicit memory biases in anxiety. *Journal of Abnormal Psychology, 98*, 131–138.

Mathews, A., Richards, A., & Eysenck, M.W. (1989). The interpretation of homophones related to threat in anxiety states. *Journal of Abnormal Psychology, 98*, 31–34.

Matthews, G., & Wells, A. (1988). Relationships between anxiety, self-consciousness, and cognitive failure. *Cognition and Emotion, 2*, 123–132.

Mattia, J.I., Heimberg, R.G., & Hope, D.A. (1993). The revised Stroop colour-naming task in social phobics: Diagnostic and treatment outcome implications. *Behaviour Research and Therapy, 31*, 305–313.

Mayo, P.R. (1983). Personality traits and the retrieval of positive and negative memories. *Personality and Individual Differences, 4*, 465–472.

Mayo, P.R. (1989). A further study of the personality-congruent recall effect. *Personality and Individual Differences, 10*, 247–252.

McAllister, H.A. (1980). Self-disclosure and liking: Effects for senders and receivers. *Journal of Personality, 48*, 409–418.

McCrae, R.R. (1982). Consensual validation of personality traits: Evidence from self-reports and ratings. *Journal of Personality and Social Psychology, 43*, 293–303.

McKeon, J., Roa, B., & Mann, A. (1984). Life events and personality traits in obsessive–compulsive neurosis. *British Journal of Psychiatry, 144*, 185–189.

McNally, R.J. (1989). Is anxiety sensitivity distinguishable from trait anxiety? Reply to Lilienfeld, Jacob, and Turner (1989). *Journal of Abnormal Psychology, 98*, 193–194.

McNally, R.J. (1990). Psychological approaches to panic disorder: A review. *Psychological Bulletin, 108*, 403–419.

McNally, R.J. (1994). *Panic disorder: A critical analysis.* New York: Guilford Press.

McNally, R.J. (1995). Automaticity and the anxiety disorders. *Behaviour Research and Therapy, 33*, 747–754.

McNally, R.J., Amir, N., Louro, C.E., Lukach, B.M., Riemann, B.C., & Calamari, J.E. (1994). Cognitive processing of idiographic emotional information in panic disorder. *Behaviour Research and Therapy, 32*, 119–122.

McNally, R.J., & Foa, E.B. (1987). Cognition and agoraphobia: Bias in the interpretation of threat. *Cognitive Therapy and Research, 11*, 567–581.

McNally, R.J., Foa, E.B., & Donnell, C.D. (1989). Memory bias for anxiety information in patients for anxiety information in patients with panic disorder. *Cognition and Emotion, 3*, 27–44.

McNally, R.J., & Lorenz, M. (1987). Anxiety sensitivity in agoraphobics. *Journal of Behavior Therapy and Experimental Psychiatry, 18*, 3–11.

McNally, R.J., Riemann, B.C., & Kim, E. (1990). Selective processing of threat cues in panic disorder. *Behaviour Research and Therapy, 28*, 407–412.

McNally, R.J., Riemann, B.C., Louro, C.E., Lukach, B.M., & Kim, E. (1992). Selective processing of emotional information in panic disorder. *Behaviour Research and Therapy, 30*, 143–149.

Menzies, R.G., & Clarke, J.C. (1993). The aetiology of childhood water phobia. *Behaviour Research and Therapy, 31*, 499–501.

Menzies, R.G., & Clarke, J.C. (1994). Retrospective studies of the origins of phobias: A review. *Anxiety, Stress, and Coping, 7*, 305–318.

Merckelbach, H., Kenemans, J.L., Dijkstra, A., & Schouten, E. (1993). No attentional bias for pictorial stimuli in spider-fearful subjects. *Journal of Psychopathology and Behavioral Assessment, 15*, 197–206.

Mersch, P.P.A. (1995). The treatment of social phobia: The differential effectiveness of exposure in vivo and an integration of exposure in vivo, rational emotive therapy, and social skills training. *Behaviour Research and Therapy, 33*, 259–269.

Miguel-Tobal, J.J., & Cano-Vindel, A. (1995). Perfiles differenciales de los trastornos de ansiedad (Differential profiles in anxiety disorders). *Ansiedad y Estres, 1*, 37–60.

Millham, J., & Kellogg, R.W. (1980). Need for social appraisal: Impression management or self-deception? *Journal of Research in Personality, 14*, 445–457.

Mogg, K. (1988). *Processing of emotional information in clinical anxiety states.* Unpublished Ph.D. thesis, University of London.

Mogg, K., Bradley, B.P., & Hallowell, N. (1994). Attentional bias to threat: Roles of trait anxiety, stressful events, and awareness. *Quarterly Journal of Experimental Psychology, 47A*, 841–864.

Mogg, K., Bradley, B.P., Millar, N., & White, J. (1995). A follow-up study of cognitive bias in generalised anxiety disorder. *Behaviour Research and Therapy, 33*, 927–935.

Mogg, K., Bradley, B.P., Miller, T., Potts, H., Glenwright, J., & Kentish, J. (1994). Interpretation of homophones related to threat: Anxiety response bias effects. *Cognitive Therapy and Research, 18*, 461–475.

Mogg, K., Bradley, B., & Williams, R. (1995). Attentional bias in anxiety and depression: The role of awareness. *British Journal of Clinical Psychology, 34*, 17–36.

Mogg, K., Bradley, B.P., Williams, R., & Mathews, A. (1993). Subliminal processing of emotional information in anxiety and depression. *Journal of Abnormal Psychology, 102*, 304–311.

Mogg, K., Kentish, J., & Bradley, B.P. (1993). Effects of anxiety and awareness on colour-identification latencies for emotional words. *Behaviour Research and Therapy, 31*, 559–567.

Mogg, K., Mathews, A., & Eysenck, M.W. (1992). Attentional bias to threat in clinical anxiety states. *Cognition and Emotion, 6*, 149–159.

Mogg, K, Mathews, A., & Weinman, J. (1987). Memory bias in clinical anxiety. *Journal of Abnormal Psychology, 96*, 94–98.

Molina, S., & Borkovec, T.D. (1994). The Penn State Worry Questionnaire: Psychometric properties and associated characteristics. In G.C.L. Davey & F. Tallis (Eds.), *Worrying: Perspectives on theory, assessment and treatment.* Chichester: Wiley.

Morris, L.W., & Liebert, R.M. (1970). Relationships of cognitive and emotional components of test anxiety to physiological arousal and academic performance. *Journal of Consulting and Clinical Psychology, 35*, 332–337.

Myers, L.B., & Brewin, C.R. (1994). Recall of early experience and the repressive coping style. *Journal of Abnormal Psychology, 103*, 288–292.

Myers, L.B., & Brewin, C.R. (1995). Repressive coping and the recall of emotional material. *Cognition and Emotion, 9*, 637–642.

Myers, L.B., & Brewin, C.R. (in press). Illusions of well-being and the repressive coping style. *British Journal of Social Psychology.*

Myers, L.B., & McKenna, F.P. (in press). The colour naming of socially threatening words. *Personality and Individual Differences.*

Naring, G.W.B., & van der Staak, C.P.F. (1995). Perception of heart rate and blood pressure: The role of alexithymia and anxiety. *Psychotherapy and Psychosomatics, 63*, 193–200.

Newton, T.L., & Contrada, R.J. (1992). Repressive coping and verbal- autonomic response dissociation: The influence of social context. *Journal of Personality and Social Psychology, 62*, 159–167.

Norton, G.R., Dorward, J., & Cox, B.J. (1986). Factors associated with panic attacks in nonclinical subjects. *Behavior Therapy, 17*, 239–252.

Nugent, K., & Mineka, S. (1994). The effect of high and low trait anxiety on implicit and explicit memory tasks. *Cognition and Emotion, 8*, 147–163.

Nutt, D.J., Glue, P., Lawson, C., & Wilson, S. (1990). Flumazenil provocation of panic attacks: Evidence for altered benzodiazepine receptor sensitivity in panic disorder. *Archives of General Psychiatry, 47*, 917–925.

O'Donohue, W., & Elliott, A. (1992). The current status of post-traumatic stress disorder as a diagnostic category: Problems and proposals. *Journal of Traumatic Stress, 5,* 421–439.

Ohman, A., Dimberg, U., & Ost, L.-G. (1985). Animal and social phobias: Biological constraints on learned fear responses. In S. Reiss & R. R. Bortzin (Eds.), *Theoretical issues in behaviour therapy.* New York: Academic Press.

Ost, L.-G. (1989). One-session treatment for specific phobics. *Behaviour Research and Therapy, 27,* 1–7.

Parkinson, B. (1994). Emotion. In A. M. Colman (Ed.), *Companion encyclopaedia of psychology* (Vol. 2). London: Routledge.

Parkinson, B. (1995). *Ideas and realities of emotion.* London: Routledge.

Parkinson, B., & Manstead, A.S.R. (1992). Appraisal as a cause of emotion. In M. S. Clark (Ed.), *Review of personality and social psychology* (Vol. 13). New York: Sage.

Paul, G.L. (1966). *Insight vs. desensitization in psychotherapy.* Stanford, CA: Stanford University Press.

Pedersen, N.L., Plomin, R., McClearn, G.E., & Friberg, L. (1988). Neuroticism, extraversion, and related traits in adult twins reared apart and reared together. *Journal of Personality and Social Psychology, 55,* 950–957.

Pennebaker, J.W. (1982). *The psychology of physical symptoms.* New York: Springer.

Perna, G., Bertani, A., Arancio, C., Ronchi, P., & Bellodi, L. (1995). Laboratory response of patients with panic and obsessive–compulsive disorders to 35% CO_2 challenges. *American Journal of Psychiatry, 152,* 85–89.

Peterson, R.A., & Reiss, S. (1987). *Anxiety sensitivity index manual.* Worthington, OH: International Diagnostic Systems.

Plutchik, R. (1980). *Emotion: A psychoevolutionary analysis.* New York: Harper & Row.

Rachman, S.J. (1977). The conditioning theory of fear acquisition: A critical examination. *Behaviour Research and Therapy, 15,* 375–388.

Rachman, S.J. (1993). A critique of cognitive therapy for anxiety disorders. *Behaviour Research and Therapy, 24,* 274–288.

Rachman, S.J., & de Silva, P. (1978). Abnormal and normal obsessions. *Behaviour Research and Therapy, 16,* 233–238.

Rainey, J.M., Frohman, C.E., Freedman, R.R., Pohl, R.B., Ettedgui, E., & Williams, M. (1984). Specificity of lactate infusion as a model of anxiety. *Psychopharmacology Bulletin, 20,* 45–49.

Rapee, R. (1991). Generalized anxiety disorder: A review of clinical features and theoretical concepts. *Clinical Psychology Review, 11,* 419–440.

Rapee, R.M. (1994). Failure to replicate a memory bias in panic disorder. *Journal of Anxiety Disorders, 8,* 291–300.

Rapee, R.M., Brown, T.A., Antony, M.M., & Barlow, D.H. (1992). Response to hyperventilation and inhalation of 5.5% carbon dioxide-enriched air across the DSM-III-R anxiety disorders. *Journal of Abnormal Psychology, 101,* 538–552.

Rapee, R.M., & Hayman, K. (1996). The effects of video feedback on the self-evaluation of performance in socially anxious subjects. *Behaviour Research and Therapy, 34,* 315–322.

Rapee, R.M., & Lim, L. (1992). Discrepancy between self- and observer ratings of performance in social phobics. *Journal of Abnormal Psychology, 101,* 728–731.

Rapee, R.M., Mattick, R., & Murrell, E. (1986). Cognitive mediation in the affective component of spontaneous panic attacks. *Journal of Behaviour Therapy and Experimental Psychiatry, 17*, 245–253.

Rapee, R.M., McCallum, S. L., Melville, L.F., Ravenscraft, H., & Rodney, J.M. (1994). Memory bias in social phobia. *Behaviour Research and Therapy, 32*, 89–99.

Rapee, R.M., & Medoro, L. (1994). Fear of physical sensations and trait anxiety as mediators of the response to hyperventilation in nonclinical subjects. *Journal of Abnormal Psychology, 103*, 693–699.

Reisenzein, R. (1983). The Schachter theory of emotion: Two decades later. *Psychological Bulletin, 94*, 239–264.

Reisenzein, R., & Gattinger, E. (1982). Salience of arousal as a mediator of mis-attribution of transferred excitation. *Motivation and Emotion, 6*, 315–328.

Richards, A., & French, C.C. (1991). Effects of encoding and anxiety on implicit and explicit memory performance. *Personality and Individual Differences, 12*, 131–139.

Richards, A., & French, C. (1992). An anxiety-related bias in semantic activation when processing threat/neutral homographs. *Quarterly Journal of Experimental Psychology, 45A*, 503–525.

Roediger, H.L., & Blaxton, T.A. (1987). Retrieval modes produce dissociations in memory for surface information. In D.S. Gorfein & R.R. Hoffman (Eds.), *Memory and cognitive processes: The Ebbinghaus centennial conference.* Hillsdale, NJ: Lawrence Erlbaum Associates Inc.

Rosenbaum, J.F., Biederman, J., Hirshfeld, D.R., Balduc, E., Faraone, S., Kagan, J., Snidman, N., & Reznick, J.S. (1991). Further evidence of an association between behavioural inhibition and anxiety disorders: Results from a family study of children from a non-clinical sample. *Journal of Psychiatric Research, 25*, 49–65.

Russell, J.A. (1991). Culture and categorisation of emotions. *Psychological Bulletin, 110*, 426–450.

Russo, R., Patterson, N., Roberson, D., Stevenson, N., & Upward, J. (1996). Emotional value of information and its relevance in the interpretation of homophones in anxiety. *Cognition and Emotion, 10*, 213–220.

Salkovskis, P.M. (1985). Obsessional–compulsive problems: A cognitive-behavioural analysis. *Behaviour Research and Therapy, 23*, 571–583.

Salkovskis, P.M. (1989). Cognitive-behavioural factors and the persistence of intrusive thoughts in obsessional problems. *Behaviour Research and Therapy, 27*, 677–682.

Salkovskis, P.M. (1991). The importance of behaviour in the maintenance of anxiety and panic: A cognitive account. *Behavioural Psychotherapy, 19*, 6–19.

Salkovskis, P.M. (1996). Cognitive-behavioural approaches to the understanding of obsessional problems. In R. M. Rapee (Ed.), *Current controversies in the anxiety disorders*. New York: Guilford Press.

Salkovskis, P.M., & Clark, D.M. (1989). Affective responses to hyperventilation: A test of the cognitive model of panic. *Behaviour Research and Therapy, 28*, 51–62.

Salkovskis, P.M., Clark, D.M., & Gelder, M.G. (1996). Cognition-behaviour links in the persistence of panic. *Behaviour Research and Therapy, 34*, 453–458.

Sanderson, W.C., Rapee, R.M., & Barlow, D.H. (1989). The influence of an illusion of control on panic attacks induced by inhalation of 5.5% carbon dioxide-enriched air. *Archives of General Psychiatry, 46*, 157–162.

Schachter, D.L. (1987). Implicit memory: History and current status. *Journal of Experimental Psychology: Learning, Memory, and Cognition, 13*, 501–518.

Schachter, S. (1964). The interaction of cognitive and physiological determinants of emotional state. In L. Festinger (Ed.), *Advances in experimental social psychology* (Vol. 1). New York: Academic Press.

Schachter, S., & Singer, J.E. (1962). Cognitive, social, and physiological determinants of emotional state. *Psychological Review, 69*, 379–399.

Schandry, R. (1981). Heart beat perception and emotional experience. *Psychophysiology, 18*, 483–488.

Scheier, M.F., & Carver, C.S. (1977). Self-focused attention and the experience of emotion: Attraction, repulsion, elation, and depression. *Journal of Personality and Social Psychology, 35*, 625–636.

Schill, T., & Althoff, M. (1968). Auditory perceptual thresholds for sensitizers, defensive and non-defensive repressors. *Perceptual and Motor Skills, 27*, 935–938.

Schwartz, G.E. (1990). Psychobiology of repression and health: A systems approach. In J. L. Singer (Ed.), *Repression and dissociation*. Chicago: University of Chicago Press.

Seger, C.A. (1994). Implicit learning. *Psychological Bulletin, 115*, 163–196.

Shields, J. (1962). *Monozygotic twins*. Oxford: Oxford University Press.

Shiori, T., Someya, T., Murashita, J., & Takahashi, S. (1996). The symptom structure of panic disorder: A trial using factor and cluster analysis. *Acta Psychiatrica Scandinavica, 93*, 80–86.

Skre, I., Onstad, S., Torgersen, S., Lygren, S., & Kringlen, E. (1993). A twin study of DSM-III-R anxiety disorders. *Acta Psychiatrica Scandinavica, 88*, 85–92.

Smith, C.A., & Lazarus, R.S. (1993). Appraisal components, core relational themes, and the emotions. *Cognition and Emotion, 7*, 233–269.

Speisman, J.C., Lazarus, R.S., Mordkoff, A., & Davison, L. (1964). Experimental reduction of stress based on ego-defence theory. *Journal of Abnormal and Social Psychology, 68*, 367–380.

Spielberger, C.D., Gonzalez, H.P., Taylor, C.J., Algaze, B., & Anton, W.D. (1978). Examination stress and test anxiety. In C.D. Spielberger & I.G. Sarason (Eds.), *Stress and anxiety* (Vol. 5). London: Halsted.

Spielberger, C.D., Gorsuch, R., & Lushene, R. (1970). *The State Trait Anxiety Inventory (STAI) test manual*. Palo Alto, CA: Consulting Psychologists Press.

Sroufe, L.A., & Waters, E. (1977). Heart rate as a convergent measure in clinical and developmental research. *Merrill-Palmer Quarterly, 23*, 3–27.

Stemberger, R.T., Turner, S.M., & Beidel, D.C. (1995). Social phobia: An analysis of possible developmental factors. *Journal of Abnormal Psychology, 104*, 526–531.

Stoler, L.S., & McNally, R.J. (1991). Cognitive bias in symptomatic and recovered agoraphobics. *Behaviour Research and Therapy, 29*, 539–545.

Stopa, L., & Clark, D.M. (1993). Cognitive processes in social phobia. *Behaviour Research and Therapy, 31*, 255–267.

Strack, F., Martin, L.L., & Stepper, S. (1988). Inhibiting and facilitating conditions of facial expressions: A non-obtrusive test of the facial feedback hypothesis. *Journal of Personality and Social Psychology, 54*, 768–776.

Streblow, H., Hoffman, J., & Kasielke, E. (1985). Experimentalpsychologische Analyse von Gedächtnisprozesse bei Phobiken. *Zeitschrift fur Psychologie, 193*, 147–161.

Tallis, F. (1995). *Obsessive compulsive disorder*. Chichester: Wiley.

Tallis, F., Eysenck, M.W., & Mathews, A. (1992). A questionnaire measure for the measurement of nonpathological worry. *Personality and Individual Differences, 13*, 161–168.

Tan, S.Y. (1982). Cognitive and cognitive-behavioural methods for pain control: A selective review. *Pain, 12*, 201–228.

Tata, P.R., Leibowitz, J. A., Prunty, M.J., Cameron, M., & Pickering, A.D. (1996). Attentional bias in obsessional compulsive disorder. *Behaviour Research and Therapy, 34*, 53–60.

Taylor, S., Koch, W.J., & Crockett, D.J. (1991). Anxiety sensitivity, trait anxiety, and the anxiety disorders. *Journal of Anxiety Disorders, 6*, 293–311.

Taylor, S., Koch, W.J., & McNally, R.J. (1992). How does anxiety sensitivity vary across the anxiety disorders? *Journal of Anxiety Disorders, 7*, 249–259.

Telch, M.J., Shermis, M.D., & Lucas, J.A. (1989). Anxiety sensitivity: Unitary construct or domain-specific appraisals? *Journal of Anxiety Disorders, 3*, 25–32.

Thorpe, S.J., & Salkovskis, P.M. (1995). Phobic beliefs: Do cognitive factors play a role in specific phobias? *Behaviour Research and Therapy, 33*, 805–816.

Torgersen, S. (1990). Genetics of anxiety and its clinical implications. In G. D. Burrows, M. Roth, & R. Noyes (Eds.), *Handbook of anxiety: Vol. 3. The neurobiology of anxiety*. Amsterdam: Elsevier.

Tulving, E., & Schachter, D.L. (1990). Priming and human memory. *Science, 247*, 301–306.

Turk, D.C., Meichenbaum, D., & Genest, M. (1983). *Pain and behavioural medicine*. New York: Guildford Press.

Turner, S.M., Beidel, D.C., & Stanley, M.A. (1992). Are obsessional thoughts and worry different cognitive phenomena? *Clinical Psychology Review, 12*, 257–270.

Turner, S.M., Beidel, D.C., & Townsley, R.M. (1990). Social phobia: Relationship to shyness. *Behaviour Research and Therapy, 28*, 497–505.

Turvey, C., & Salovey, P. (1993). Measures of repression: Converging on the same construct? *Imagination, Cognition and Personality, 13*, 279–289.

Tversky, A., & Kahneman, D. (1973). Availability: A heuristic for judging frequency and probability. *Cognitive Psychology, 5*, 207–232.

Ullmann, L.P. (1962). An empirically derived MMPI scale which measures facilitation-inhibition of recognition of threatening stimuli. *Journal of Clinical Psychology, 18*, 127–132.

Usala, P.D., & Hertzog, C. (1991). Evidence of differential stability of state and trait anxiety in adults. *Journal of Personality and Social Psychology, 60*, 471–479.

Valins, S. (1966). Cognitive effects of false heart-rate feedback. *Journal of Personality and Social Psychology, 4*, 400–408.

van den Hout, M., Arntz, A., & Hoekstra, R. (1994). Exposure reduced agoraphobia, but not panic, and cognitive therapy reduced panic but not agoraphobia. *Behaviour Research and Therapy, 32*, 447–451.

van den Hout, M., Tenney, N., Huygens, K., Merckelbach, H., & Kindt, M. (1995). Responding to subliminal threat cues is related to trait anxiety and emotional vulnerability: A successful replication of MacLeod and Hagan (1992). *Behaviour Research and Therapy, 33*, 451–454.

van der Molen, G.M., van den Hout, M.A., Vroemen, J., Lousberg, H., & Griez, E. (1986). Cognitive determinants of lactate-induced anxiety. *Behaviour Research and Therapy, 24*, 677–680.

van Oppen, P., & Arntz, A. (1994). Cognitive therapy for obsessive–compulsive disorder. *Behaviour Research and Therapy, 32*, 79–87.

van Oppen, P., de Haan, E., van Balkom, A.J.L.M., Spinhoven, P., Hoogduin, K., & van Dyck, R. (1995). Cognitive therapy and exposure in vivo in the treatment of obsessive–compulsive disorder. *Behaviour Research and Therapy, 33*, 379–390.

Veltman, D.J., van Zijderveld, G.A., & van Dyck, R. (1994). Fear of fear, trait anxiety and aerobic fitness in relation to state anxiety during adrenalin provocation. *Anxiety, Stress, and Coping, 7*, 279–289.

Verburg, K., Griez, E., Meijer, J., & Pols, H. (1995a). Respiratory disorders as a possible predisposing factor for panic disorder. *Journal of Affective Disorders, 33*, 129–134.

Verburg, K., Griez, E., Meijer, J., & Pols, H. (1995b). Discrimination panic disorder and generalised anxiety disorder by 35% carbon dioxide challenge. *American Journal of Psychiatry, 152*, 1081–1083.

Walsh, J.J., Eysenck, M.W., Wilding, J., & Valentine, J. (1994). Type A, neuroticism, and physiological functioning (actual and reported). *Personality and Individual Differences, 16*, 959–965.

Watson, D., & Clark, L.A. (1984). Negative affectivity: The disposition to experience aversive emotional states. *Psychological Bulletin, 96*, 465–490.

Watson, D., Clark, L.A., & Carey, G. (1988). Positive and negative affect and their relation to anxiety and depressive disorders. *Journal of Abnormal Psychology, 97*, 346–353.

Watson, D., & Friend, R. (1969). Measurement of social-evaluative anxiety. *Journal of Consulting and Clinical Psychology, 33*, 448–457.

Watson, D., Weber, K., Assenheimer, J.S., Clark, L.A., Strauss, M.E., & McCormick, R.A. (1995). Testing a tripartite model: 1. Evaluating the convergent and discriminant validity of anxiety and depression symptom scales. *Journal of Abnormal Psychology, 104*, 3–14.

Watson, J.B., & Rayner, R. (1920). Conditioned emotional reactions. *Journal of Experimental Psychology, 3*, 1–14.

Watts, F.N., Trezise, L., & Sharrock, R. (1986). Processing of phobic stimuli. *British Journal of Clinical Psychology, 25*, 253–261.

Weinberger, D.A. (1990). The construct validity of the repressive coping style. In J.L. Singer (Ed.), *Repression and dissociation: Implications for personality theory, psychopathology, and health*. Chicago: University of Chicago Press.

Weinberger, D.A., & Schwartz, G.E. (1990). Distress and restraint on superordinate dimensions of self-reported adjustment: A typological perspective. *Journal of Personality, 58*, 381–417.

Weinberger, D.A., Schwartz, G.E, & Davidson, J.R. (1979). Low-anxious, high-anxious, and repressive coping styles: Psychometric patterns and behavioural and physiological responses to stress. *Journal of Abnormal Psychology, 88*, 369–380.

Wells, A. (1990). Panic disorder in association with relaxation induced anxiety: An attentional training approach to treatment. *Behavior Therapy, 21*, 273–280.

Wells, A., Clark, D.M., Salkovskis, P., Ludgate, J., Hackmann, A., & Gelder, M. (1995). Social phobia: The role of in-situation safety behaviours in maintaining anxiety and negative beliefs. *Behavior Therapy, 26*, 153–161.

Wells, A., & Matthews, G. (1994). *Attention and emotion: A clinical perspective*. Hove, UK: Lawrence Erlbaum Associates Ltd.

Wells, A., & Morrison, A.P. (1994). Qualitative dimensions of normal worry and normal obsessions: A comparative study. *Behaviour Research and Therapy, 32*, 867–870.

Westling, B.E., & Ost, L.-G. (1995). Cognitive bias in panic disorder patients and changes after cognitive-behavioural treatments. *Behaviour Research and Therapy, 33*, 585–588.

White, P.D., & Nias, D.K.B. (1994). A comparison of self-report and relative ratings of personality. *Personality and Individual Differences, 16*, 801–803.

Wilhelm, S., McNally, R.J., Baer, L., & Florin, I. (1996). Directed forgetting in obsessive–compulsive disorder. *Behaviour Research and Therapy, 34*, 633–641.

Williams, J.M.G., Watts, F.N., MacLeod, C., & Mathews, A. (1988). *Cognitive psychology and emotional disorders.* Chichester: Wiley.

Williams, J.M.G., Watts, F.N., MacLeod, C., & Mathews, A. (1997). *Cognitive psychology and emotional disorders* (2nd ed.). Chichester: Wiley.

Williams, S.L., & Falbo, J. (1996). Cognitive and performance-based treatments for panic attacks in people with varying degrees of agoraphobic disability. *Behaviour Research and Therapy, 34*, 253–264.

Woods, S.W., Charney, D.S., Goodman, W.K., & Heninger, G.R. (1988). Carbon dioxide-induced anxiety: Behavioural, physiologic and biochemical effects of carbon dioxide in patients with panic disorders and in healthy subjects. *Archives of General Psychiatry, 45*, 43–52.

Woody, S.R. (1996). Effects of focus of attention of anxiety levels and social performance of individuals with social phobia. *Journal of Abnormal Psychology, 105*, 61–69.

Yeragani, V.K., Balon, R., & Pohl, R. (1989). Lactate infusions in panic disorder patients and normal controls: Autonomic measures and subjective anxiety. *Acta Psychiatrica Scandinavica, 79*, 32–40.

Young, G.C.D., & Martin, M. (1981). Processing of information about self by neurotics. *British Journal of Clinical Psychology, 20*, 205–212.

Zajonc, R.B., Murphy, S.T., & Inglehart, M. (1989). Feeling and facial efference: Implications of the vascular theory of emotion. *Psychological Review, 96*, 395–416.

Zanbergen, J., Bright, M., Pols, H., Fernandez, I., De Loof, C., & Griez, E. (1991). Higher lifetime prevalence of respiratory diseases in panic disorder? *American Journal of Psychiatry, 148*, 1583–1585.

Zinbarg, R.E., & Barlow, D.H. (1996). Structure of anxiety and the anxiety disorders. *Journal of Abnormal Psychology, 105*, 181–193.

Zoellner, L.A., Craske, M.G., & Rapee, R.M. (1996). Stability of catastrophic cognitions in panic disorder. *Behaviour Research and Therapy, 34*, 399–402.

Zuckerman, M. (1987). All parents are environmentalists until they have their second child. *Behavioral and Brain Sciences, 10*, 42–44.

Author index

Subject index